In the Studio is a series from Hauser & Wirth Publishers that gives readers a behind-the-scenes view of artists at work. Generously illustrated and written by a leading scholar or critic, each book focuses on a major artist and offers an overview of their influences, materials, and techniques.

Explore the series:
Phyllida Barlow by Frances Morris
Lee Lozano by Lucrezia Calabrò Visconti
Jack Whitten by Yinka Elujoba

Mika Yoshitake is an independent curator specializing in postwar Japanese and contemporary art. She earned her PhD in Art History at the University of California, Los Angeles, which culminated in the AICA Award–winning exhibition *Requiem for the Sun: The Art of Mono-ha* (2012) at Blum & Poe, Los Angeles. Formerly a curator at the Hirshhorn Museum and Sculpture Garden in Washington, DC, she has organized retrospectives, there and elsewhere, of Lee Ufan, Yayoi Kusama, and Yoshitomo Nara; and milestone exhibitions, among them *Parergon: Japanese Art of the 1980s and 1990s* (2019), that shed light on transformative art practices and underground Japanese music. In 2024–25, her exhibition *Breath(e): Toward Climate and Social Justice*, co-curated with Glenn Kaino, was on view at the Hammer Museum, Los Angeles.

In the Studio

Mika
Yoshitake

Takesada Matsutani

Hauser & Wirth Publishers

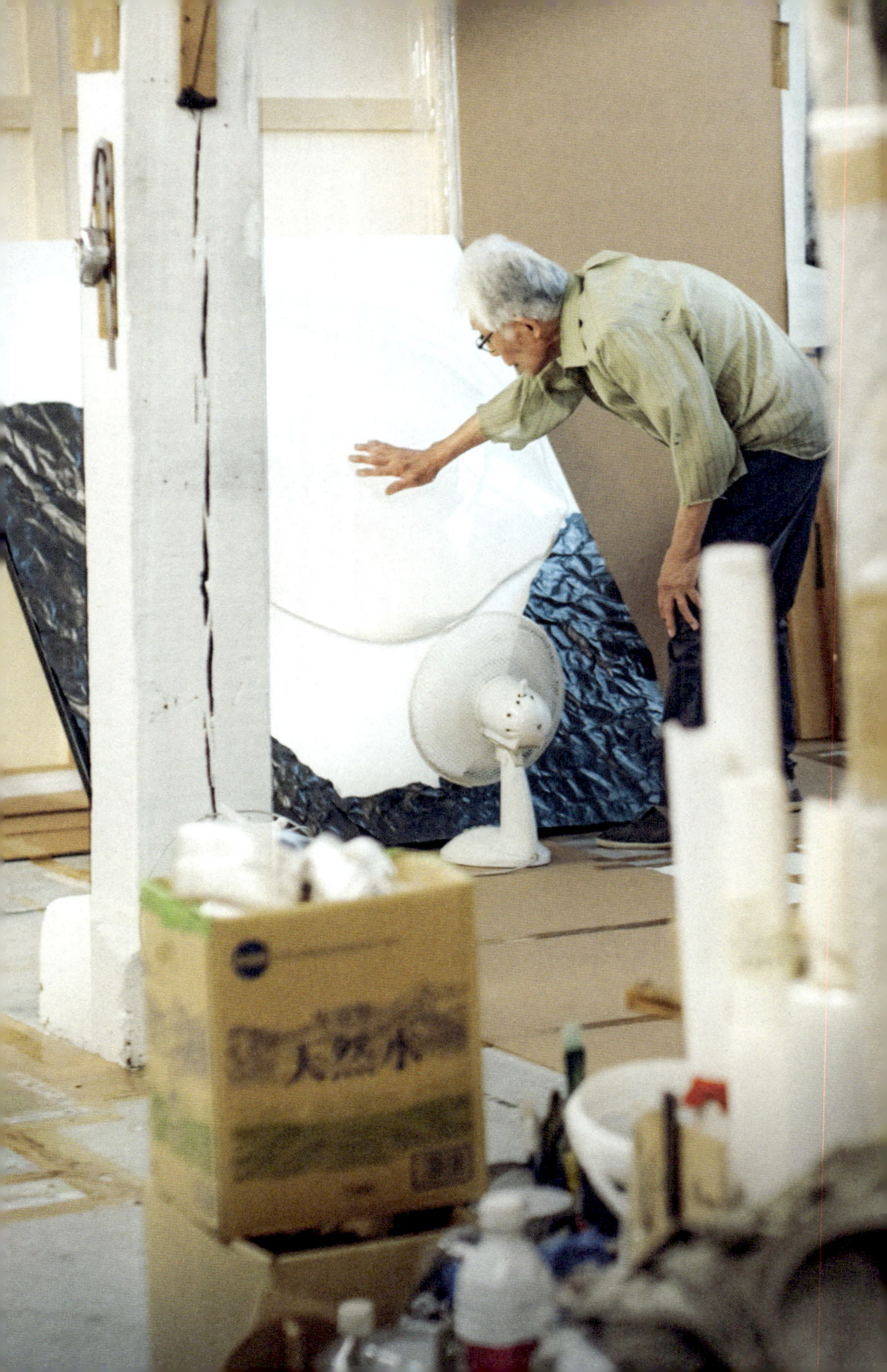
天然水

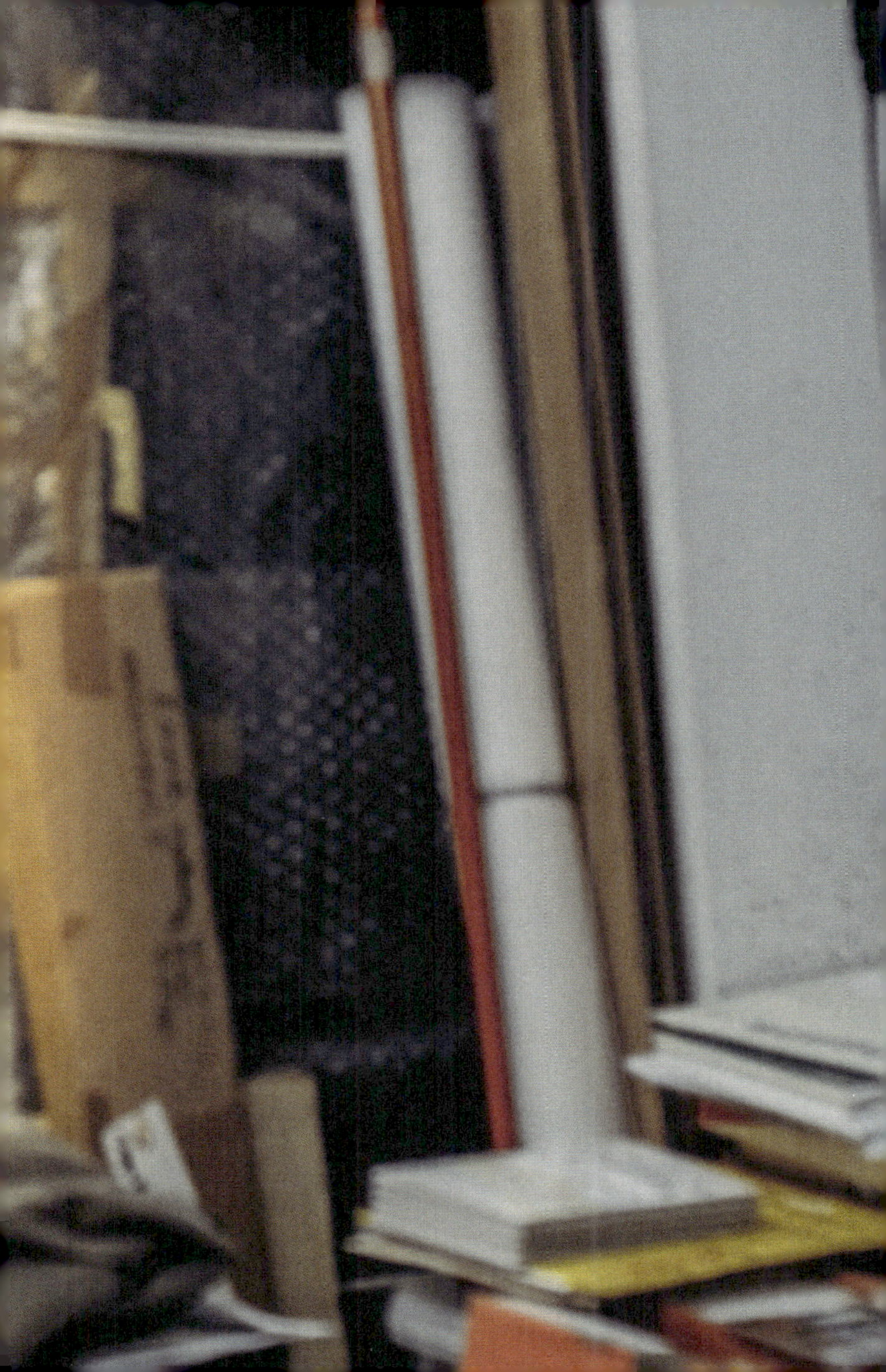

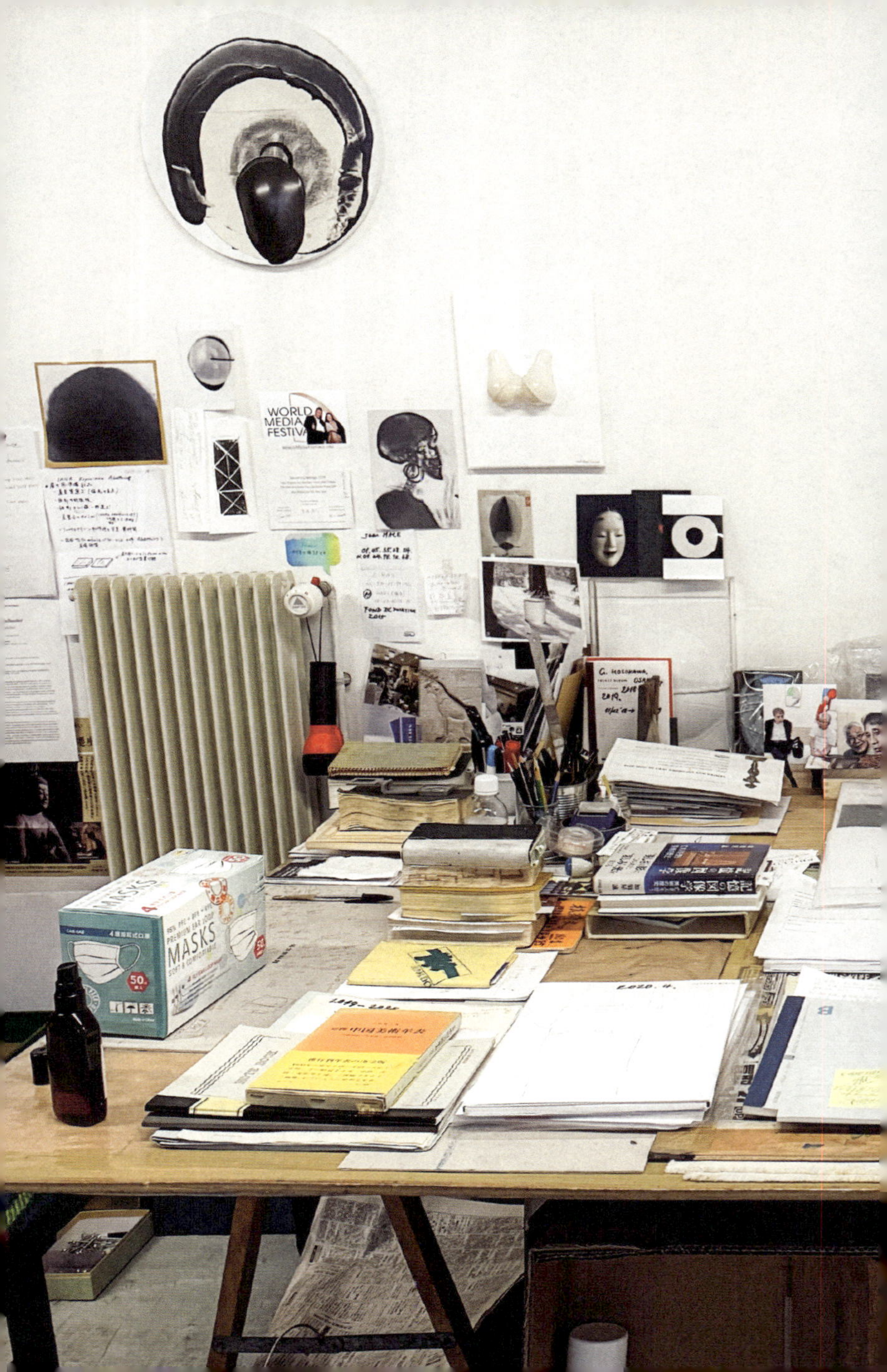
WORLD
MEDIA
MASKS
PREMIUM EAR LOOP
MASKS
SOFT & COMFORTABLE
2020. 4.

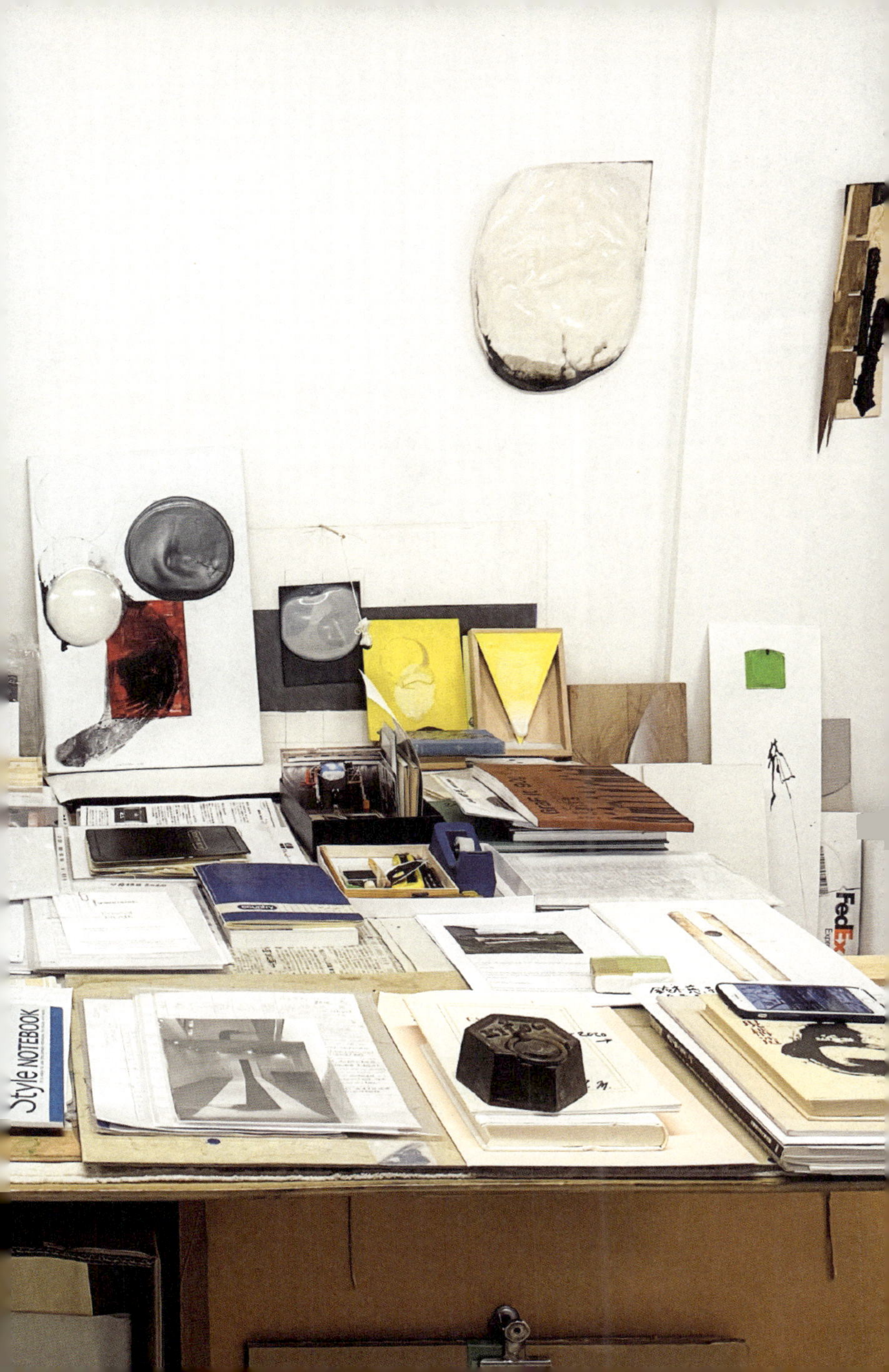
Style NOTEBOOK
FedEx

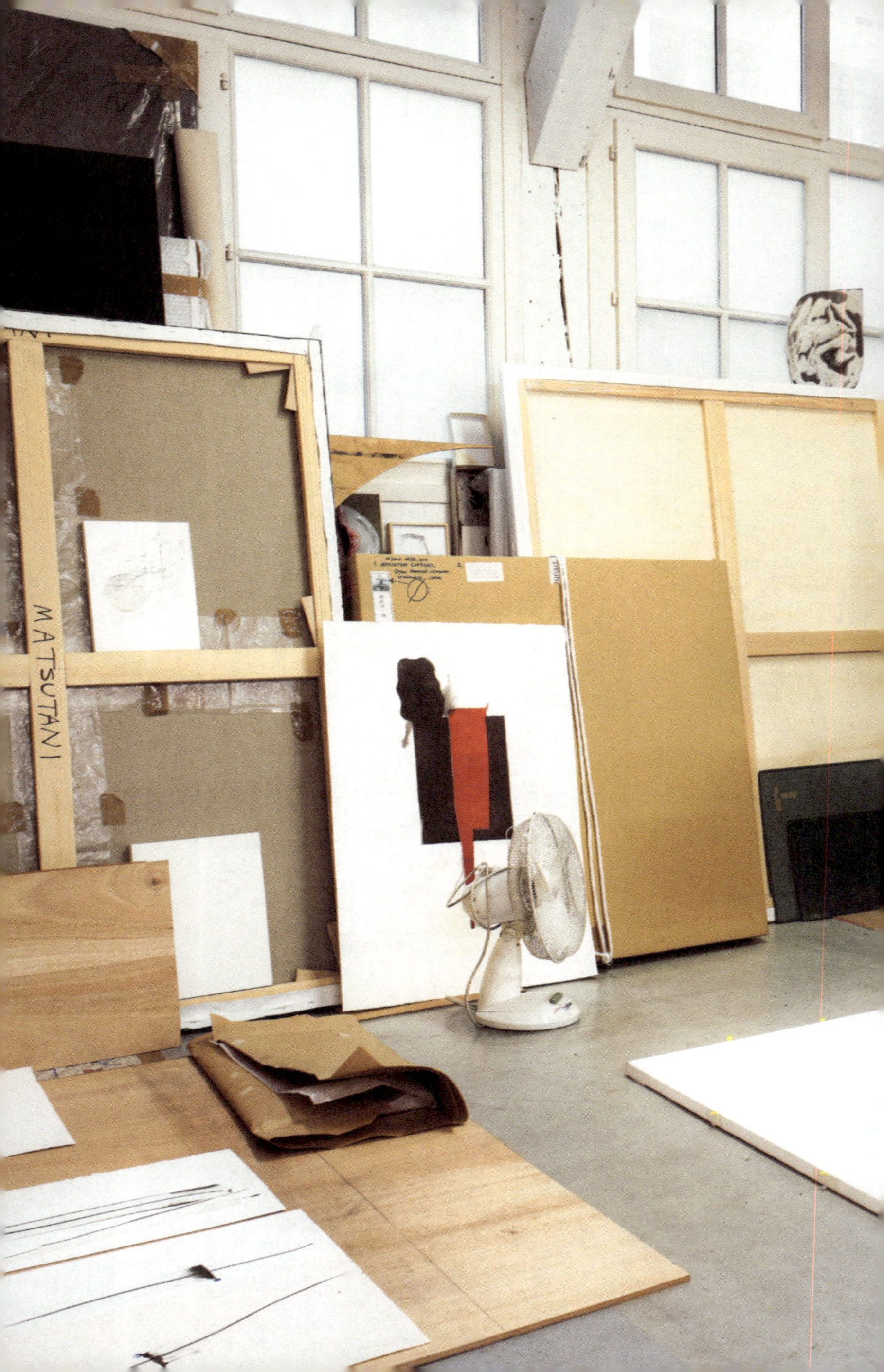
MATSUTANI

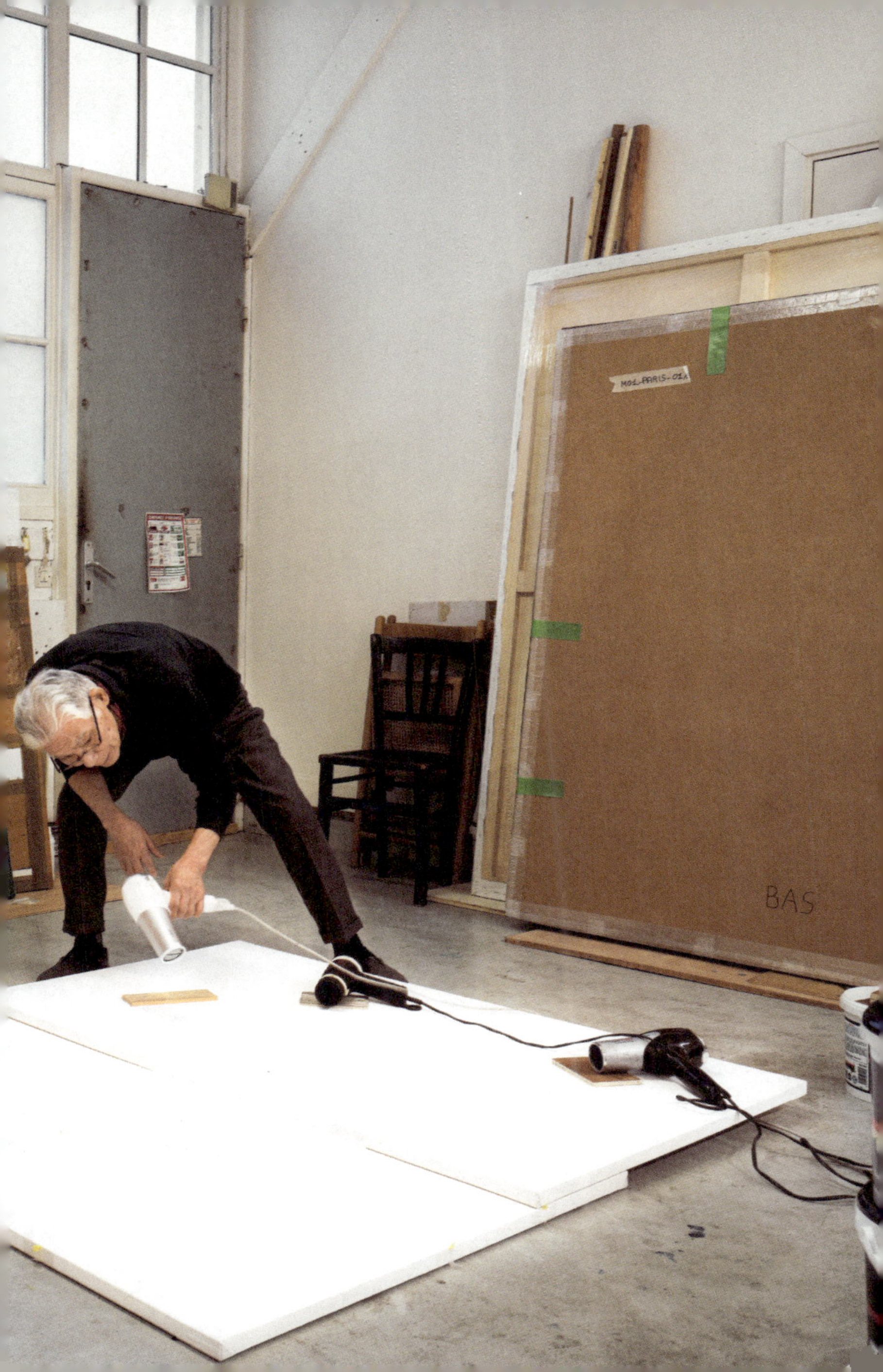
BAS

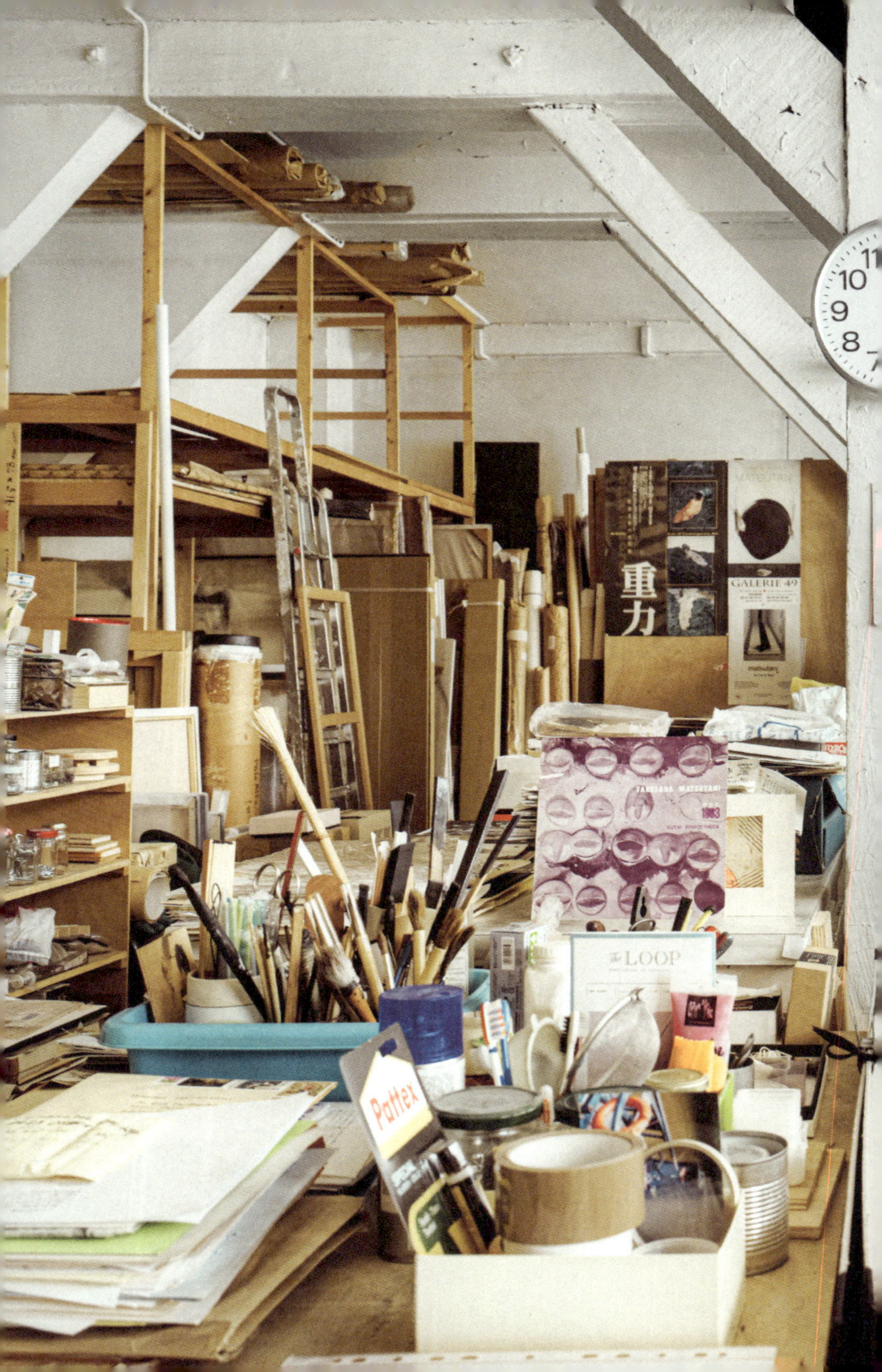

重力
GALERIE 49
TAKESADA MATSUTANI
The LOOP
Pattex

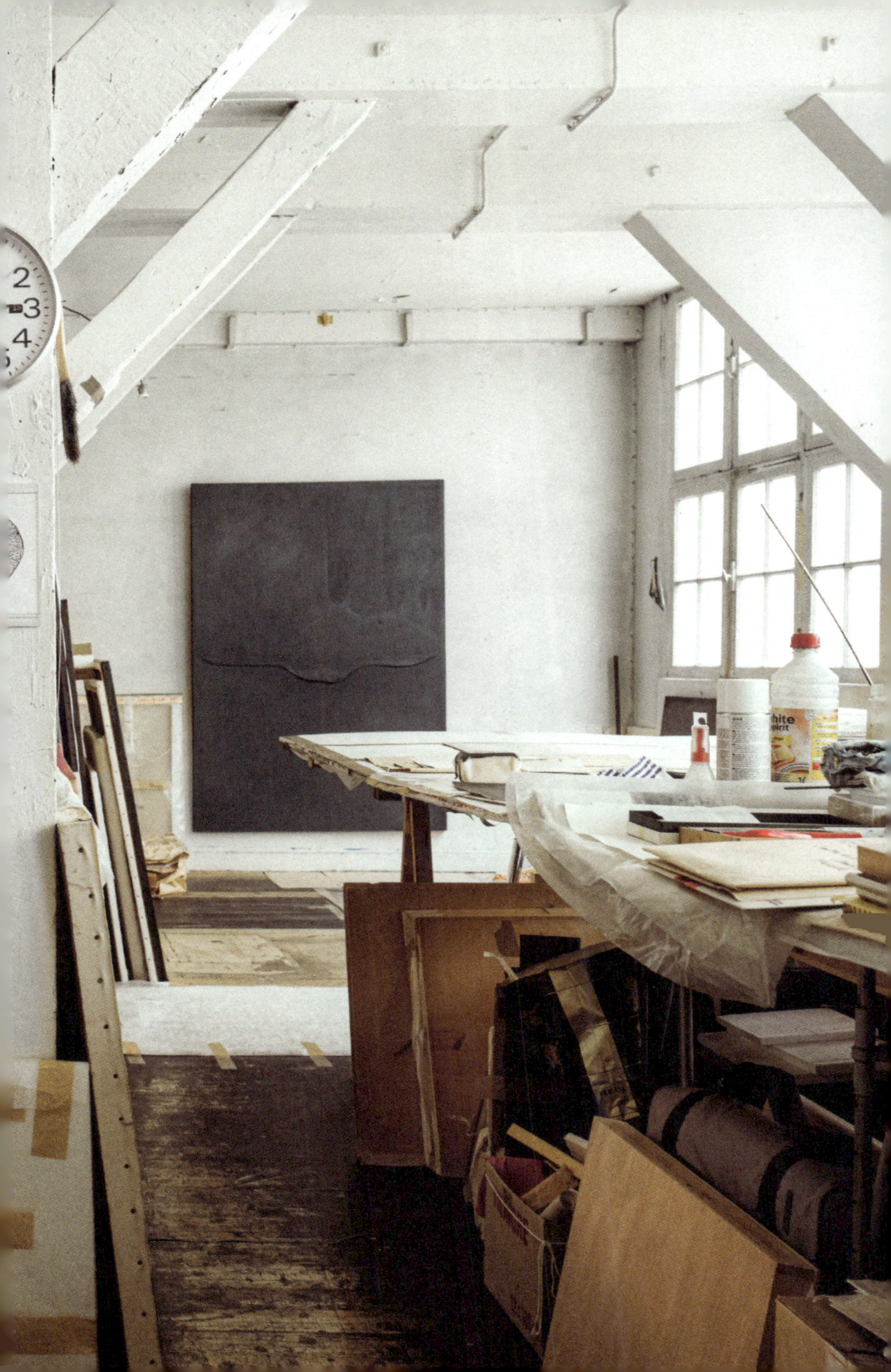

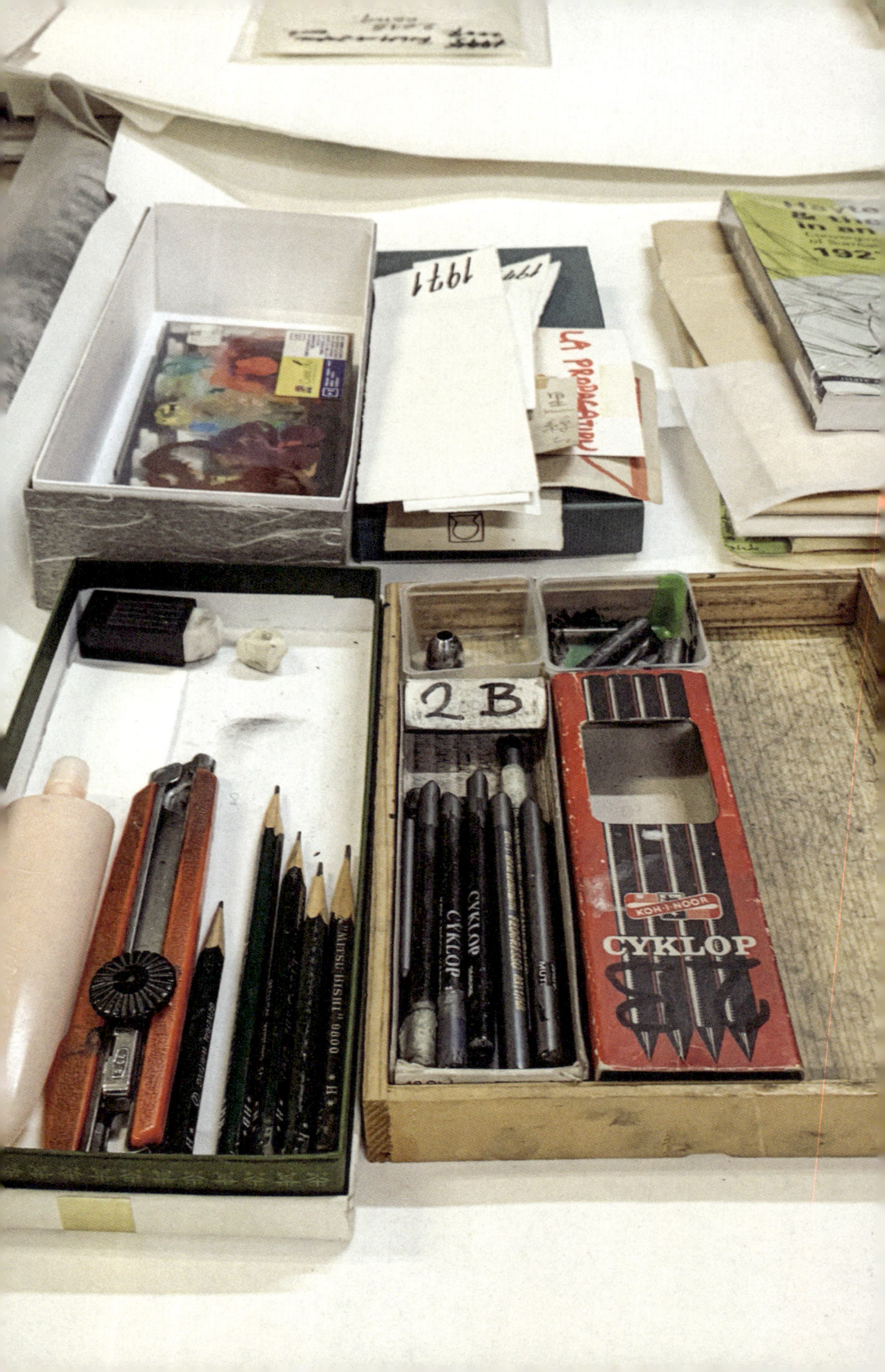
1971
LA PROPAGATION
2 B
CYKLOP
KOH-I-NOOR
CYKLOP

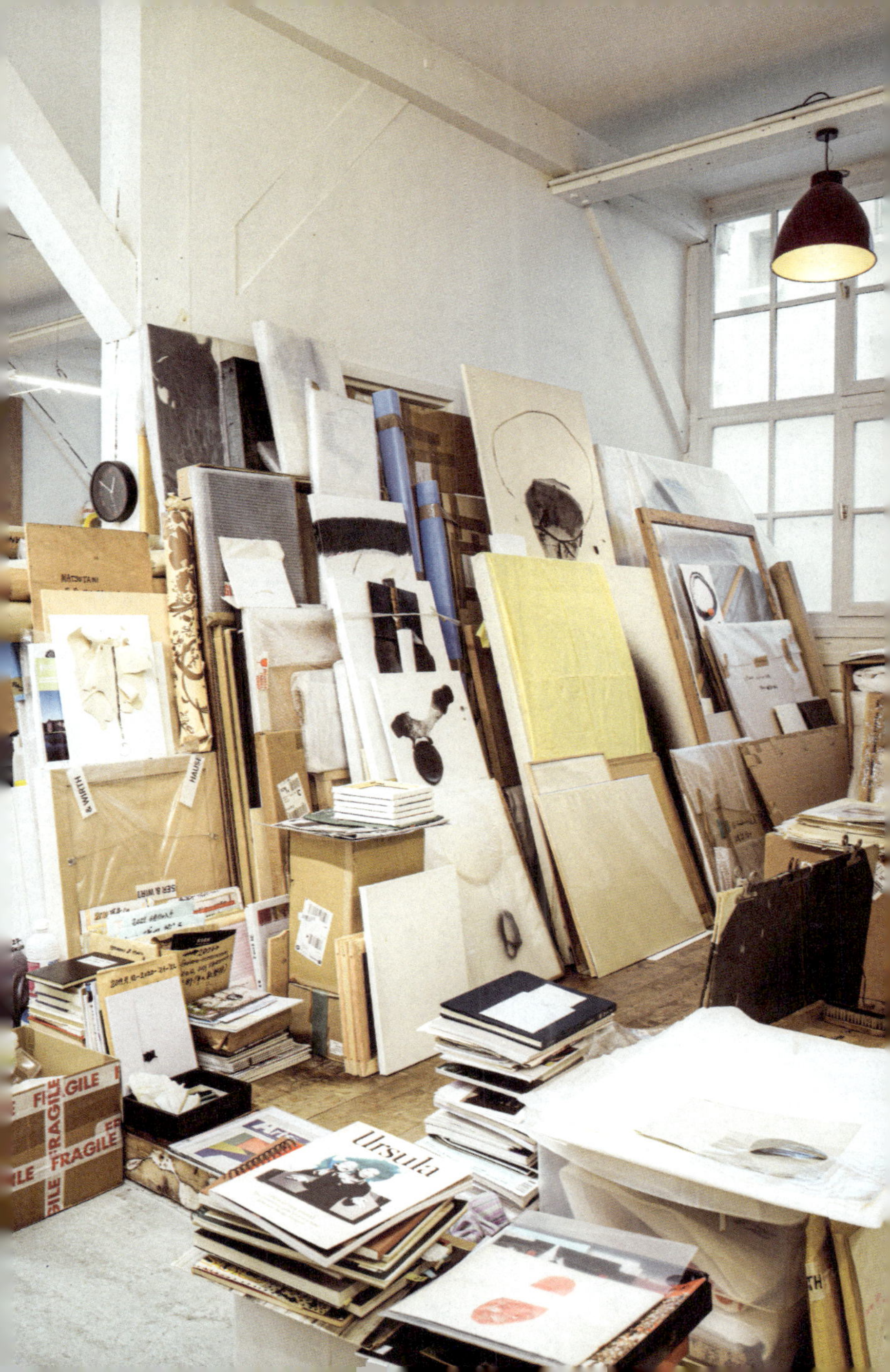
Ursula
FRAGILE

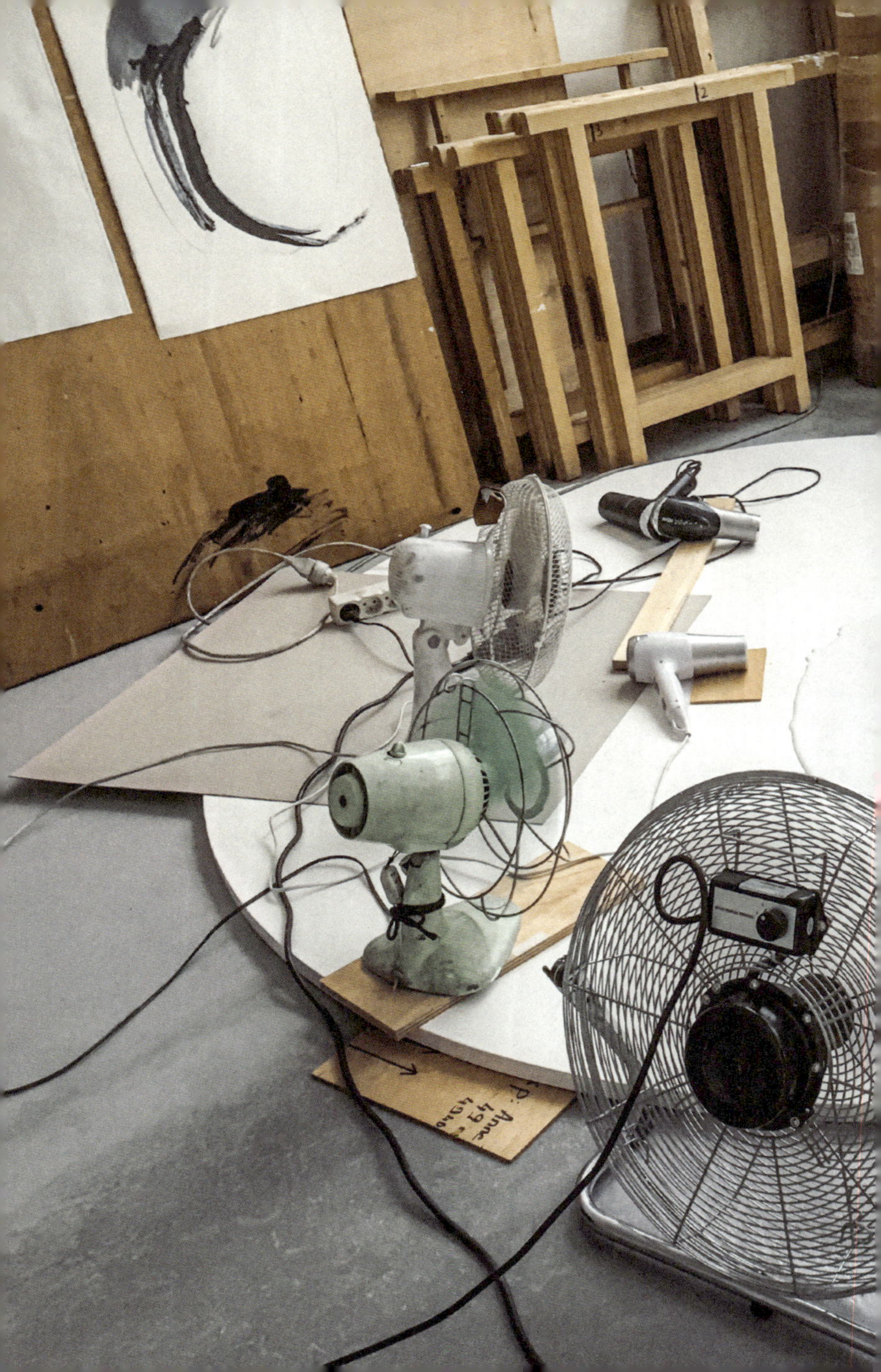

"Art is special, and it never goes away, I hope. When humans are finished maybe it will die, but while humans are alive, art is also."

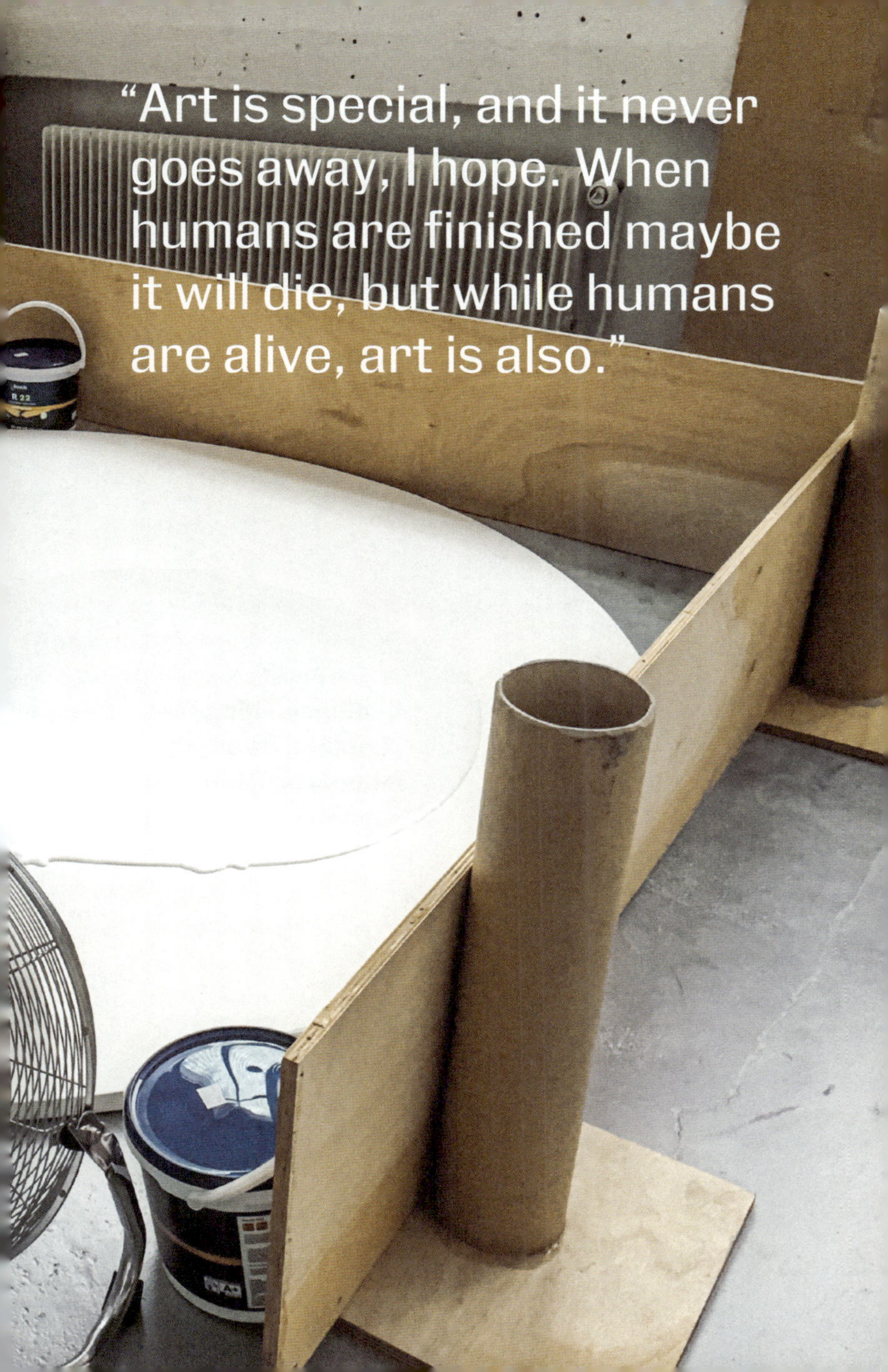

Contents

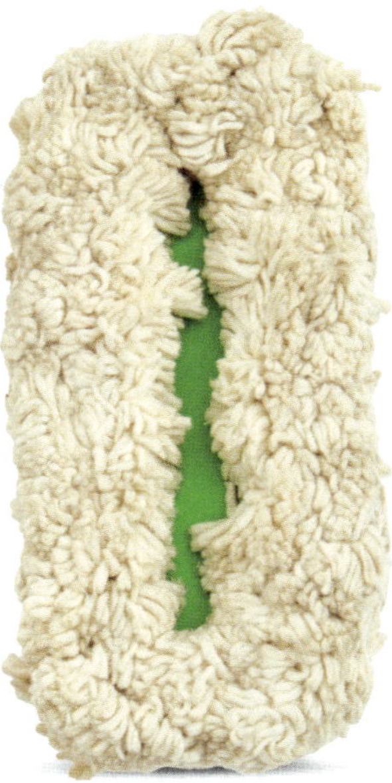

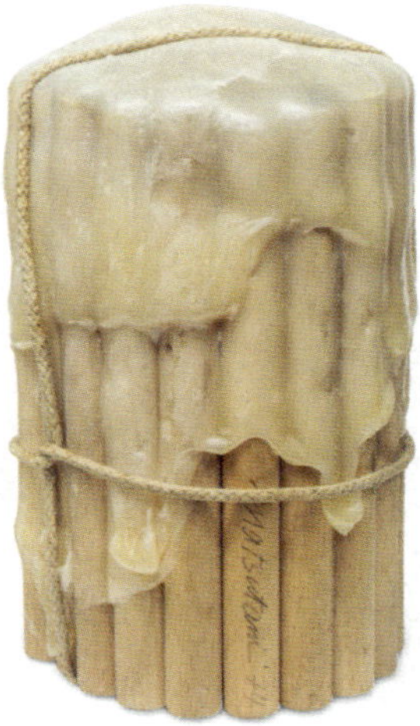

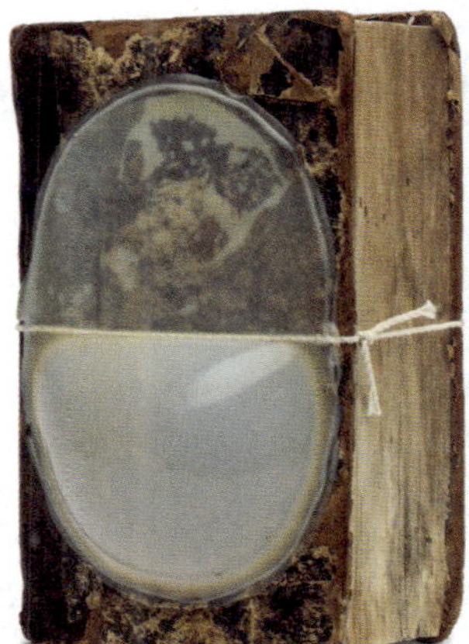

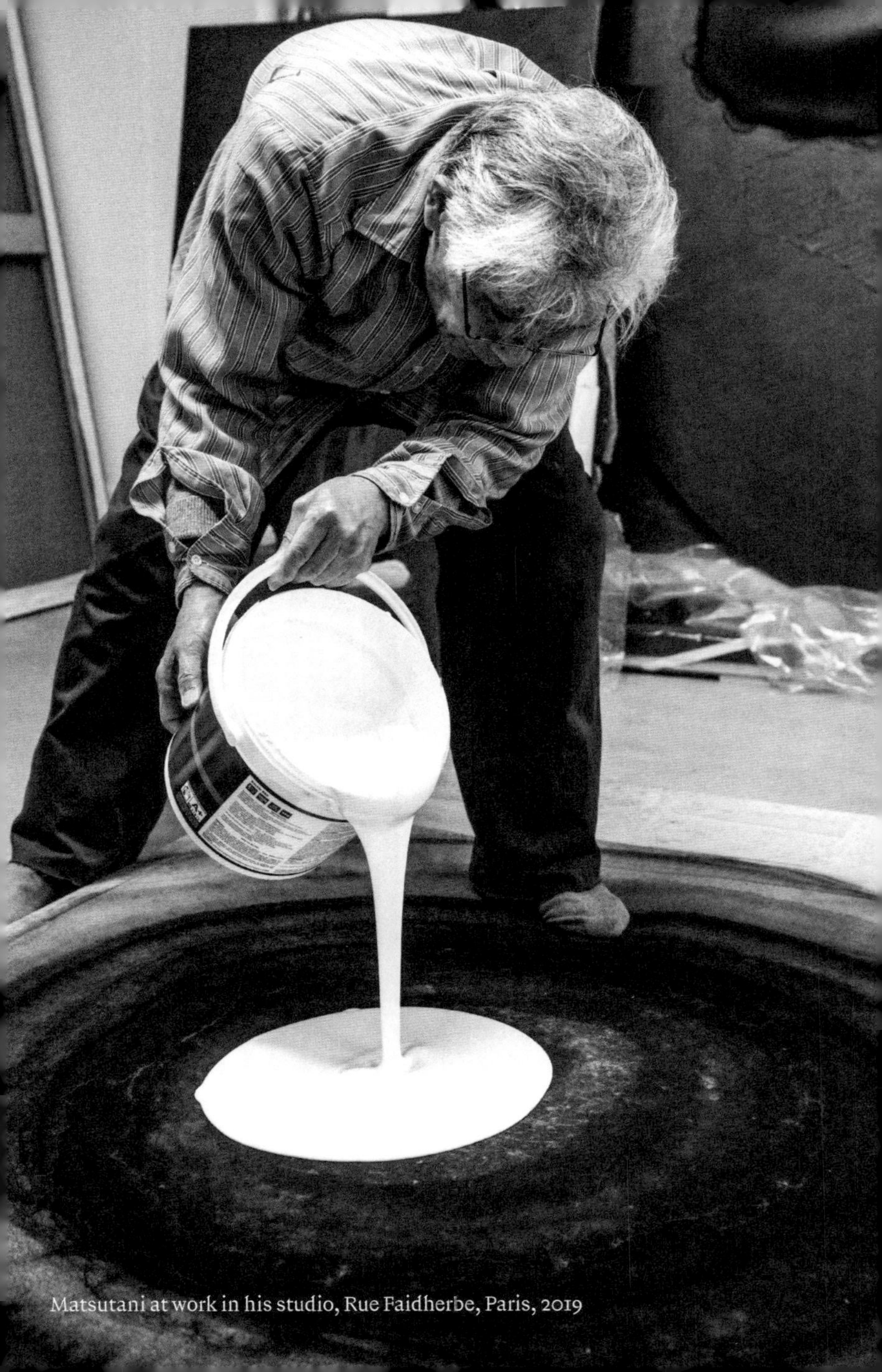

Matsutani at work in his studio, Rue Faidherbe, Paris, 2019

Process, Patience, Presence

Through a lifelong commitment to process, patience, and presence, Takesada Matsutani has created a body of work that continues to expand the language of contemporary art, evoking the profound complexities of existence with grace and rigor.

Emerging in the early 1960s as a member of the Gutai Art Association, he embraced the group's radical emphasis on the physical engagement with matter, creating works in which glue, air, and gravity became active agents in his artistic process. His signature vinyl glue reliefs—formed by inflating, drying, and sometimes puncturing bulbous membranes on a canvas ground—capture the tension between organic growth and decay, evoking bodily and visceral associations while revealing the material's unpredictable behavior.

After moving to Paris in 1966, where he worked with painter and printmaker Stanley William Hayter at Atelier 17, he became drawn to hard-edge abstraction, which he pursued alongside his Gutai activities and printmaking before eventually turning to a startling series of works in graphite on long rolls of paper.

Matsutani continued to experiment with form and surface, absorbing influences from Western abstraction while remaining deeply connected to the meditative discipline of Japanese aesthetics. Over time, his practice evolved into a more restrained exploration of repetition, time, and the mark, particularly through his large-scale graphite drawings and installations. The color black took on a renewed importance in his work, going on to play a key role in his performances with ink and stones, where the act of drawing is transformed into a durational and spiritual process that merges endurance with introspection.

Some sixty years after his arrival in Paris, Matsutani is widely celebrated for his inventive use of materials and profound engagement with the act of making, the senses, and the passage of time. His journey has encompassed painting, sculpture, printmaking, and installation, each medium bearing witness to recurring conceptual explorations. Through his evolving practice, Matsutani invites viewers to slow down, attend to subtle shifts of surface and form, and reflect on the enduring possibilities of renewal and change. Certain themes—material transformation, embodiment, time, emptiness, memory, and cross-cultural dialogue—consistently animate his work, offering critical insight into his creative intentions and artistic legacy. These themes coalesce into a practice that is both radically experimental and deeply contemplative. Matsutani's work stands as a testament to the persistence of matter and human touch, bridging the experimental fervor of postwar Japan with a universal search for balance and transcendence in the material world.

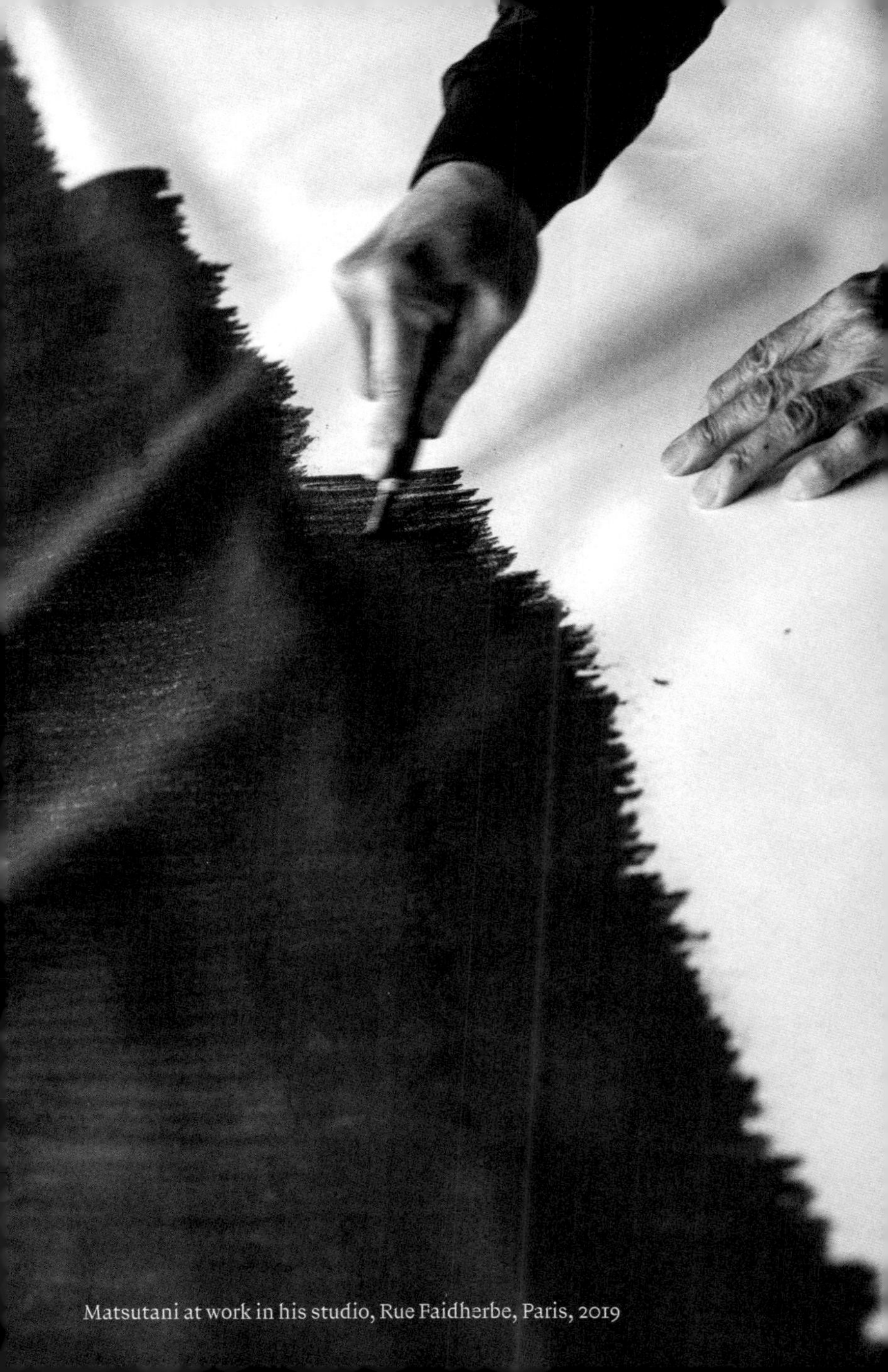

Matsutani at work in his studio, Rue Faidherbe, Paris, 2019

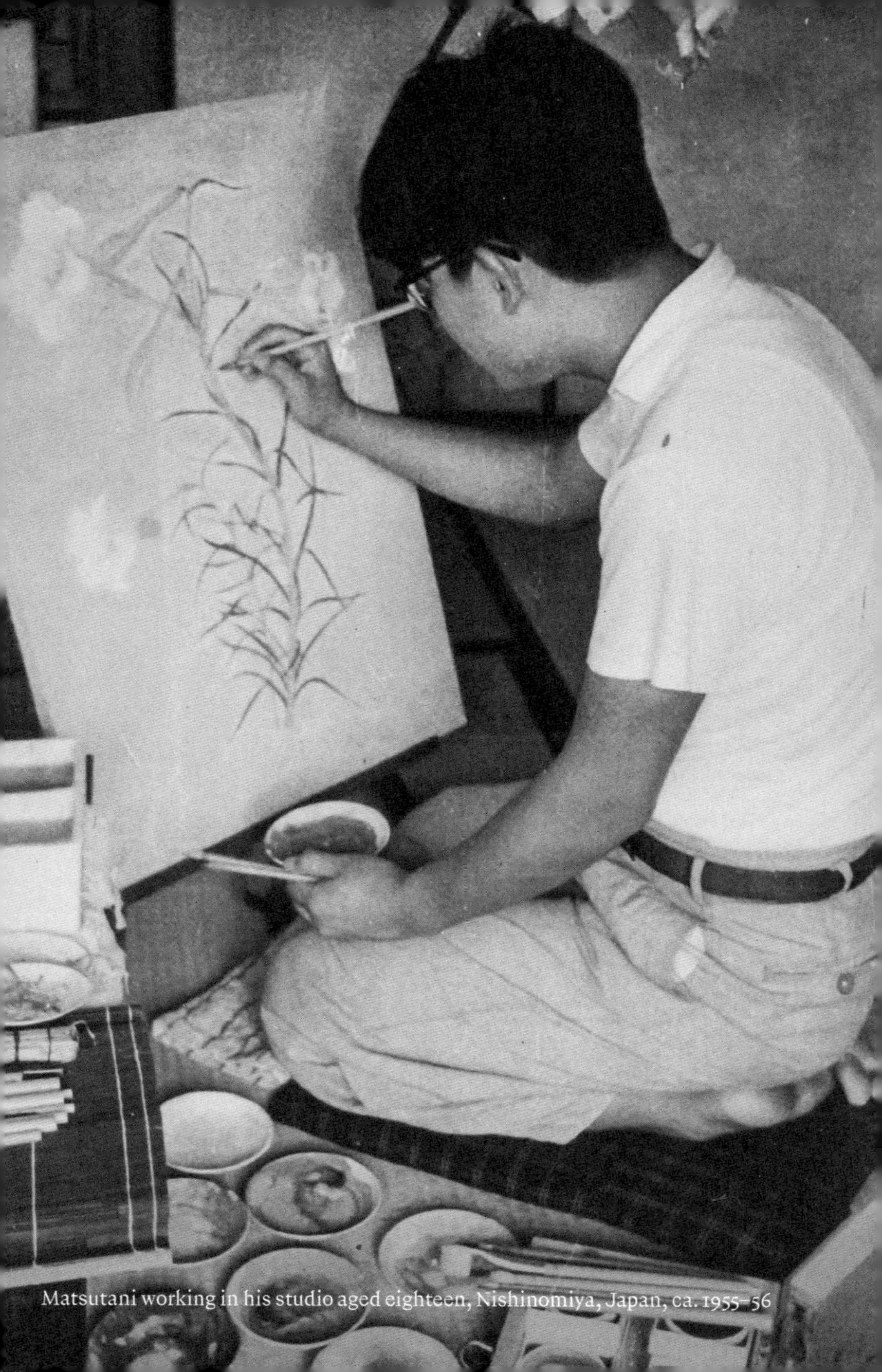

Matsutani working in his studio aged eighteen, Nishinomiya, Japan, ca. 1955–56

Early Years: From Nihonga to Gutai

Matsutani was born in Osaka on January 1, 1937. His family moved many times within the Kansai region due to his father's frequent job transfers at a life insurance company. Nevertheless, Matsutani would have been exposed to the cosmopolitan culture of the area before World War II, when it was a hub of fashionable living and artistic innovation. Cafés, department stores, jazz, theater, cinema, and Art Deco–inspired architecture all contributed to the renown of so-called Hanshinkan Modernism. But the world was on the brink of war; one of Matsutani's clearest childhood memories is of American B29 bombers flying high in the sky, unperturbed by ineffectual ground fire.

Eventually, the Matsutanis settled in Nishinomiya, Hyōgo Prefecture, in 1952. The year before, when Matsutani was fourteen years old, he had contracted tuberculosis, which he would not overcome completely until he was twenty-two. In 1954, he entered the nihonga (Japanese painting) department of the Osaka Municipal High School of Crafts and Arts, but following a relapse, he was forced to withdraw. He endured long days of confinement and social isolation. As he later recalled: "I spent my uneasy adolescence sketching the plants that I kept and the movements of the birds in the aviary I built and my pet cat." He continued to pursue nihonga, practicing traditional painting techniques using mineral pigments, and began to absorb Japanese art magazines focusing on Fauvism and Cubism in Europe. His teenage years already gave indications of the attributes that would become key to his artistic production: a deep curiosity and reverence for life, physical sensation, and the human body.

In 1957, when Matsutani was twenty years old, he submitted his landscape painting *The Rock's Surface* (1956), depicting the local Rokkō mountain range, to the Eighth Nishinomiya City Exhibition (nihonga). One of the jurors was Shōsaku Arao (p. 66), a nihonga painter whose work reflected a radical transition in the genre toward Cubism and abstraction. After seeing Matsutani's work, which was accepted into the exhibition, Arao contacted him by postcard, writing: "For a twenty-year old, your work is too serious. Why don't you stop by my atelier?"

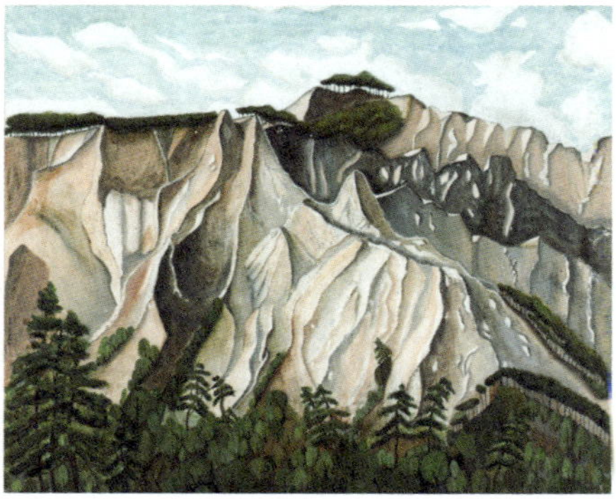

The Rock's Surface, 1956. Mineral pigments on Japanese paper mounted on plywood, 28 × 35 in. (71.2 × 89 cm)

Matsutani took him up on his offer, and through Arao, he learned about the idea of *shinshō*—inner imagery—which became a guiding concept for his practice (p. 109). In a series of drawings from 1957, Matsutani sketched the wood grain of his bedroom ceiling while bedridden. As he later described the experience: "One evening, I was looking up at the ceiling unable to sleep and the streaks of straight grain caught my attention. The following morning, I sketched them right away. From within the streaks of straight grain, I began picturing a face that expressed the intense suppression that I felt from the long period of illness, my sense of inferiority from not being able to attend school, my worries about living on, and everything else. In my works . . . , I outwardly expressed my inner conflict and attempted to brush aside this heavy burden. In such ways, I shifted from realism to abstraction via my own inner image."

The imagery from the woodgrain also emerged, for example, in the vivid peacock feathers or moth wings that double as a weakened pair of lungs or heart with "eyes" in *Résistance (Pressure)*. This 1958 nihonga painting allows us to see how mimicry functions as an evolutionary strategy for survival. While evoking the visceral experiences the artist had during his traumatic eight-year bout with tuberculosis, its overlapping biomorphic forms also reveal Matsutani's attraction to the potential of Surrealism to access dreamlike states of the unconscious mind.

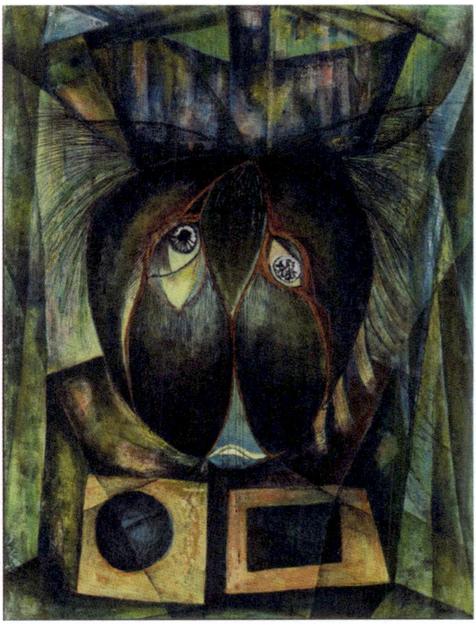

Résistance (Pressure), 1958. Mineral pigments on Japanese paper mounted on plywood, 45 3/8 × 35 1/4 in. (115.2 × 89.4 cm)

Realism in Postwar Japan

In the post-atomic moment during the Allied occupation of Japan (1945–52), the ethics of representation revolved around one key question: How to reconcile the psychosocial aspect of defeat through a reconceptualization of "realism." The work of the Surrealist painter Masao Tsuruoka, for example, was a reaction against desensitized, photorealistic depictions of war atrocities, as well as the documentary and propagandistic paintings commissioned by the postwar military government. In hindsight, Matsutani's *The Modern in the Ancient* (1958) unconsciously resonates with Tsuruoka's *Heavy Hand* (1949), a landmark painting depicting a large hand devouring a human figure. Matsutani found Tsuruoka's take on the harsh reality of postwar Japan too "severe," although the colossal cyclops in his own painting comparably captures the heavy weight of the moment in a Surrealist abstract mode.

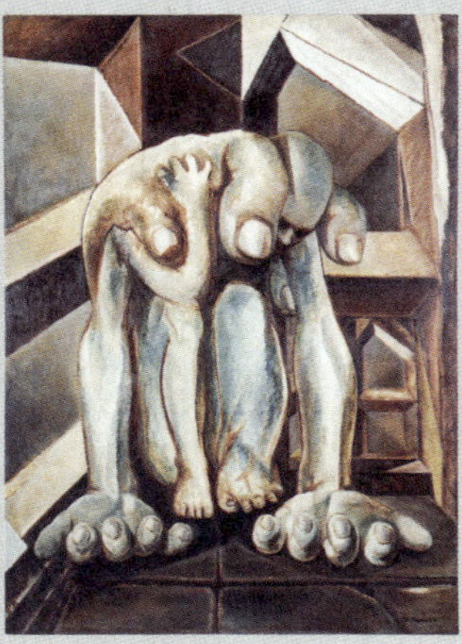

Masao Tsuruoka, *Heavy Hand*, 1949. Oil on canvas, 51⅛ × 38¼ in. (130 × 97 cm)

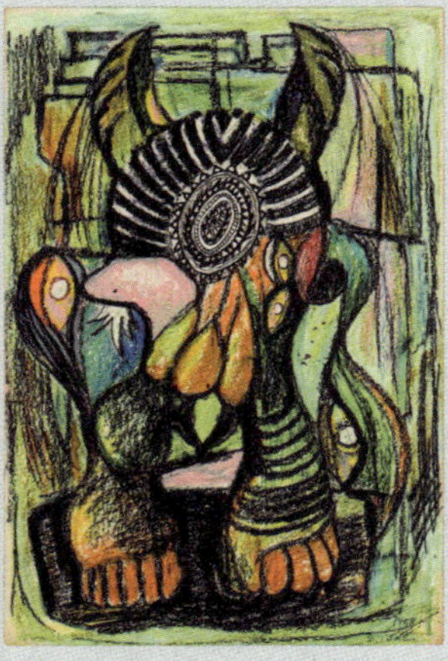

The Modern in the Ancient, 1958. Oil pastel, pencil, and ink on paper, 14¼ × 9⅞ in. (36.2 × 25.2 cm)

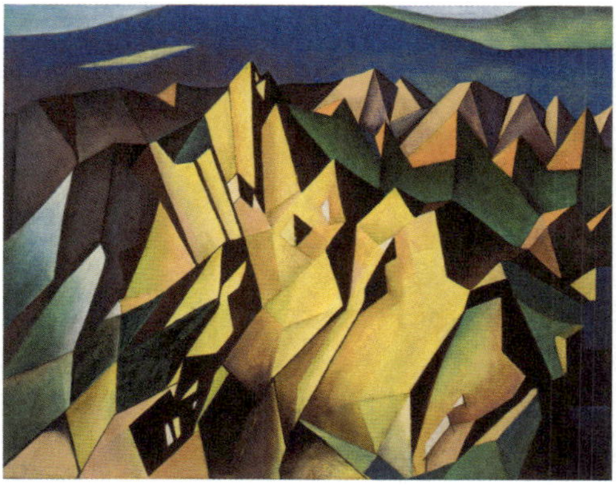

The Setting Sun (Sunny Rock), 1957. Mineral pigments on Japanese paper mounted on plywood, 35⅝ × 45⅞ in. (90.5 × 116.5 cm)

As his tuberculosis was going into remission in 1959, Matsutani began to receive greater recognition, earning awards for his figurative nihonga paintings that contained hallucinatory imagery and elements of deformed abstraction. Several were shown in regional open-call exhibitions, which local governments were promoting after the war as part of the country's democratization and social education efforts. That same year, Matsutani also began attending the Nishinomiya Civic Art Class. His instructors included leading avant-garde calligraphic painters Kokuta Suda and Waichi Tsutaka, who had been shaped by their active participation in the Kansai-based Genbi Group, an interdisciplinary study and discussion group that explored the meaning of modernism in Japan. There he met the renowned Gutai artist Sadamasa Motonaga.

Integrating nihonga, Surrealism, and abstraction, Matsutani's practice at the time was gravitating toward both the heightened observation of natural phenomena and material experimentation. Although he was familiar with Gutai through the group's extensive press coverage, he had not been impressed at first. In his own words:

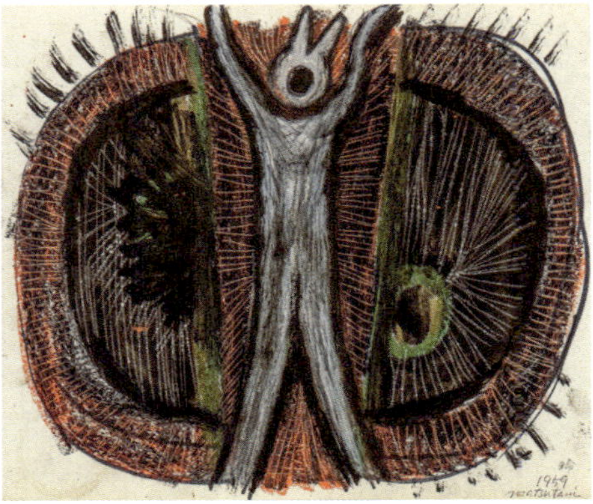

Life, 1959. Sumi ink, felt pen, pastel, and scratching on paper, 10 × 11⅞ in. (25.2 × 35.6 cm)

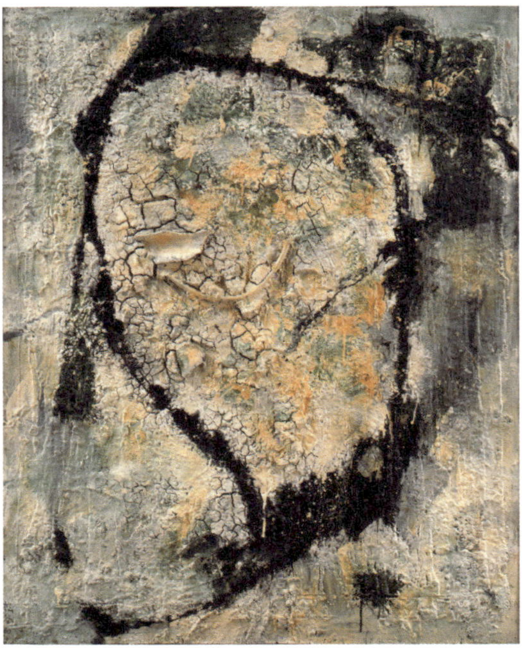

Work, 1960. Oil, cement, and mixed media on plywood, 63 × 51½ in. (160 × 130.8 cm)

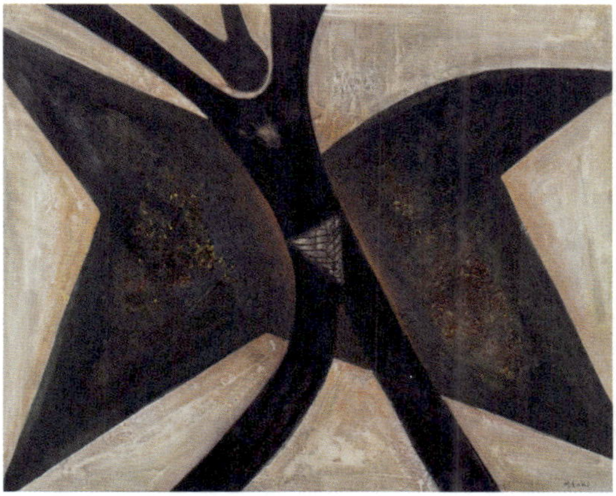

Life-B, 1959. Mineral pigments and varnish on Japanese paper mounted on plywood, 31 × 39 in. (78.8 × 99 cm)

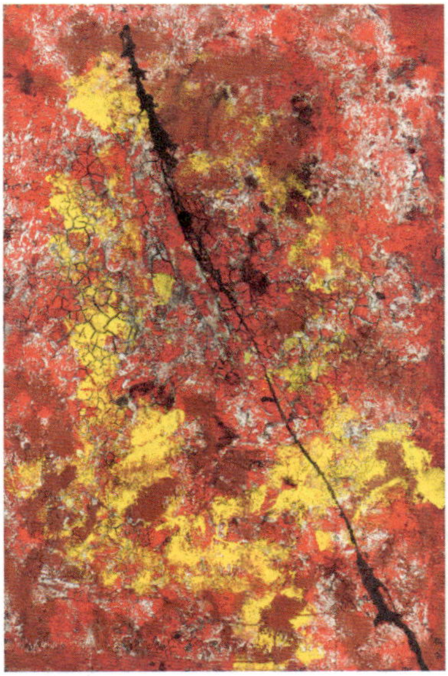

Work-60, 1960. Cement, acrylic, and oil on plywood, 72⅛ × 48⅛ in. (183.2 × 122.1 cm)

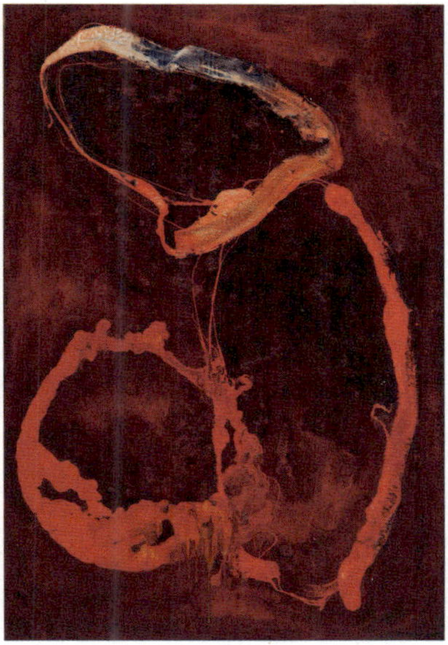

Work-B-62, 1962. Oil on canvas, 73¼ × 49¾ in. (186.1 × 126.5 cm)

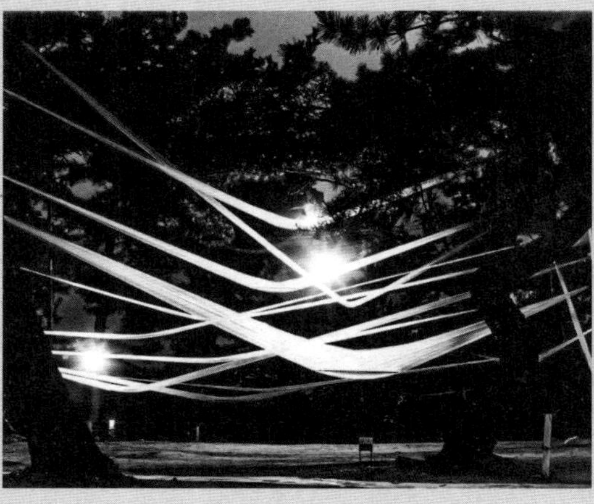

Sadamasa Motonaga's *Work (Water)* installed at the outdoor Gutai exhibition in Ashiya Park, 1956

Gutai

The Gutai Art Association was established in 1954 under the leadership of Jirō Yoshihara. In Gutai ("concrete body") art, Yoshihara declared, "the human spirit and matter shake hands with each other while keeping their distance." Breaking with traditional painting and sculpture, members staged performances and experimented with materials such as water, sand, smoke, and industrial paints, sometimes tearing or puncturing surfaces to let the material "act" freely. They mounted outdoor exhibitions as a way to explore the interactions between art, environment, and chance. In *Work (Water)* (1956), for example, Sadamasa Motonaga filled plastic tubes with colored water and slung them like hammocks between trees. Gutai artists embraced technology, mail art, and unconventional tools, incorporating ropes, pulleys, and even fire or explosions into their work. In their journal *Gutai*, they emphasized the liberation of materials, the importance of action, and art as an encounter between human will and material autonomy.

Many Gutai artists embraced the spectacle of destruction-as-creation. Saburō Murakami ran straight through a series of sheets of paper stretched across multiple frames. Shōzō Shimamoto fired paint-filled objects from a cannon onto canvases, and on another occasion filled hundreds of glass bottles with seeds, fruit skins, hair, ash, paper, sand, cigarette butts, and dead insects mixed with synthetic paint, which he then smashed onto a large stone atop an unstretched canvas. In 1955, Kazuo Shiraga created *Challenging Mud* (1955), for which he repeatedly hurled his body into a heap of wet mud. A 1956 restaging of the work was shown on Japanese national television, cementing Gutai's reputation for radical, bodily experimentation.

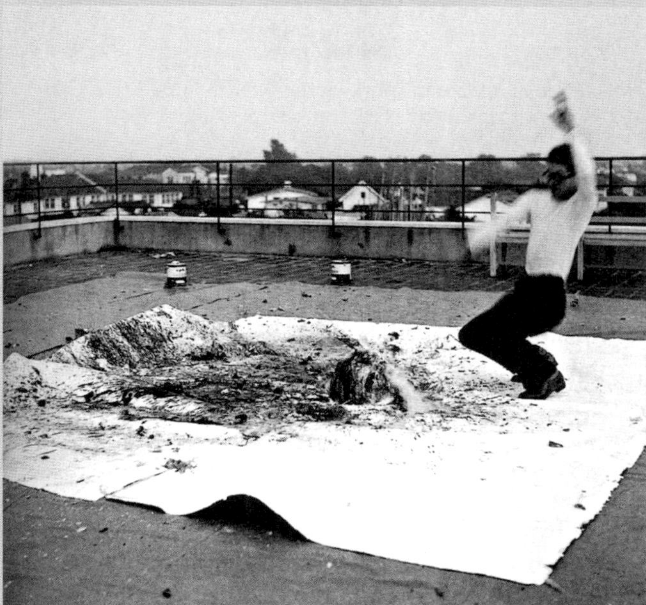

Shōzō Shimamoto painting by throwing bottles of paint onto canvas at the Second Gutai Art Exhibition, Ohara Kaikan Hall, Tokyo, 1956

"In all honesty, I did not like what they were doing and thought, 'This is not art. It's blasphemy.'" He was, however, drawn to Motonaga's towering and charismatic personality. Thanks to him, Matsutani learned about the Gutai group's central philosophy of bridging art and the human spirit.

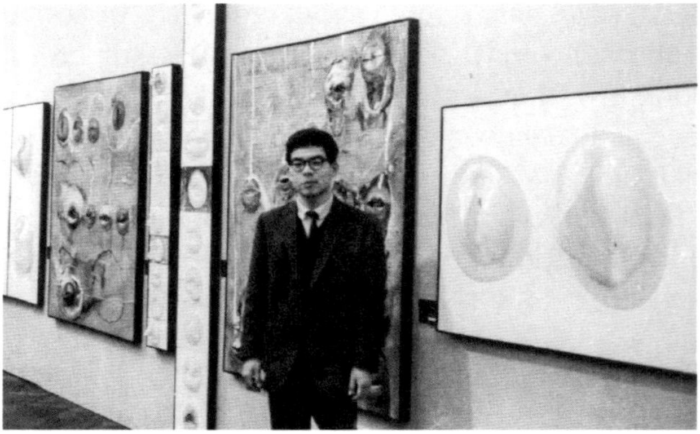

Matsutani in front of his works at the Twelfth Gutai Art Exhibition, Takashimaya department store, Tokyo, 1963

Motonaga introduced Matsutani to Gutai's leader, Jirō Yoshihara, in 1960. That same year, Matsutani participated in the Ninth Gutai Art Exhibition, showing canvases caked with soil or cement that had dried and cracked (p. 28). He was, however, disappointed that his work was exhibited in a corner, and it took three years of trial and error for him to find a way past the highly expressive, gestural abstraction of what the Japanese press was starting to call "Informel shock." The term gained popularity in the wake of the success of French critic and curator Michel Tapié's touring exhibition *Art of Today's World*, which, in 1956, had offered Japanese audiences a first glimpse of the experimental practices of artists such as Georges Mathieu, Jean Fautrier, and Sam Francis.

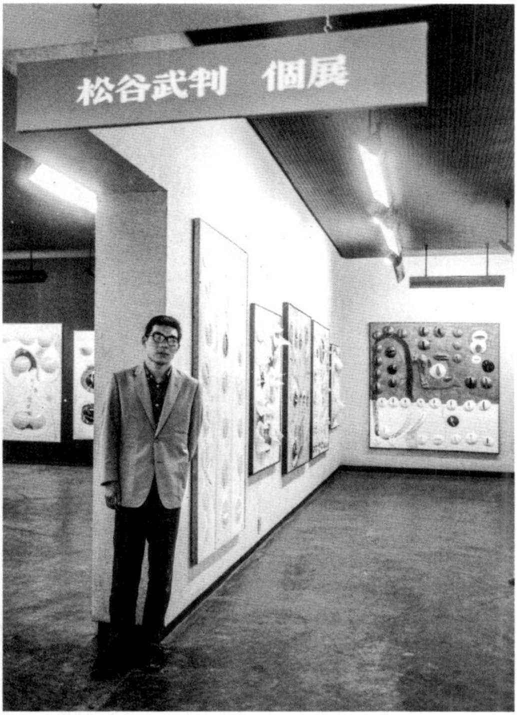

Matsutani at his solo exhibition at the Gutai Pinacotheca, Osaka, October 1963

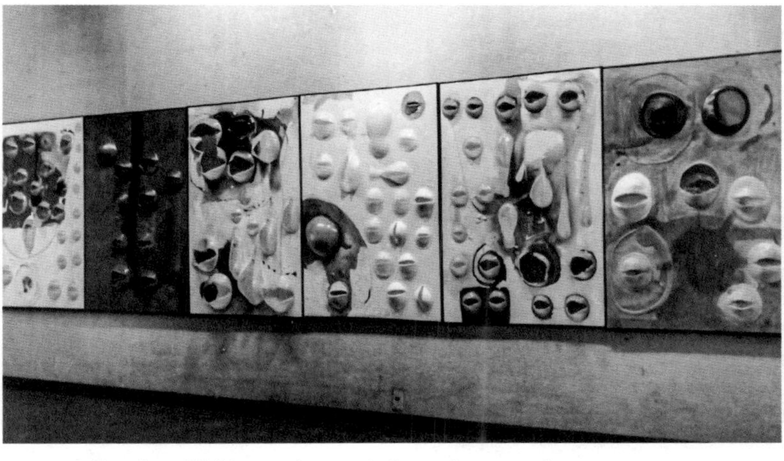

Matsutani's solo exhibition at the Gutai Pinacotheca, Osaka, 1963

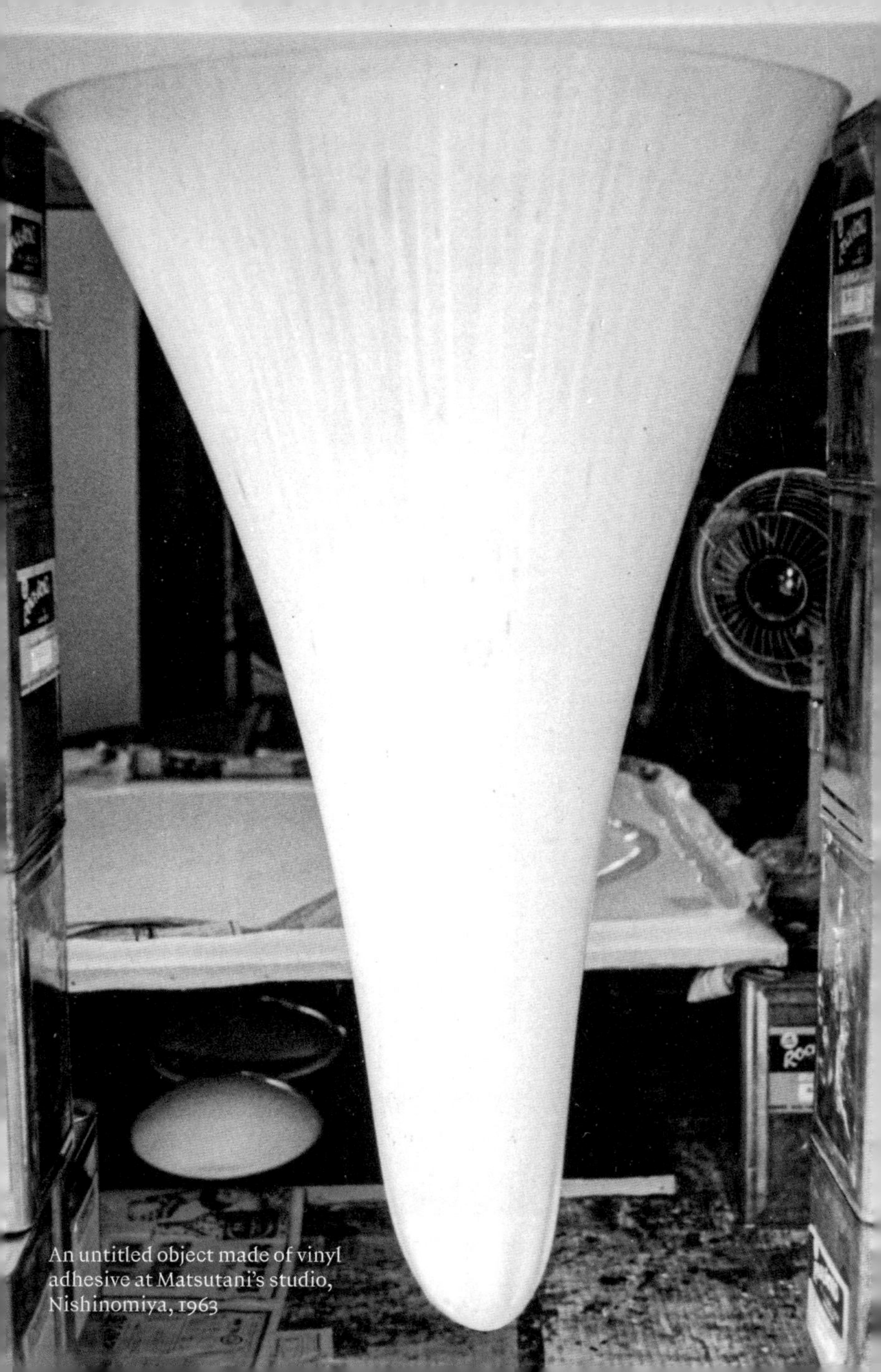

An untitled object made of vinyl adhesive at Matsutani's studio, Nishinomiya, 1963

Material Transformation

A friend of Matsutani's who was studying medicine at Kobe University once let him observe blood samples under a microscope. The artist was inspired by their supple, organic forms, which he sketched as he wondered how to make them three-dimensional. This led to his innovative use of polyvinyl acetate glue—a synthetic polymer adhesive of the kind known in the United States as Elmer's glue—which would become his signature medium.

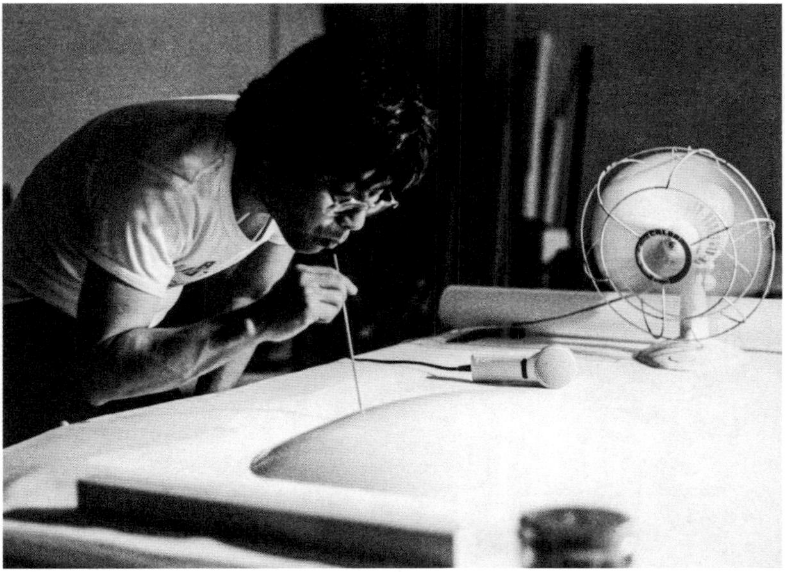

Matsutani inflating vinyl glue with a straw while using a fan to dry its surface in his Paris studio at Passage de la Bonne Graine, 1981

Vinyl glue was commercially developed in the 1920s–30s and became popular as an adhesive for woodworking, bookbinding, and general industrial use by the 1940s. By the early 1960s, as neon, lightbulbs, and resin were

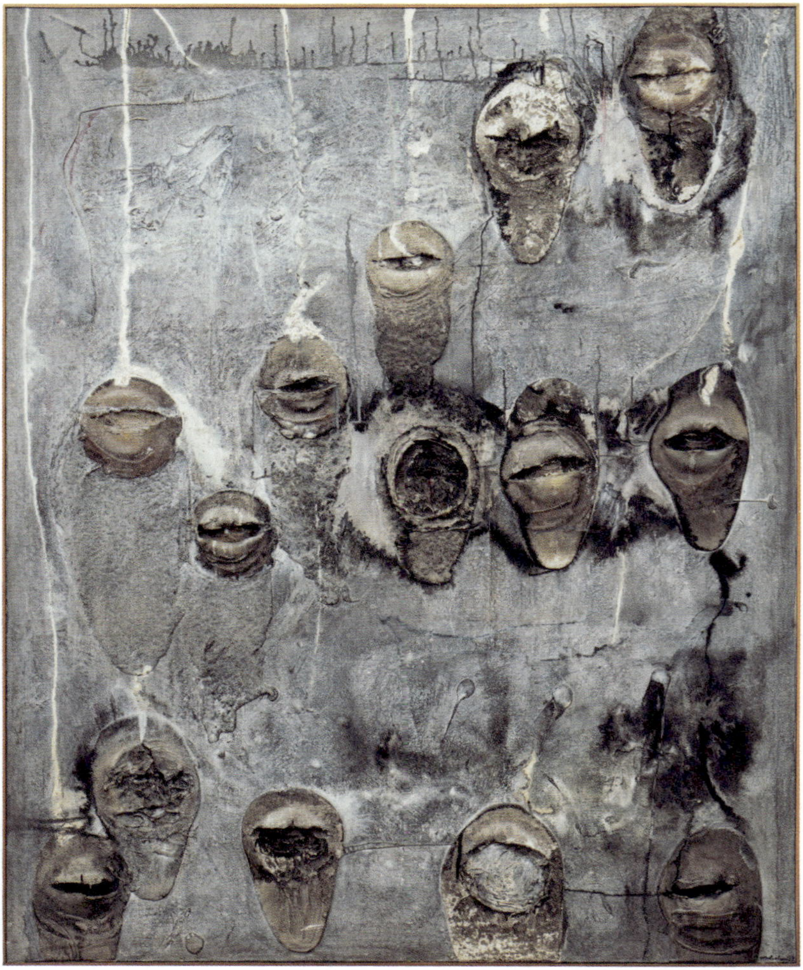

Propagation B (Grey), 1963. Vinyl adhesive, acrylic, and oil on canvas, 62½ × 52½ in. (158.8 × 133.4 cm)

becoming material staples in contemporaneous art practices, vinyl glue had become available in Japan, which was entering the height of its postwar technological innovation and economic growth.

Matsutani's discovery of this material in 1962 was serendipitous: "By chance," he recalled in a 2022 interview, "I started to use a special glue called vinyl glue and that was for me something very interesting and organic. I would throw the glue on the canvas on a nice clear but windy day and leave it to dry. The wind made it half dry and there was dripping similar to shapes found in caves. It was interesting to see these forms create three-dimensional shapes. But the wind was too much of a chance, so I started using a fan or a hair dryer. Following the drying process, I would try to make a shape. Sometimes I would start shaping the material in [a] half-dry state, as the vinyl glue is very soft and based on water."

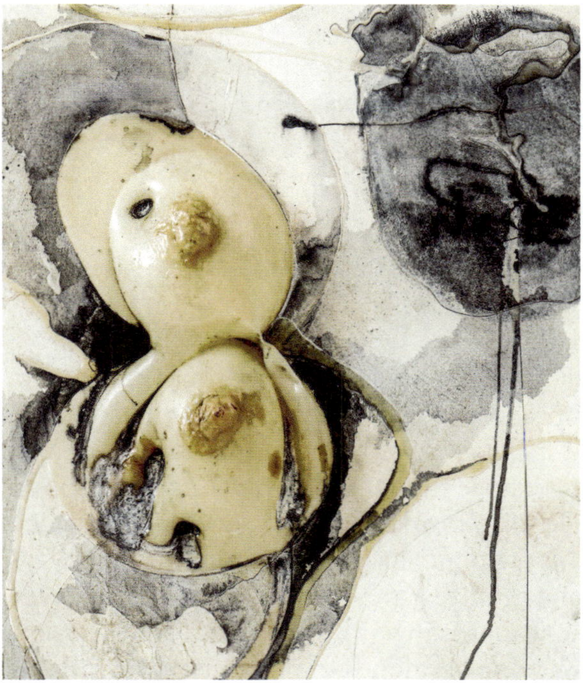

Work 63-9 (detail), 1963 (p. 38)

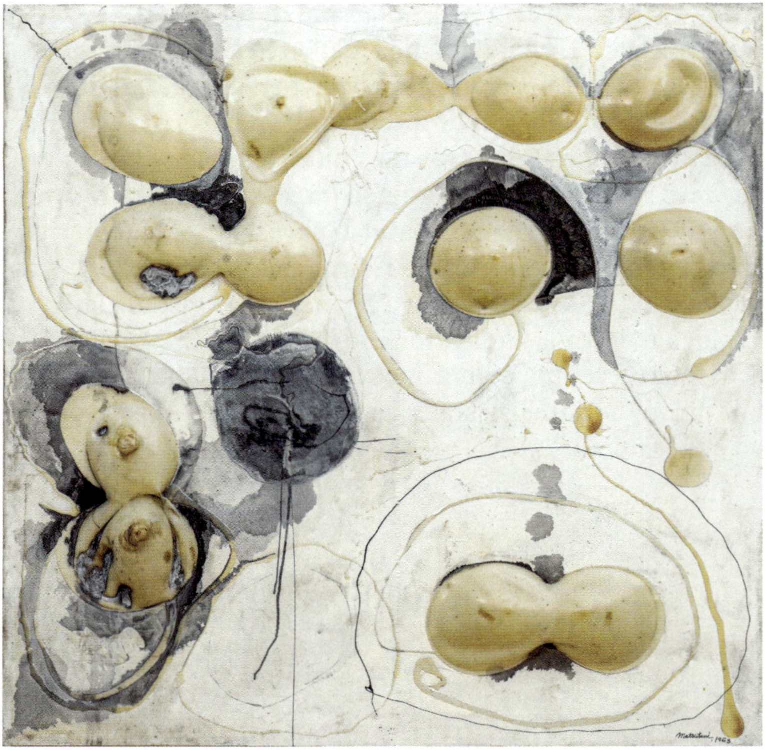

Work 63-9, 1963. Vinyl adhesive, oil, and acrylic on canvas, 73⅝ × 75⅝ in. (187 × 192 cm)

Fascinated by the glue's ability to form a translucent, skin-like membrane as it dries, Matsutani found additional ways to exploit its physical properties, such as stretching and inflating it across the canvas by blowing into it through a straw. He was drawn to its stretchy viscosity, which allowed him to pour, layer, and manipulate it in ways that emphasized gesture, chance, and material presence. This radical approach epitomized the Gutai ethos of "do what no one has done before" while foregrounding the unpredictability and autonomy of the medium itself.

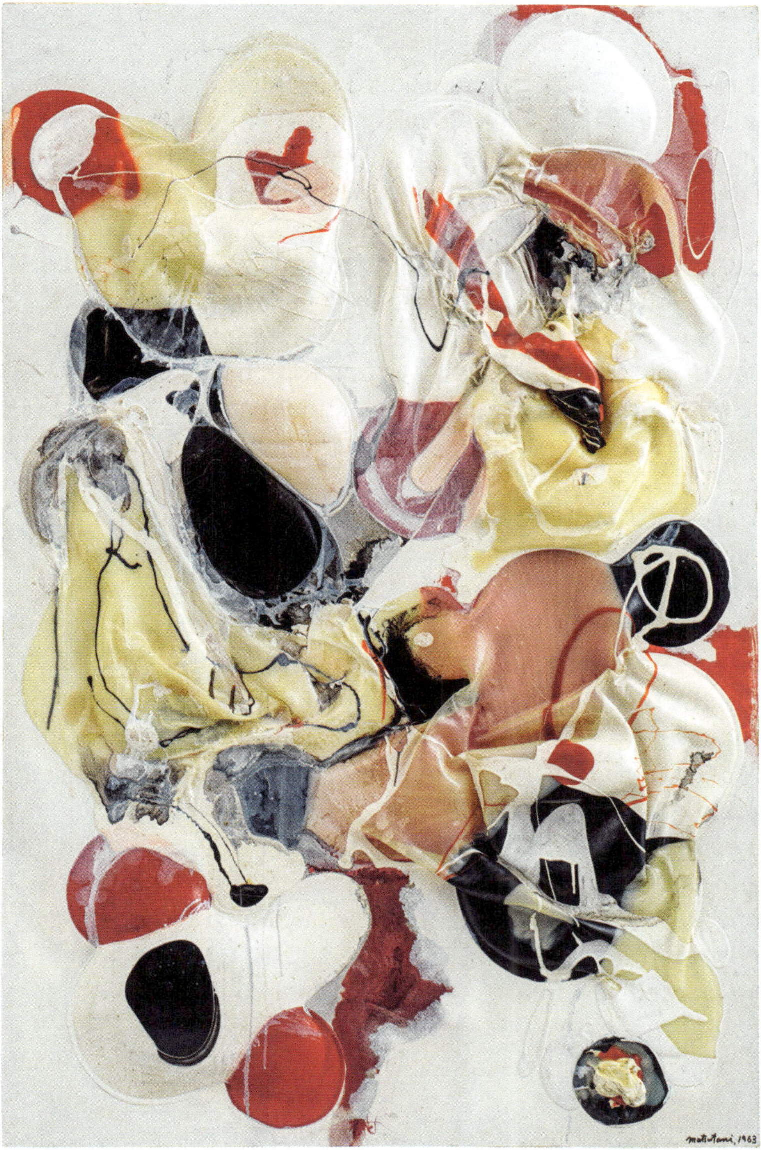

Work-Pile, 1963. Vinyl adhesive, oil, and acrylic on canvas mounted on plywood, $72\frac{1}{4} \times 48\frac{3}{8} \times 4\frac{1}{2}$ in. (183.5 × 123 × 11.5 cm)

Work 63-K (1963)

Work 63-K is one of the earliest examples of Matsutani's exploration of the organic potential of vinyl glue. Inspired by a pivotal experience using a microscope with the help of a friend who was in medical school, Matsutani attempted to re-create the forms of blood cells in glue by carefully pouring liquid adhesive over painted canvas, forming thirty circular pools, each resembling a mochi rice cake. As the emulsion began to dry, he blew air into each circle using a thin straw, creating bubbles. After the glue hardened, he sliced the sacs to reveal the various layers of red, blue, and eggshell white paint beneath.

The palette, with its deep reds, murky blues, and faint yellows, suggests a conscious engagement with gestural abstraction. And yet the repetitive slashes, opening wide in the center and tapering toward the edges, point to a morphological obsession with ruptures and wounds, bulbous sacs, and swollen blisters, while also evoking the sensual realm of human orifices—optical, oral, vaginal, anal. As the artist later explained: "I realized that I had an organic side to my mind, *un peu sensuel*, *un peu érotique*. . . . I discovered myself, by chance, in action." On another occasion, he said, "At the time, a lot of people were repelled. Even now, women often say so. They say it looks like buttocks, or genitals, or the belly of a pregnant woman. I personally feel embarrassed about it, even now. I learned to use words such as 'sensual,' but that was after I had made the works."

Work 63-K was first shown to the public in Matsutani's solo exhibition at the Gutai Pinacotheca in Osaka in October 1963.

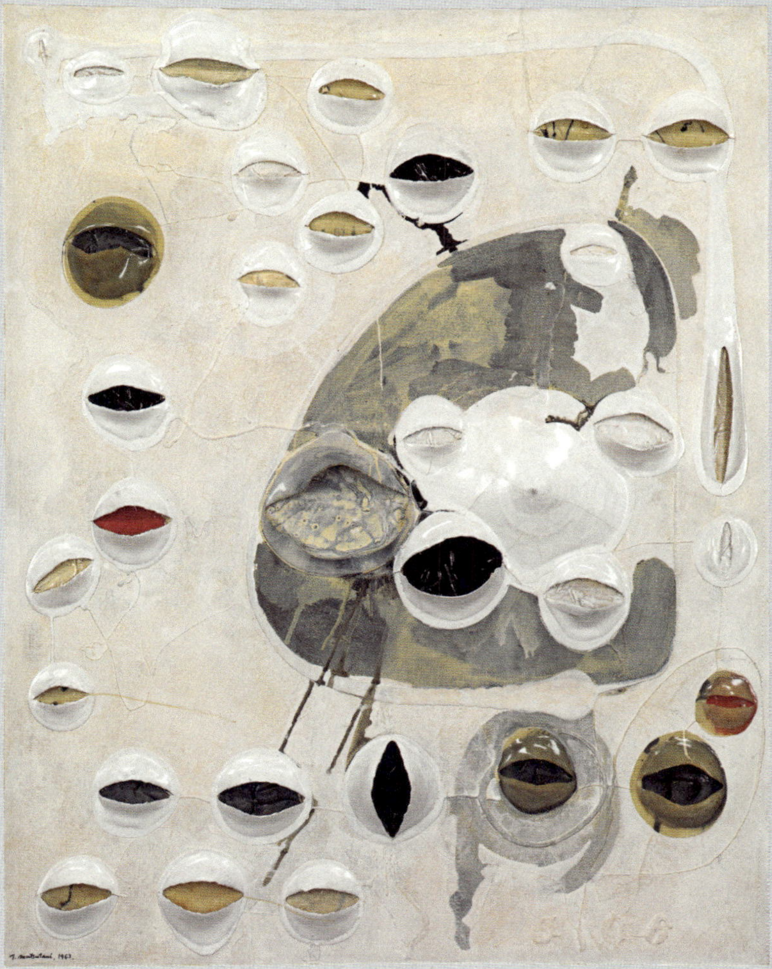

Work 63-K, 1963. Vinyl adhesive, acrylic, and oil on canvas, 64 × 51 3/8 × 3 7/8 in. (162.6 × 130.6 × 10 cm)

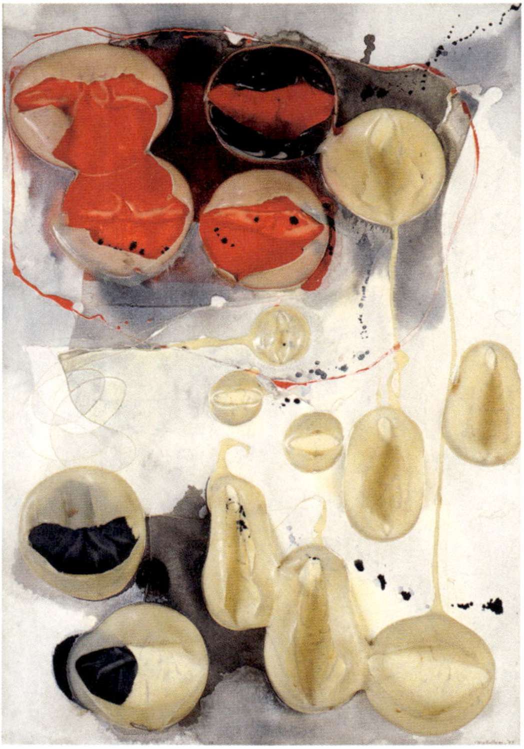

Work 63-A-36, 1963. Vinyl adhesive, oil, and acrylic on canvas mounted on plywood, 51 3/8 × 36 1/8 in. (130.5 × 91.8 cm)

Encouraged by Gutai artists Saburō Murakami and Shūji Mukai, Matsutani gained the courage to show some of the earliest works made with this new technique to Yoshihara, who liked what he saw, saying it was "lively." After further developing this body of work, Matsutani was officially invited to join Gutai in 1963, when both Yoshihara and Tapié, who had been visiting Japan, praised his innovative use of an unconventional medium. That year Matsutani also had a solo exhibition at the Gutai Pinacotheca, where he showed a series of forty works made using vinyl glue. From that point on, Matsutani would continue to participate in every Gutai group exhibition until the association's dissolution in 1972.

“All of a sudden everything was plastic and plastic seemed wonderful. We loved it. We got rid of anything else.”

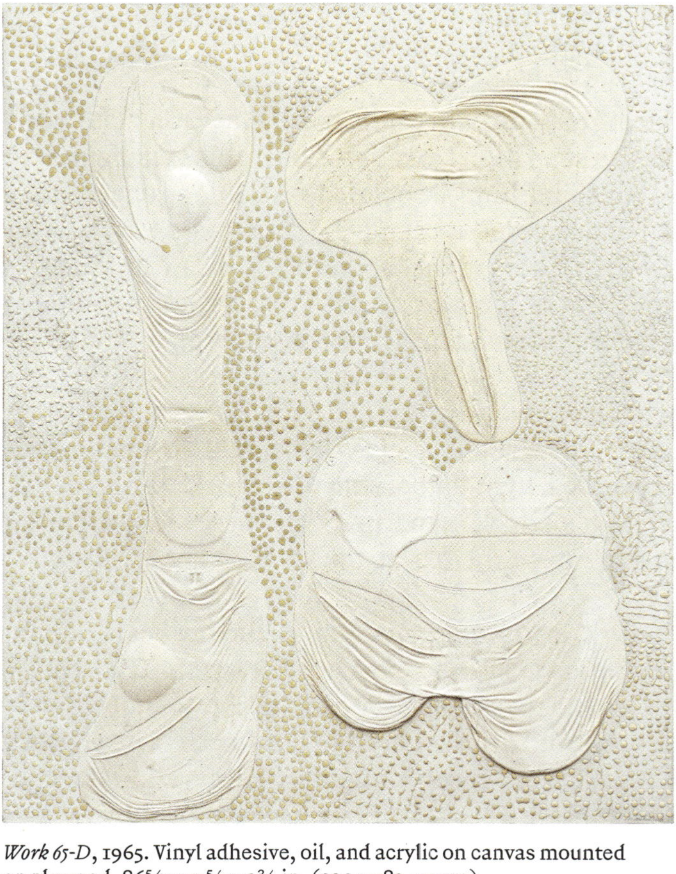

Work 65-D, 1965. Vinyl adhesive, oil, and acrylic on canvas mounted on plywood, 86⅝ × 71⅝ × 2¾ in. (220 × 182 × 7 cm)

Ordinary Things

In 1965, Matsutani made the following statement on the occasion of the Fifteenth Gutai Art Exhibition at the Gutai Pinacotheca in Osaka:

I am often startled or gladdened by the most ordinary things. What sorts of things startle me the most forcefully? Things like gaping holes, dark alleys between buildings, thick-trunked leafless trees on a dark road at night, and long, dark earthen walls.

On the other hand, what things make me feel glad? Unlike the sensation I just described, this is not a fleeting state, but something associated with things I have long sought or desired. For example, I often visit a friend who works with tissues in the laboratory of a cancer ward, and the sight of the various glass vessels, and organs and glands preserved in alcohol, is pleasing to my eye.

Some such things are more common sights: advertising balloons, party balloons, glass balls, vehicle headlights, vacuum tubes, light bulbs, shiny parts of pots and pans, spherical gas tanks. Sometimes when I see these, I feel the urge to touch them or to take a closer look.

In my work, my primary material is vinyl adhesive. I enjoy its flexible viscosity and capacity to expand. The game begins when I pour out the adhesive. The opaque, pure white liquid flows and drips silently, like stalactites in a limestone cave. After a while it settles on the canvas, and when air is blown into it with a straw, it takes on an uncanny tension, swelling at times into a transparent sphere, at other times into something resembling a breast.

These living creatures, whose essence is incomprehensible, cling to the surface, slick and breathing, taking on various guises as the game continues. As vigorous and active as cells or blood vessels, they sometimes break free of the ground and take over the entire space, provoking a pressing desire to lick them all over.

This game no doubt appears utterly ridiculous to those on the outside, but I am completely absorbed in it. In fact, I aim for something even more absurd and pointless. For me, making something new goes beyond brilliant words and ideas. Unless those are brilliantly expressed in the work, words and ideas—and the artist—say and mean nothing. Or so I believe.

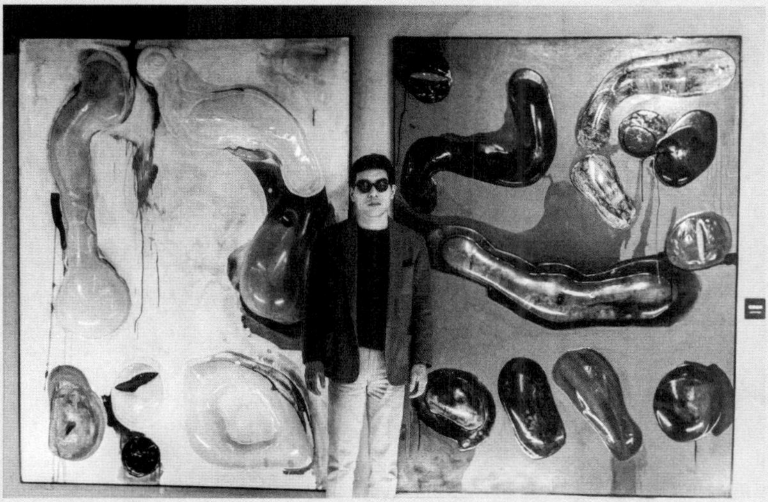

Matsutani with his work at the Fourteenth Gutai Art Exhibition, Takashimaya department store, Osaka, 1964

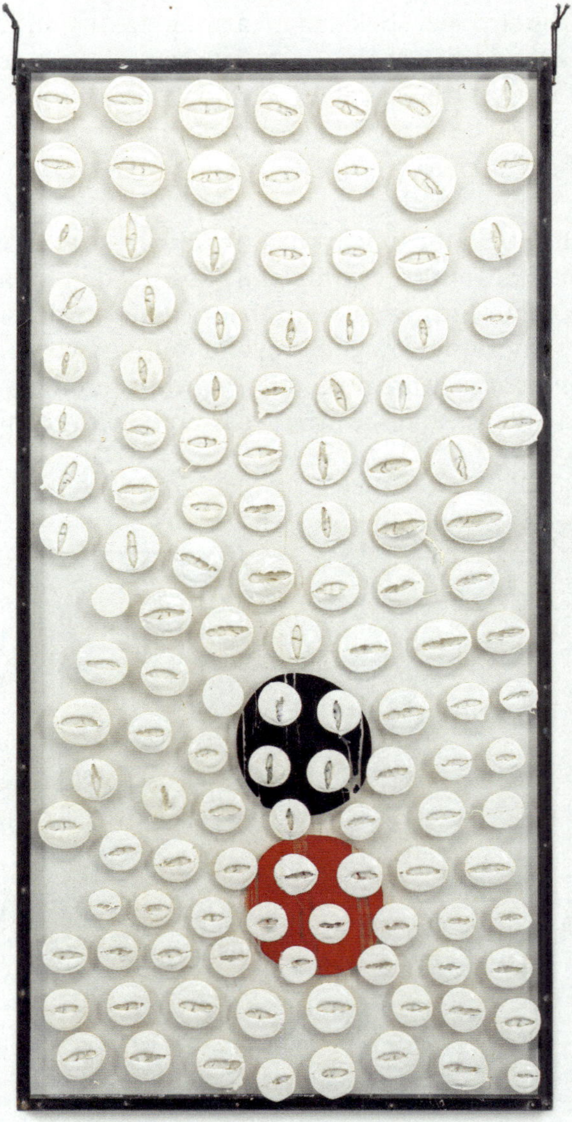

Propagation, 1964. Vinyl adhesive, acrylic, and oil on plexiglass, 78¾ × 39⅜ × 1¾ in. (200 × 100 × 4.5 cm)

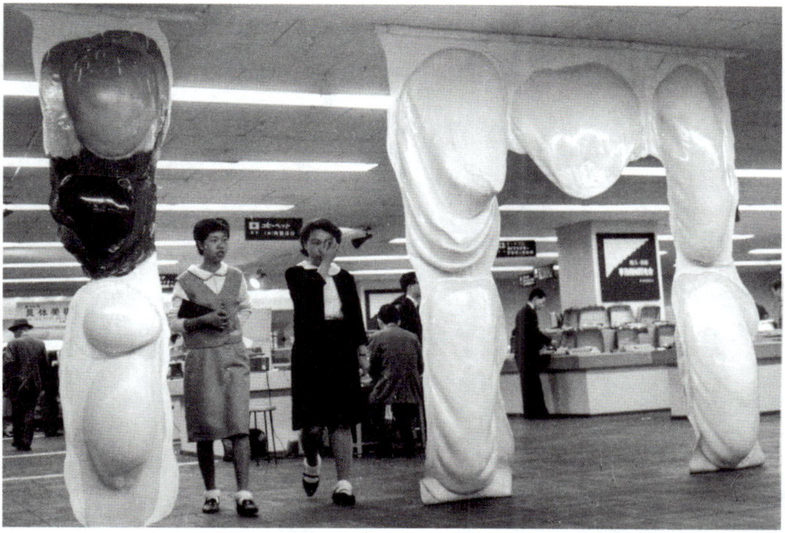

The Fourteenth Gutai Art Exhibition, Takashimaya department store, Osaka, 1964, with Matsutani's *The Gate* on right

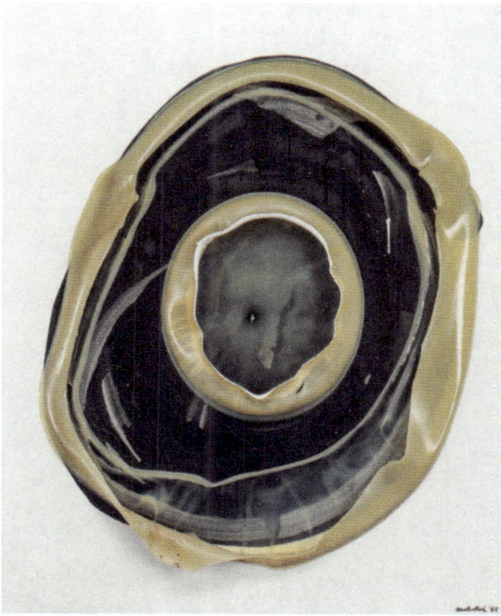

Circle-2, 1965. Vinyl adhesive, acrylic, and oil on canvas mounted on plywood, 43¼ × 36¼ × 2¾ in. (110 × 92 × 7 cm)

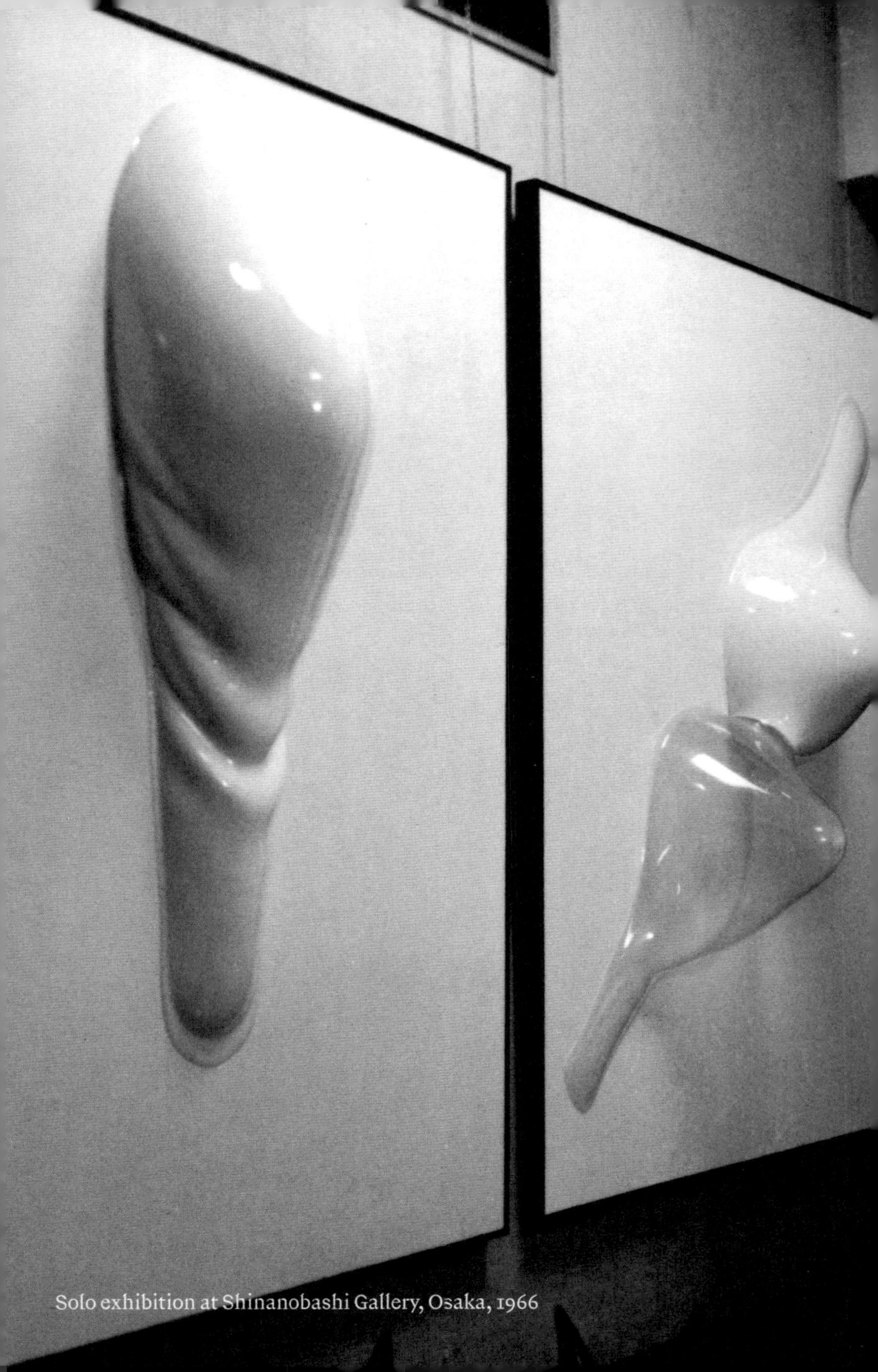

Solo exhibition at Shinanobashi Gallery, Osaka, 1966

The Body and Glue

The fluid, skin-like quality of the vinyl glue that Matsutani began using in the early 1960s, and its hardening, liquid emulsion, proved it a material capable of evoking numerous symbolic and metaphoric associations, from the corporeal and sensual to the fantastic and otherworldly. The transformations that the glue undergoes—dripping, drying, bulging, shrinking—become a metaphor for organic growth, decay, and the ever-shifting boundaries between control and chance.

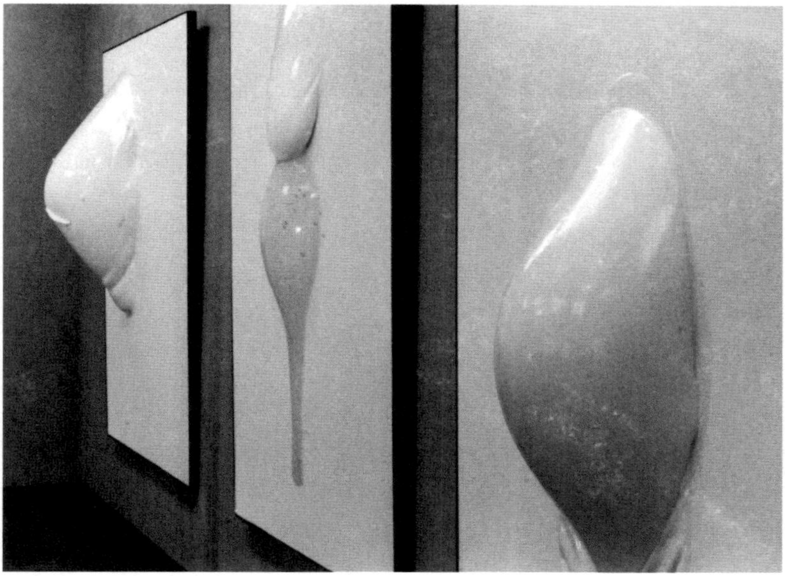

Solo exhibition at Kiyamachi Gallery, Kyoto, 1966

The bulbous forms and glossy surfaces of Matsutani's early works suggest skin, wounds, and body parts, evoking both attraction and discomfort. His process—blowing air into the glue to form protruding blisters, then slicing, pressing,

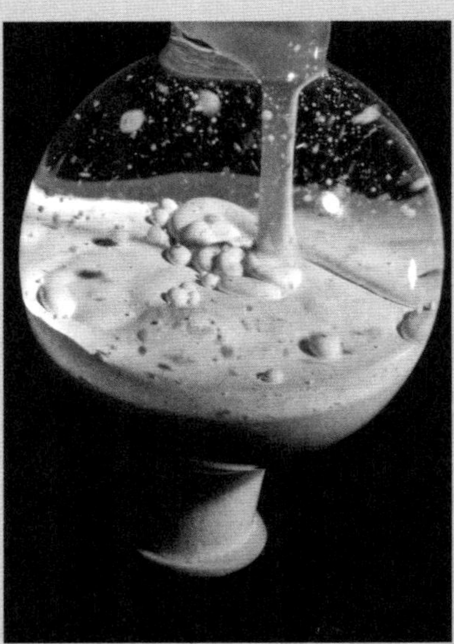 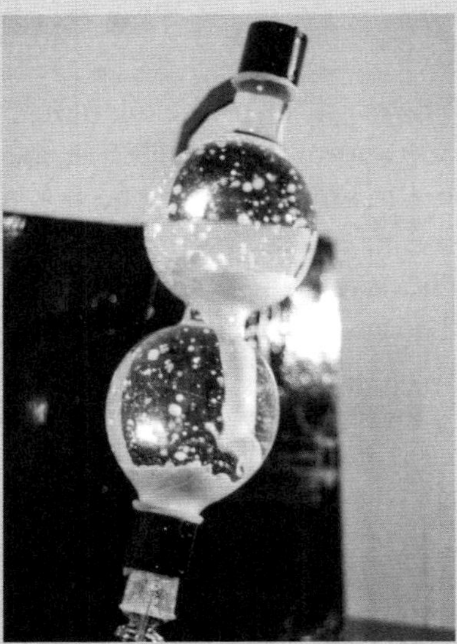

Kaiten (Rotation), 1966. Oil paint, water, glass, and motor, dimensions unknown

Kinetic Art

As he was becoming increasingly known as a Gutai artist, Matsutani created *Kaiten (Rotation)* (1966), a kinetic work that reflected his interest in materiality, transformation, and the dynamic interplay of forms. It consisted of two interconnected glass spheres filled with water, into which he poured white oil-based house paint. A motorized mechanism gently rotated the containers, causing the paint within to rise and fall in an ever-changing circular movement. This now lost experimental work exemplifies Matsutani's exploration of physical phenomena—gravity, motion, suspension—and his engagement with Gutai's broader ethos of activating matter through direct, performative interaction. The result was a living system of visual and sensory engagement, where the boundary between painting and sculpture dissolved into a space of continual becoming.

or binding them—creates a compelling analogue for organic processes: birth, healing, scarring, and transformation.

In this context, the body serves as both subject and tool. Matsutani's own physical actions, his breath, and the weight of his hands are inscribed into the work, making each piece an index of lived experience and embodied energy. The viewer, too, is implicated—drawn in by the visceral tactility and palpable tension of the surface. To explain his process, he again turned to the idea of the "inner image" (p. 109).

Matsutani's work maintains Gutai's tenet of activating materials on equal terms with the human spirit while simultaneously transforming the utilitarian character of the glue, pushing it into an evocative and animistic space defined by gravity and rupture. Matsutani wrestled with Gutai's early painting principles, which reflected a denial of the literary, the figurative, and the symbolic, emphasizing the embodiment of material as "a 'work' of nature itself." Unlike the iconic actions and events executed by his elder colleagues, Matsutani's process was slow and deliberate, which proved crucial to how his materials revealed their transformative nature.

Both in his earlier, smaller works and in his later large-scale works that focus entirely on gravity's pull on the vinyl glue as it stabilizes mid-drip, the fluid emulsion and skin-like membrane of the adhesive share a kinship with the sensuous, glistening, gigantic tubes filled with colored water in his mentor Motonaga's *Work (Water)* (1956; p. 30).

具体美術協会会員
アートクラブ会員
松 谷 武 判 個 人 展

1965. 12. 2 → 12. 15
AM. 10→PM. 6（木曜休）
神　戸　画　廊
神戸元町2角 (33) 8877

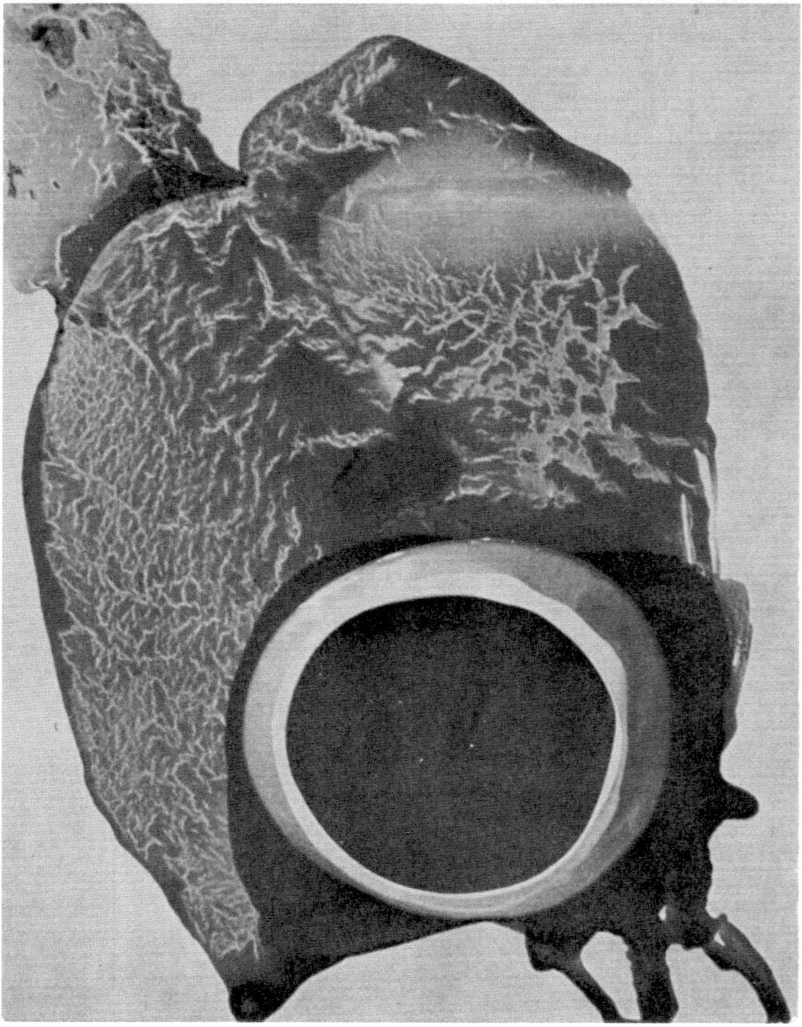

Invitation card for Matsutani's solo show at the Kobe Gallery, Kobe, 1965

Un Parisien Japonais

In 1966, Matsutani participated in the First Mainichi Art Competition, co-organized by the Kyoto branch of the Institut Français and *Mainichi Shimbun*, one of Japan's major newspapers. Matsutani submitted *White Circle/Object 6-B* and *Work 66-2* (both 1966; pp. 54, 55) and received the grand prize—a grant from the French government to live and work for six months in Paris. Both paintings reflect Matsutani's signature process of working with vinyl glue in a way that combines breath and erasure. A work on canvas made using a similar technique, likewise featuring the carefully cut outline of a vinyl glue circle, had been reproduced in black and white on the invitation card for the artist's 1965 solo exhibition at Kobe Gallery.

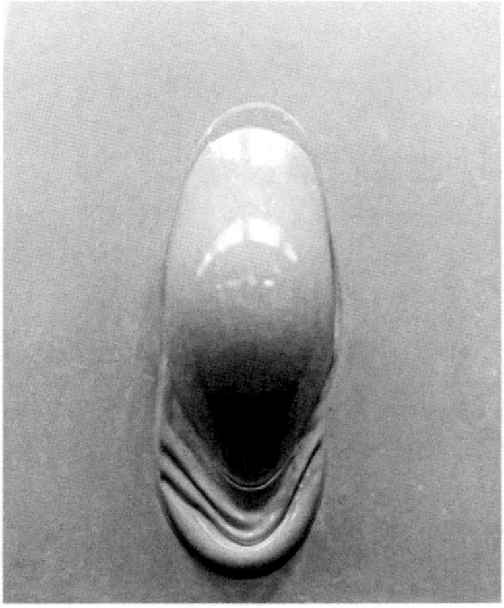

Work 6-P, 1966, as originally exhibited

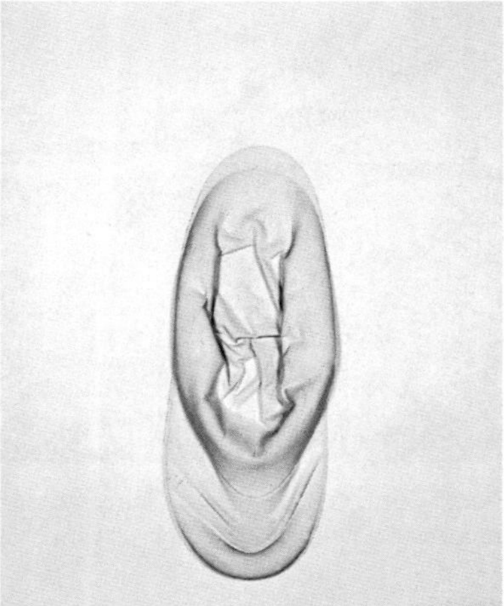

Work 6-P, 1966, after the air was released

White Circle/Object 6-B and *Work 66-2* are composed around circular forms made up of the translucent residue of a glue bubble that seems to have been popped and cut

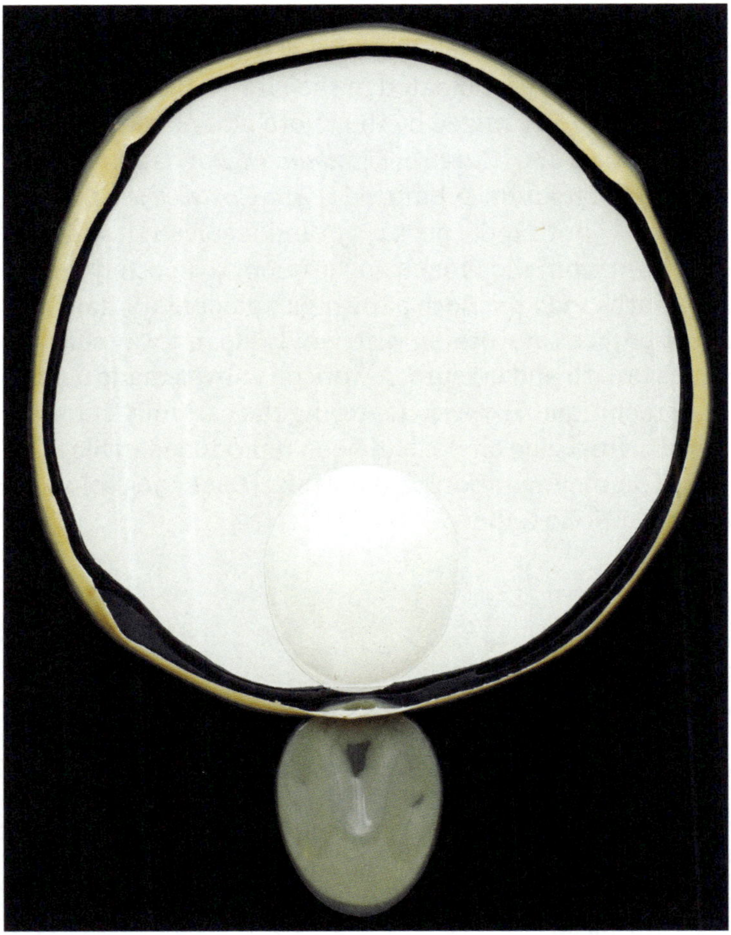

White Circle/Object 6-B, 1966. Vinyl adhesive, oil, and acrylic on canvas mounted on plywood, 63⅞ × 51⅛ × 4⅛ in. (162.3 × 129.9 × 10.5 cm)

along the edges. In contrast to the former, whose tension arises, in part, from the interplay of inside and outside, the latter features a large lightbulb-shaped bubble that drips down the center of the dominant black oval. This "teardrop" bubble has captured the artist's breath while

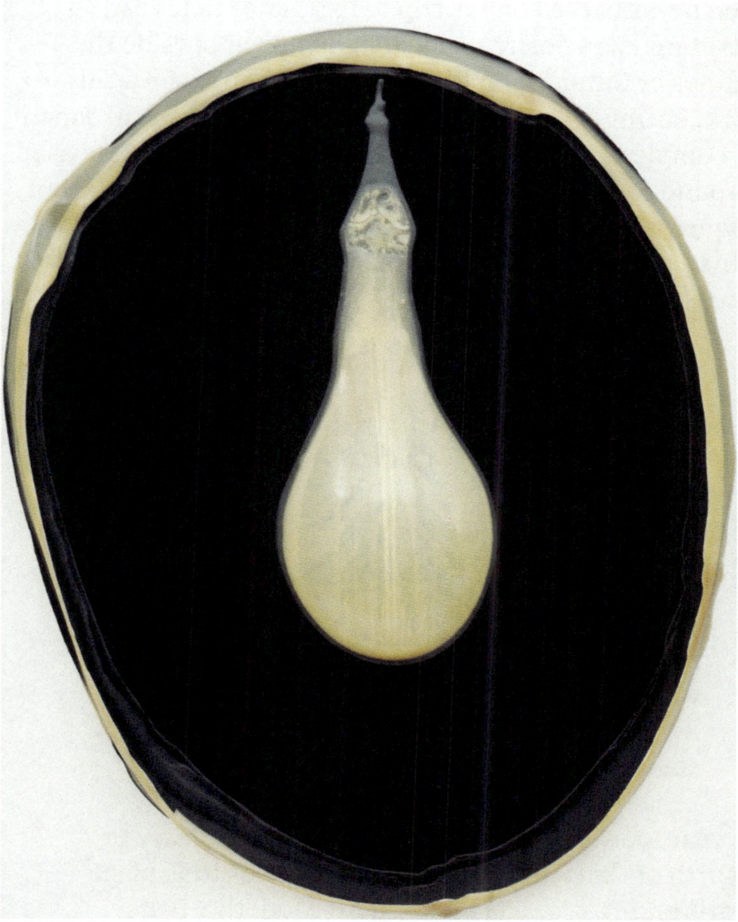

Work 66-2, 1966. Vinyl adhesive, oil, and acrylic on canvas mounted on plywood, 63¾ × 51⅛ × 4¾ in. (161.8 × 129.8 × 12.2 cm)

the larger bubble that contains it indexes a breath that has since disappeared into thin air. These two spatiotemporal moments exist simultaneously in the piece, and the materiality of the glue itself leaves one with the impression of a kinetic energy that has been frozen in time.

When he embarked on his trip to Paris later that year, Matsutani felt a desire to challenge himself outside the confines of Gutai. Upon his arrival he experienced a culture shock, noting, "The Europe I had in my mind back in Japan was completely different to what I . . . experienced." He used this period to explore the origins of European culture, from antiquity to the Renaissance, and sought to visit landmark art historical sites, traveling to Luxor in Egypt as well as to Greece and Italy.

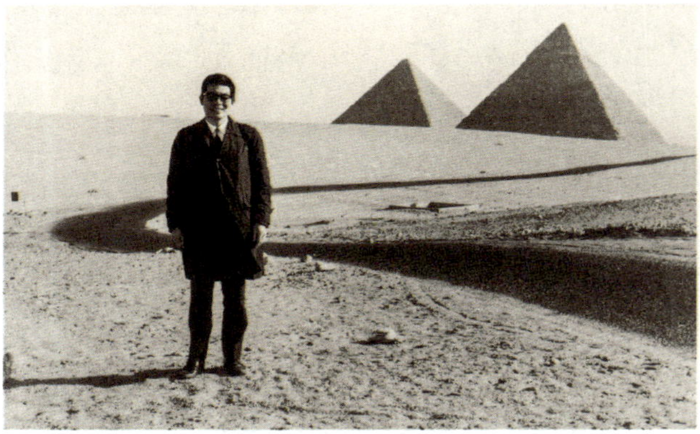

Matsutani in Egypt, December 24, 1966

The year 1966 also marked the fiftieth anniversary of the birth of Dada, and major retrospectives took place in Paris and Tokyo. The Musée d'Art Moderne, Paris, presented *Dada: 50 ans après* (Dada: 50 Years After), framing the movement as a foundational chapter in European modernism that paved the way for Surrealism, Abstract Expressionism, and the postwar neo-avant-gardes. This show had a profound impact on Matsutani, making him feel as if every radical idea had already been accomplished. Interestingly, *Dada 1916–1966*, which Matsutani did not see, took place the same year at the National Museum of Modern

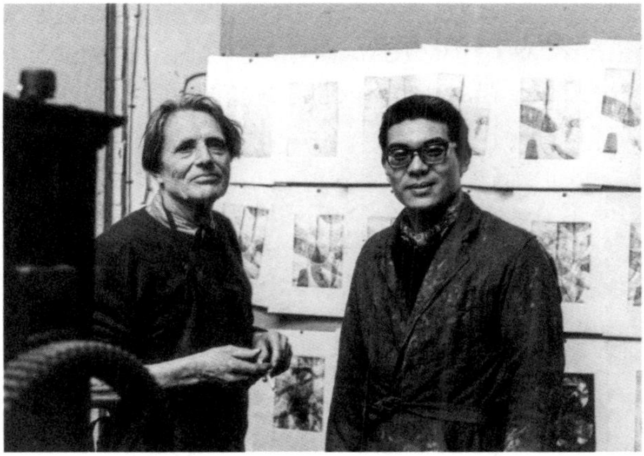

Matsutani and Stanley William Hayter at Atelier 17, Paris, 1967

Art, Tokyo, and introduced the movement not as a historical fait accompli but as a living model of experimentation, encouraging postwar Japanese avant-garde artists to see their own radical practices as part of a global lineage.

Having prioritized learning French and traveling, Matsutani began to feel a renewed desire to make art. He recalled reading about Atelier 17, the renowned printmaking studio directed by Stanley William Hayter, whose abstract prints with vibrant kinetic lines and organic shapes he had first encountered in Osaka in the 1960s. Hayter had worked at an oil company but wanted to be a painter, so he had moved from London to Paris and, in 1926, opened a studio near Alberto Giacometti's atelier in Montparnasse. In 1967, Hayter invited Matsutani to be his studio assistant, attending Atelier 17 during the day while continuing his language studies in the evenings. Another Japanese artist, Kenji Yoshida, was also working at Hayter's studio, and Matsutani learned etching and zinc-plating techniques from him. Matsutani also met his future wife,

Kate Van Houten, an American artist who became a central inspiration for his shift to printmaking and his later turn to graphite. They married in 1976 and continue to live in Paris to this day.

In his time at Atelier 17, Matsutani began to redeploy the forms he made with vinyl glue onto flat copper plates, as etchings. Depicting round organic forms reminiscent of cell structures, these works—like some of his vinyl adhesive canvases of the early 1960s—were given the title *Propagation*. As Matsutani studied aquatint and burin engraving techniques at Hayter's studio, his thinking and his practice were deepened and refined by his experiences and observations, as well as by engagement with Hayter's spatial theories. For Hayter, the human perception of space is inherently linked to motion, and in art, the movement of line allows for the depiction of space to be infused with time—effectively creating a form of "four-dimensional" space. In a way that proleptically resonates with Matsutani's future work, spatial expression was understood to encompass temporal dimensions through the dynamic flow of line.

One of the works of this time, *La propagation-noire* (Propagation-Black, 1967) evokes the origins of human life: Negative and positive shapes bring to mind black sperm entering the lining of an elongated, abstracted egg cell. The sliced vinyl forms of his preceding body of work here become diagrammatic in a series of square outlines that gradually get smaller toward the left edge, anticipating the perspectival illusionism that would become more pronounced in a subsequent series of monumental acrylic on canvas works (p. 73). *La propagation-noire* is also an early example of Matsutani's experiments with variations of black. The printer's ink is "very heavily pressed, and strong," he once noted, with reference to this body of work. "It is sharper than black that is painted. The black color impressed me." In particular, the deep impressions of the black engraved lines in these copperplate prints allowed him to experiment with spatial depth and movement in ways he previously could not in the realm of painting. In some etchings from this period, he used aquatint to create metallic purples and yellows reminiscent of the rainbow sheen of an oil spill on water.

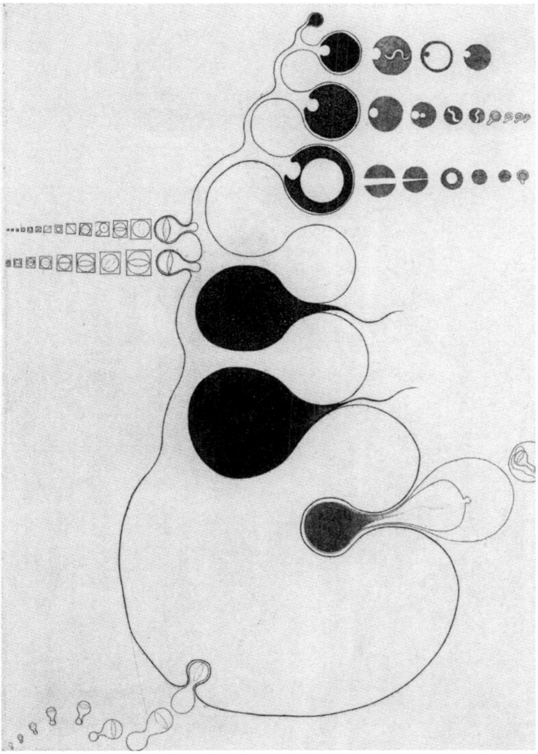

La propagation-noire (Propagation-Black), 1967. Aquatint and burin on BFK paper, 17¼ × 12½ in. (43.8 × 31.8 cm)

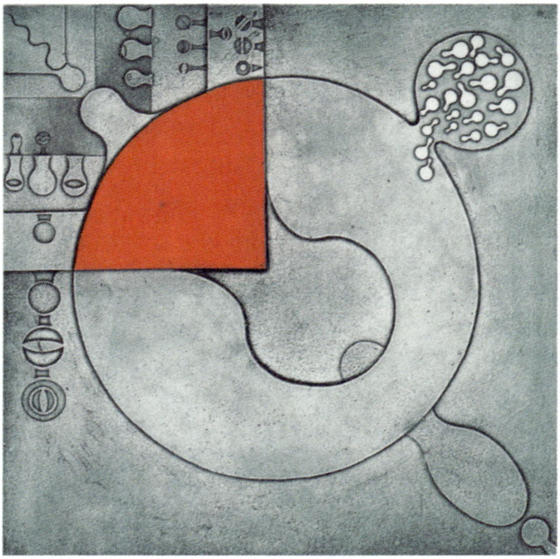

La propagation-10, 1967.
Etching on BFK paper,
$25^{3}/_{8} \times 19^{1}/_{2}$ in.
(64.5×49.5 cm)

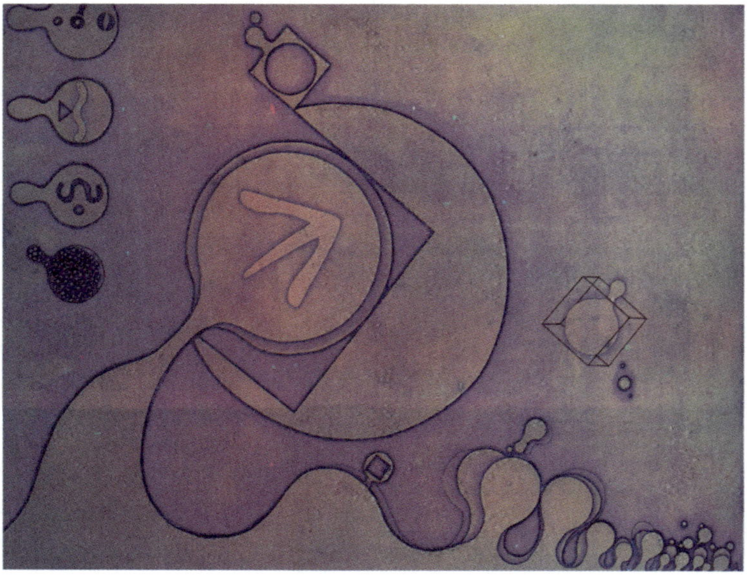

La propagation-15, 1967. Etching, aquatint, and burin on BFK paper,
$11^{3}/_{4} \times 15^{3}/_{8}$ in. (29.7×39.1 cm)

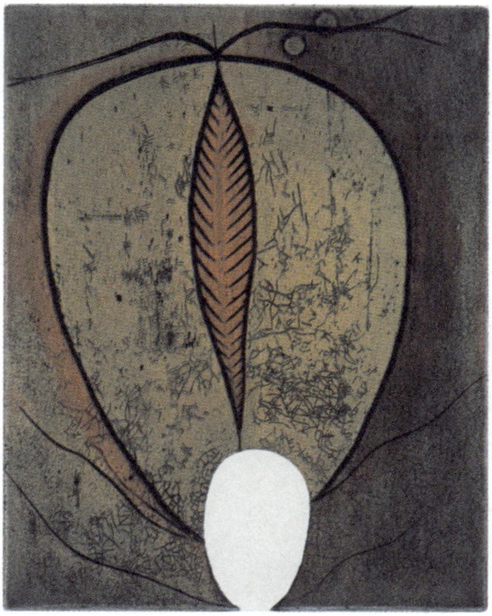

La propagation-50, 1967. Etching, burin, and stencil on BFK paper, 9⅝ × 7¾ in. (24.4 × 19.8 cm)

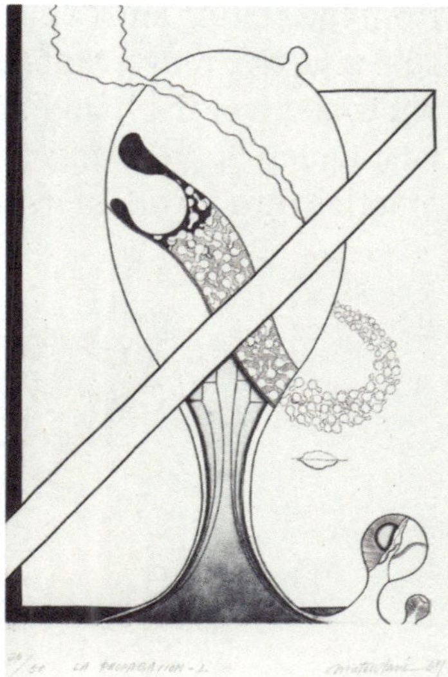

La propagation-L, 1967. Burin and aquatint on BFK paper, 13⅜ × 9¾ in. (33.9 × 24.7 cm)

For Matsutani's breakthrough exhibition in 1968, with painter Mittsu Sugai at Galerie Zunini in Montparnasse, he showed both works on canvas and vinyl glue objects, each in different ways bringing into play the chance accidents and oozing gravitational pull of his signature medium. After a brief hiatus from the vinyl glue works, Matsutani had resumed making them, using vinyl glue shipped by sea from Japan. The assemblages he presented at Galerie Zunini picked up on the column of vertical baubles and the *torii* gate structure made out of vinyl glue he placed at the entrance to the Fourteenth Gutai Art exhibition in 1964 (p. 47). The new works were more refined in technique than their more raw, ovular, and sagging precursors, however. One of them was a large column of almost spherical vinyl bubbles, which were suspended from the ceiling and could be seen from the street. In a self-reflexive move, Matsutani also used an installation photograph of the hanging sculpture to make a blue-hued zincograph (p. 76), thus turning the documentation of his practice into a work in its own right.

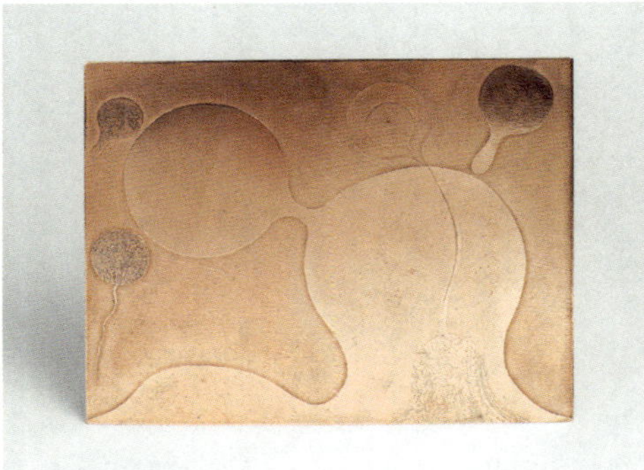

Copperplate for *La propagation-5*, 1967

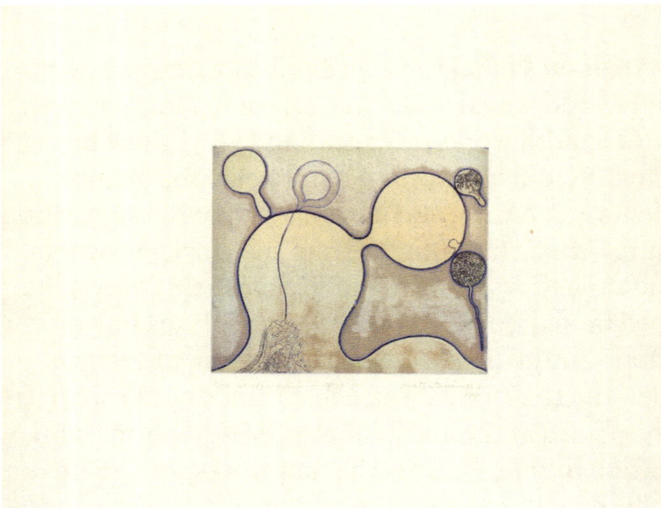

La propagation-5, 1967. Etching and burin on BFK paper, 8½ × 10½ in. (21.6 × 26.7 cm)

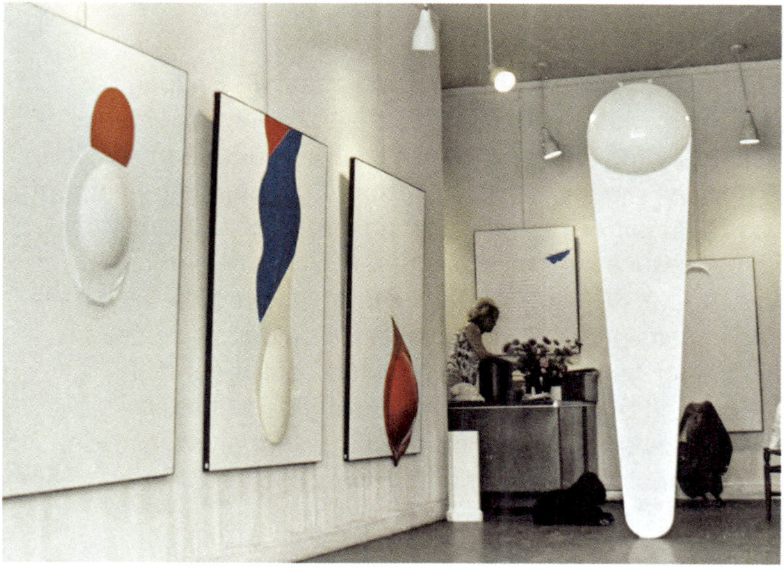

Installation view of the two-person show *Matsutani/Mittsu*, Galerie Zunini, Paris, 1968

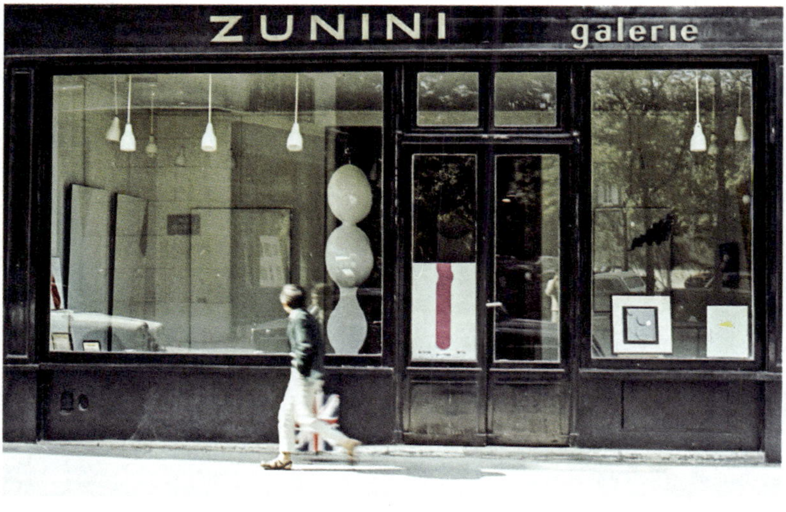

Galerie Zunini, Paris, 1968

Influences

Matsutani's development as an artist was shaped by his engagement with multiple trajectories of postwar art, including Japan's postwar reexamination of tradition, American modernist abstraction, European engagements with biomorphism, and the transnational exchange of ideas fostered in Paris. Alongside the major influence of Gutai (p. 30) and its charismatic leader Jirō Yoshihara, the figures presented in the following pages represent a broader network of aesthetic and philosophical influences through which Matsutani developed his distinctive synthesis of materiality, spatial awareness, and embodied expression.

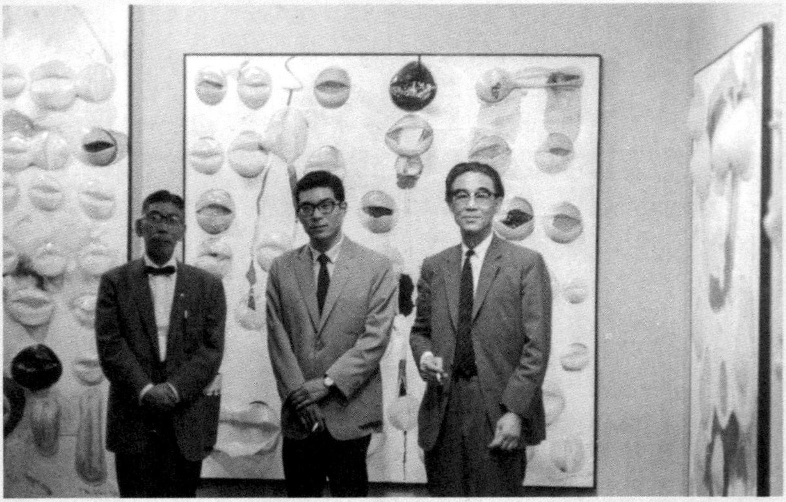

Matsutani with his father (left) and Gutai founder Jirō Yoshihara (right) at the Gutai Pinacotheca, Osaka, October 1963

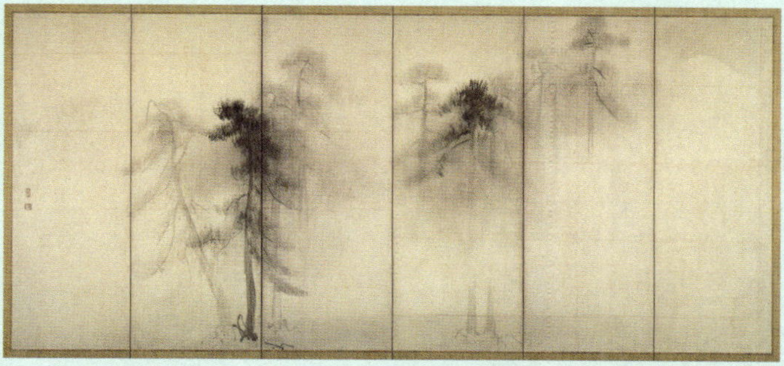

One of the two screens making up Tōhaku Hasegawa's *Pine Trees*, ca. 1580

Tōhaku Hasegawa (1539–1610)

Matsutani absorbed and reinterpreted the qualities of emptiness, atmosphere, and restraint from the sixteenth-century master Tōhaku Hasegawa, whom he considers the artist with the greatest influence on his work. He keeps a reproduction of Hasegawa's legendary *Pine Trees* (ca. 1580), a pair of six-panel folding screens, next to his desk. Hasegawa deftly depicts pine trees swaying in and out of space, with vast areas of blank space (*ma*) evoking mist, depth, and the unseen. Matsutani found in this a model for how *yohaku* (empty space and its balance to filled space) itself could carry expressive weight. In his own works—especially the graphite on paper works and many of his larger canvases—he embraces expanses of unmarked surface, setting them against dense areas composed of labor-intensive marks or glue forms. Hasegawa's balancing of fullness and void offered Matsutani a historical model for using empty space as an active, expressive element. Filtered through his postwar encounter with Gutai, Western abstraction, and Zen thought, this principle echoes throughout Matsutani's oeuvre, creating a dialogue between presence and absence that resonates across centuries.

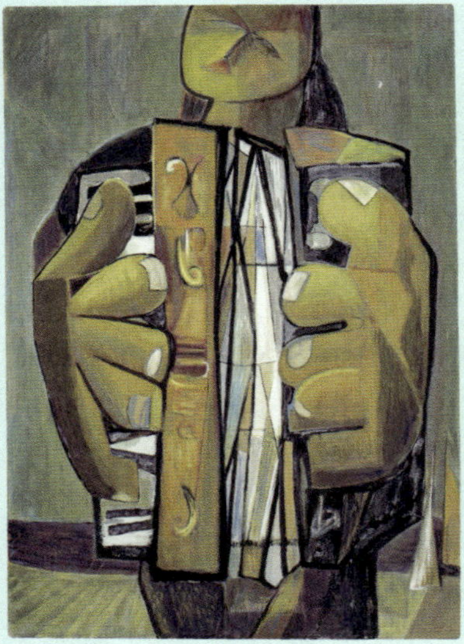

Shōsaku Arao, *Crépuscule (Dusk)*, 1955. Oil on canvas, 35¾ × 25⅝ in. (90.7 × 65 cm)

Shōsaku Arao (1906–1964)

Trained in nihonga, Shōsaku Arao explored the intersection of figuration and abstraction and often engaged with Western-style subjects. He first encountered Matsutani's work at the Eighth Nishinomiya City Art Exhibition, and invited him to visit his studio. While his works drew from everyday life, Arao's treatment of form and space conveys a psychological and expressive intensity informed by the concept of *shinshō* (inner imagery), which would become a guiding principle in Matsutani's own practice. Their meetings soon became a regular, almost weekly, occurrence. Without their relationship ever being formally that of teacher and student, Matsutani regularly sought out Arao's insight into contemporary art movements and aesthetic theory, using their discussions to supplement his self-directed education. After Arao's death in 1964, Matsutani continued his friendship with Arao's son, Jun Arao, a photographer.

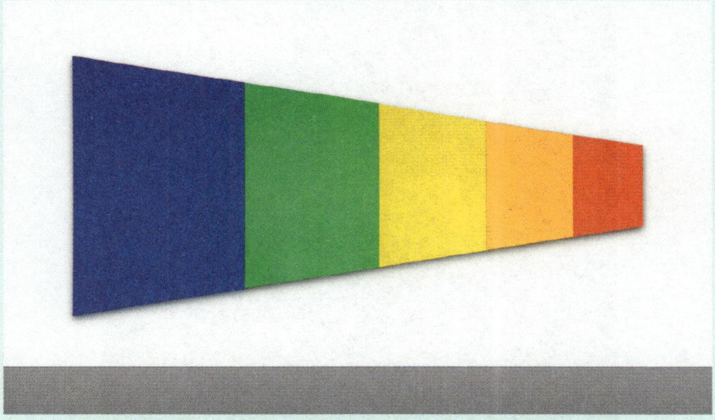

Ellsworth Kelly, *Blue Green Yellow Orange Red (Blue panel)*, 1968.
Oil on canvas, overall 120 × 272 in. (304.8 × 690.9 cm)

Ellsworth Kelly (1923–2015)

After serving in a special camouflage unit of the US Army in World War II in France, Ellsworth Kelly lived in Paris from 1948 to 1954, where he became an abstract artist after absorbing modernist works by Henri Matisse, Pablo Picasso, and Jean (Hans) Arp. His observations of shadows and buildings drew him to Romanesque and Byzantine art and architecture, which he appreciated for their anonymous craftsmanship, emphasis on space and monumental scale, and use of simple, powerful forms. By eliminating the artist's subjective decisions through chance and impersonal abstraction, Kelly aimed to produce pure, objective objects. Back home in the US, his practice offered an alternative to Abstract Expressionism, paving the way for Minimalism and Color Field painting with a style based on empirical observation, blocks of color, and geometric forms. Critics soon associated him with a nascent movement dubbed "hard-edge painting." Some of his works create illusions of three-dimensionality comparable to those Matsutani also explored (p. 71).

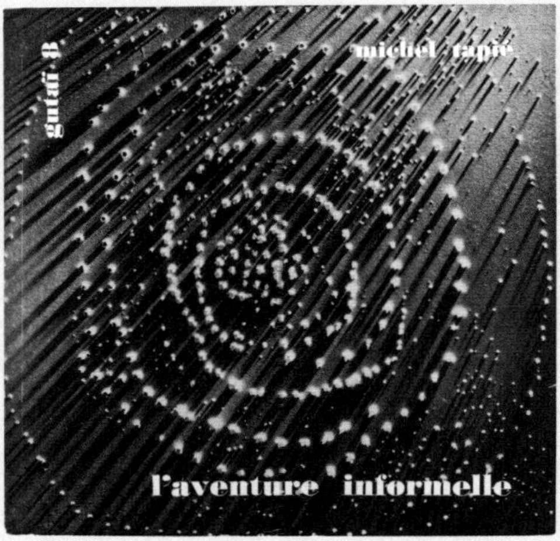

Cover of *Gutai*, no. 8 (1957), special issue "*L'aventure informelle*," edited by Michel Tapié and Jirō Yoshihara, featuring a work by Lucio Fontana

Lucio Fontana (1899–1968)

Matsutani first learned about Lucio Fontana's practice in Japan, where the Italian artist's work was admired by the Gutai group, who once even featured it on the cover of their journal. Matsutani has expressed admiration not only for Fontana's viscerally sliced canvases but also for his large-scale sculptural works and ceramics. In addition to using cuts, the two artists were both interested in puncturing space and playing with air, as in Fontana's *Concetto spaziale* (Spatial Concept, 1952), which was first hung in midair to show rays of light filtering through the holes in the canvas. Fontana's relationship to Matsutani and to Gutai more generally was a striking consequence of an internationalist time when many felt, in the words of painter and sculptor Antoni Tàpies, that "artistic creation addressed the great problems of our times as though in a great common explosion, and no-one thought of borders."

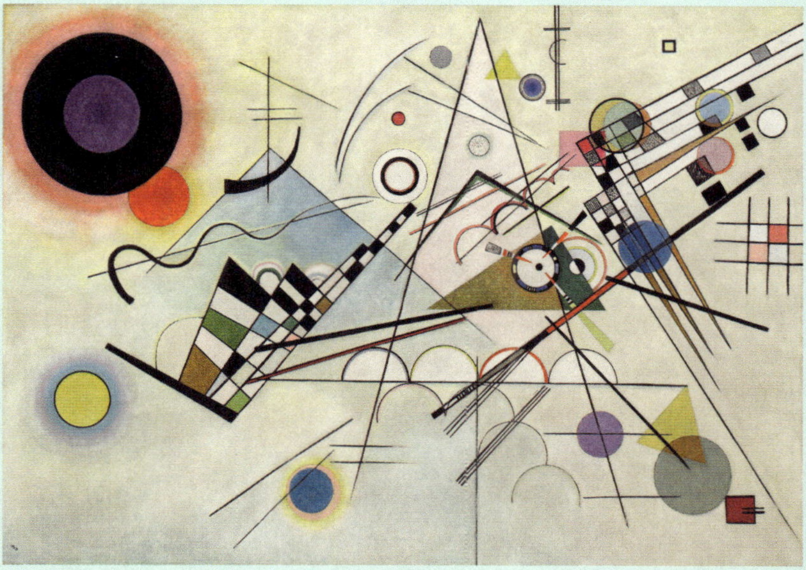

Vasily Kandinsky, *Composition*, 1923. Oil on canvas. $55^{1}/_{8} \times 79^{1}/_{8}$ in. (140 × 201 cm)

Vasily Kandinsky (1866–1944)

Among the many art publications and translated writings from Europe and America that Matsutani absorbed during Japan's cultural reconstruction, Vasily Kandinsky's book *Point and Line to Plane* (1926) became a touchstone for him. It was thanks to Kandinsky that Matsutani came to recognize the constraints of merely replicating the external world and instead turned to inner experience as the true point of departure for his practice. Matsutani's encounter with Kandinsky's abstract paintings—especially their quasi-cellular motifs—catalyzed his own shift toward the vitality of organic life and themes of impermanence and death. Kandinsky's influence can be felt in the preoccupation with biological forms and processes of propagation that would define many of Matsutani's organic and hard-edge works of the mid-1960s.

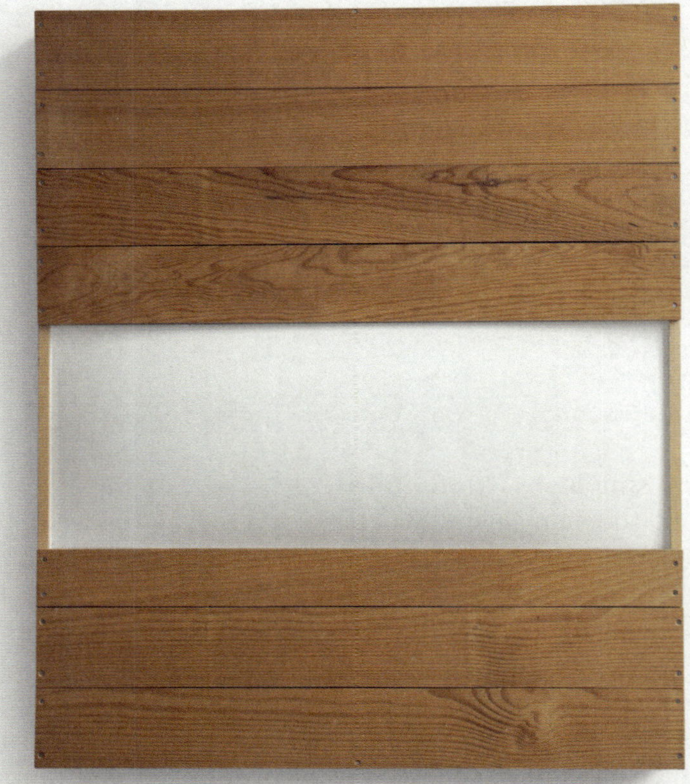

Object Box, 1976. Vinyl adhesive, acrylic, and wood, 52 3/8 × 34 5/8 × 5 7/8 in. (133 × 88 × 15 cm)

From Hard-Edge to "Soft and Hard"

In the late 1960s, Matsutani made another significant breakthrough that was inspired in part by his encounter with Ellsworth Kelly's hard-edge abstraction and use of pure, geometrically shaped color fields (p. 67). Kelly's clarity of form and economy of means encouraged Matsutani to strip away excess and focus on restraint, repetition, and spatial precision in a group of works that stood in decisive contrast to his Gutai-era vinyl glue works and their emphasis on organic materiality and chance. An engagement with Kelly's legacy is above all visible in Matsutani's prints and paintings of this time, where surface and line are pared down to essentials and create spatial illusions between two- and three-dimensionality. Kelly effectively helped Matsutani transition from Gutai's focus on material experimentation toward a disciplined minimalism.

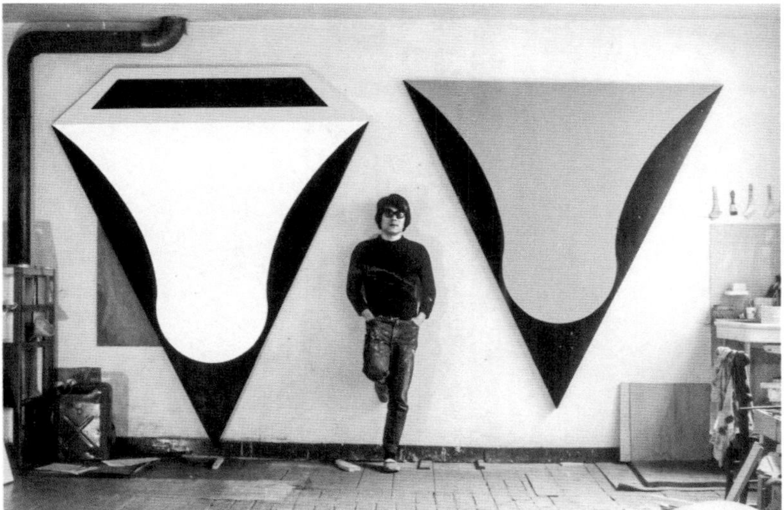

Matsutani between *Work-B* and *Work-D* in his studio, Paris, 1972

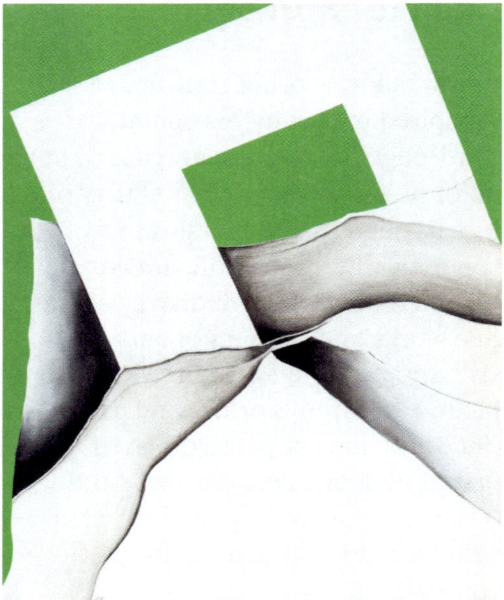

Object-8. P.F, 1975. Acrylic on canvas, 25¼ × 21⅛ × ¾ in. (64.2 × 53.6 × 2 cm)

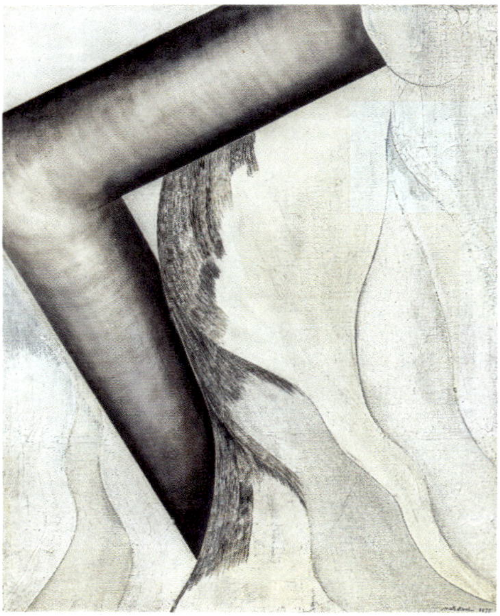

Object P-6, 1975. Acrylic on canvas, 28¼ × 23⅝ × ¾ in. (71.9 × 59.9 × 2 cm)

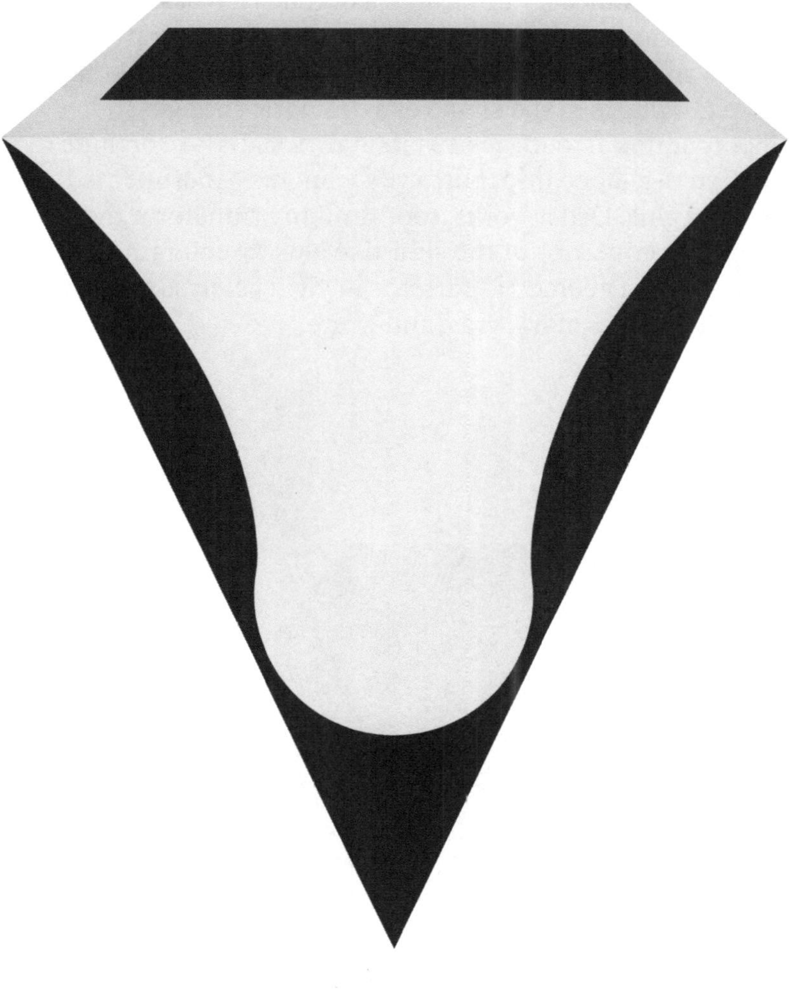

Work-D, 1971. Acrylic on canvas, 78¾ × 94½ in. (200 × 240 cm)

These seemingly divergent tendencies could, however, come together to spectacular effect, not least in a group of monumental acrylic-on-shaped-canvas works from the early 1970s, characterized by precise geometric forms and receding trapezoidal lines. *Work-D* (1972; p. 73), for example, is in the shape of a dramatic triangle and incorporates an outline of Matsutani's signature organic poured U-shaped drip, borrowed from his experiments in vinyl glue. Other works, too, similarly transform the material properties of the skin-like glue by enlarging them into stylized geometric patterns in vivid palettes of crimson, sky blue, ocher, navy, gray, and white.

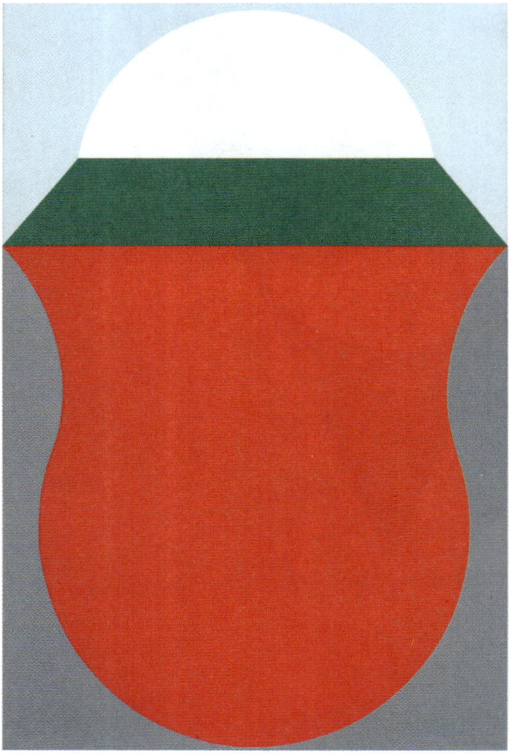

Box of Hope, 1972. Acrylic on canvas, 51¼ × 35⅛ in. (130.2 × 89.3 cm)

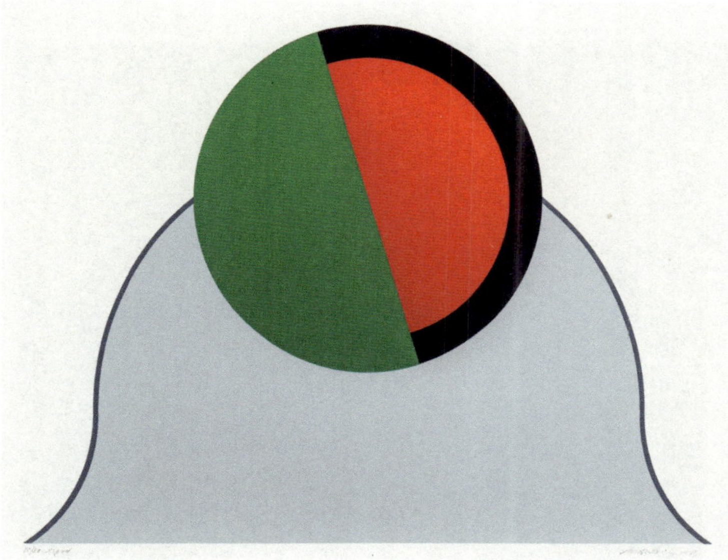

Signal, 1971. Silkscreen on offset paper, 19⅞ × 25½ in. (50.5 × 64.8 cm)

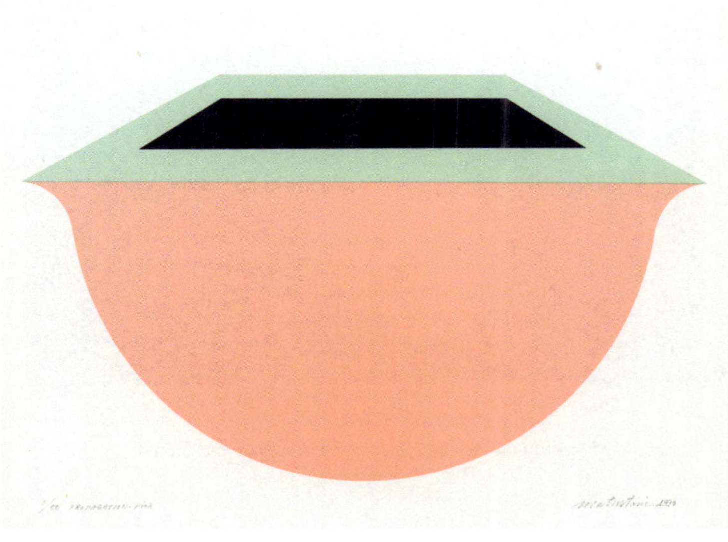

Propagation-Pink, 1970. Silkscreen on offset paper, 22 × 29⅞ in. (56 × 75.8 cm)

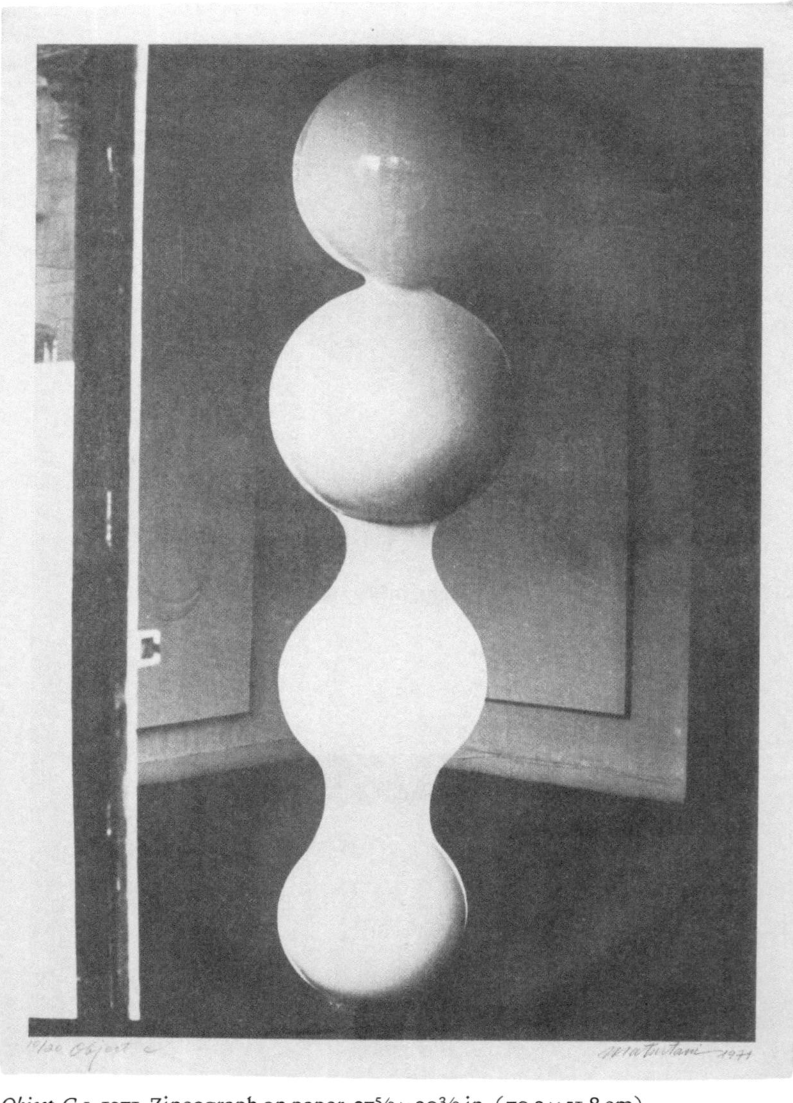

Object-C-1, 1971. Zincograph on paper, 27⅝ × 20⅜ in. (70.2 × 51.8 cm)

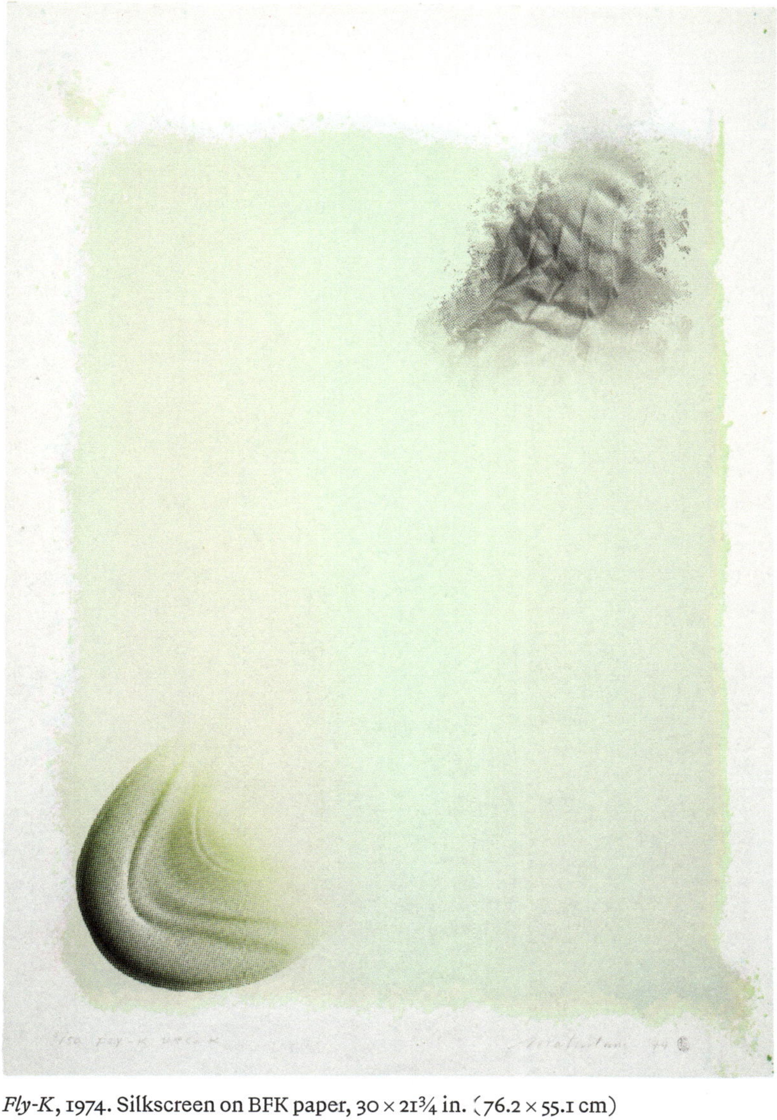

Fly-K, 1974. Silkscreen on BFK paper, 30 × 21¾ in. (76.2 × 55.1 cm)

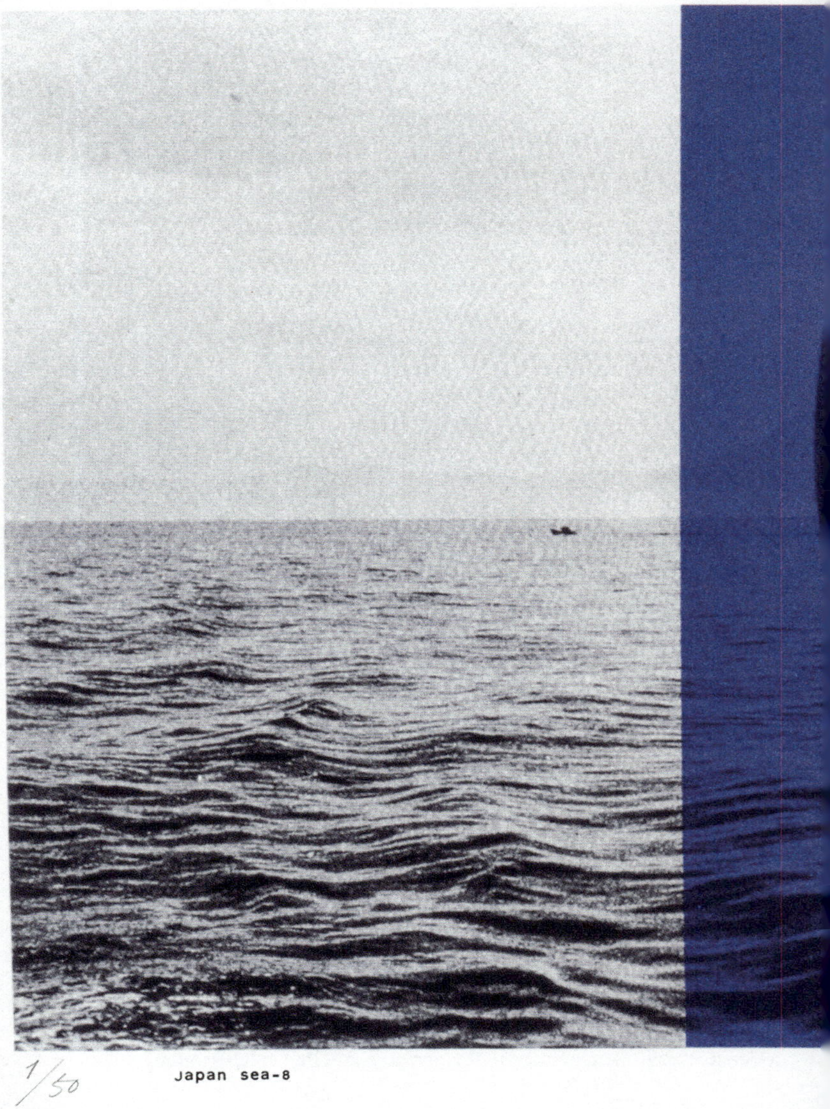

Japan Sea-8, 1978. Silkscreen on paper, 14⅜ × 22¾ in. (36.5 × 57.9 cm)

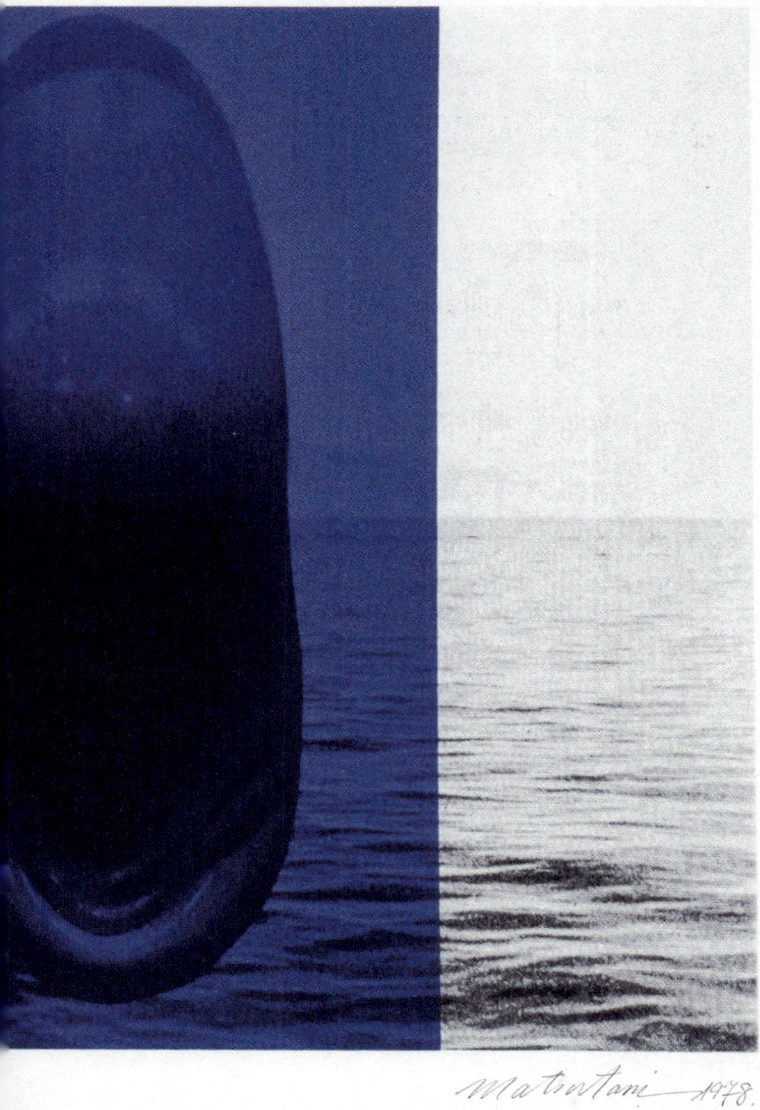
Matsutani 1978.

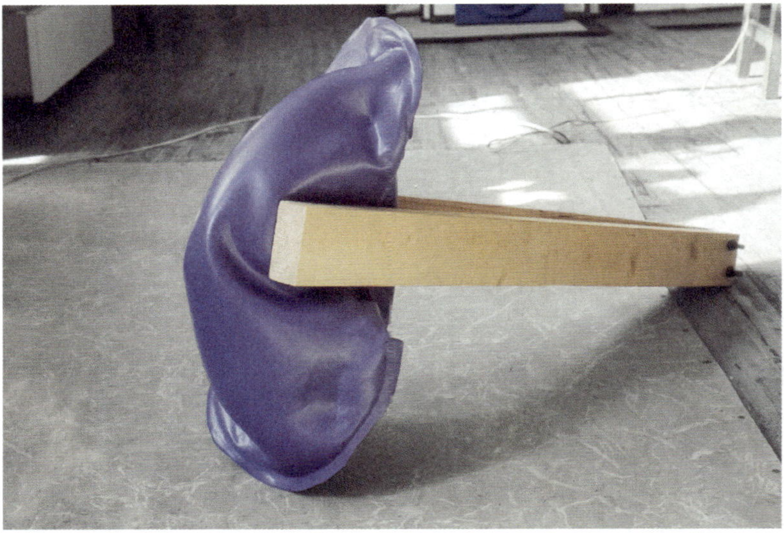

Object-M, 1976. Vinyl adhesive, paint, and wood, 39³⁄8 × 19¾ in. (100 × 50 cm)

From 1970 on Matsutani also began working alongside Van Houten in a new silkscreen studio in Montparnasse. He printed the works of other artists while making his own, which retained elements of hard-edge abstraction while integrating photographic reproductions of vinyl glue reliefs (pp. 75–79). The process he used to generate montaged compositions in photo-silkscreen printing with benday dots represented a deliberate effort to analyze and reengage what he calls his "primal images." Matsutani's silkscreens were exhibited widely in international print festivals throughout the 1970s across Europe, including in an exhibition of graphic art that was a key part of the Venice Biennale in 1972, as well as in Tunisia, Mexico, Hong Kong, and Japan.

Faced with limited financial resources but ample time to think, Matsutani reevaluated his connection to art and the history of Gutai, turning his focus back to the creative process and the expression of an inner image. During this time of great self-reflection, Matsutani was working through a concept he termed “soft and hard,” examining the tension between pliable forms compressed by rigid structures or bound by tight bands. The resulting works were not purely visual: They engage dimensions of touch, pain, and bodily awareness. Although certain motifs carry sadistic overtones, the works are more playful than aggressive. Matsutani grounded his imagery in his own bodily experience, seeking to awaken the full range of human perception. Rather than pouring his emotions into his works, he allowed the material properties to interact and convey sensations that effectively mediate formal relationships into steady, thoughtful expressions that seem to have absorbed both Japanese influences and European intellectual traditions.

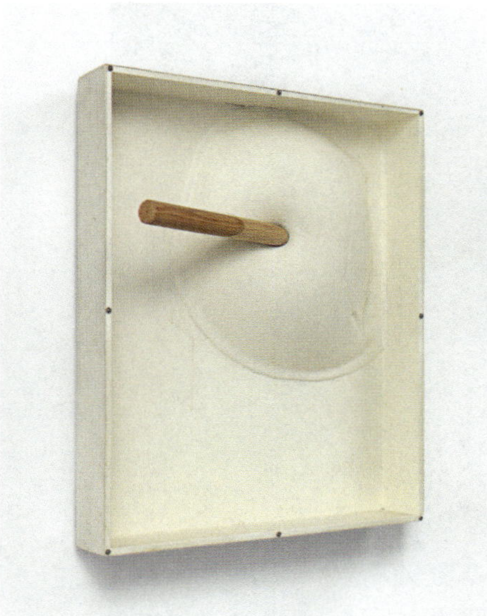

Object-P, 1975. Vinyl adhesive, acrylic, and wood, 27½ × 23⅝ × 7½ in. (70 × 60 × 19 cm)

Objects

In his 1965 artist's statement (p. 44), Matsutani reflected upon how he often gets "startled or gladdened by the most ordinary things." Since early in life, he has always been a close observer of quotidian objects, which he has kept in his studio and transformed into bricolage-like assemblages. Almost representing poetic sketches of his larger practice, his interventions on these objects include attaching vinyl glue bubbles to the covers or inside pages of vintage books, melting vinyl glue over a bundle of wooden pencils like a candle, piercing a stack of burnt paper with a nail, and coiling a thickly twisted jute rope into a metal container.

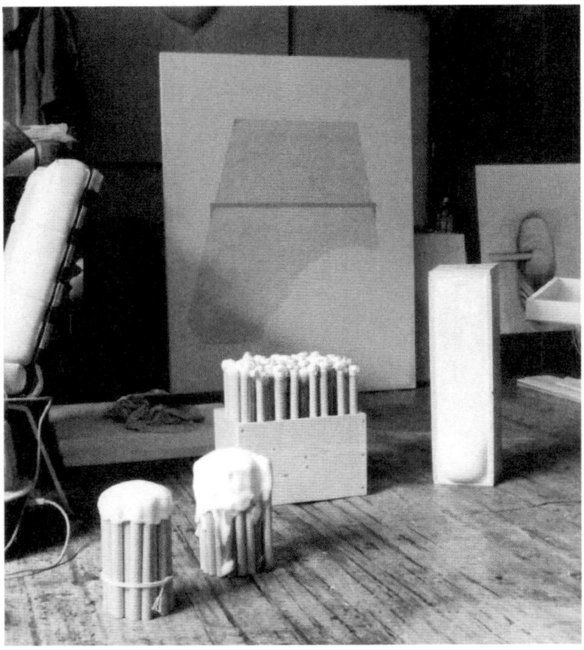

Matsutani's studio, Bastille, Paris, with works from the 1970s

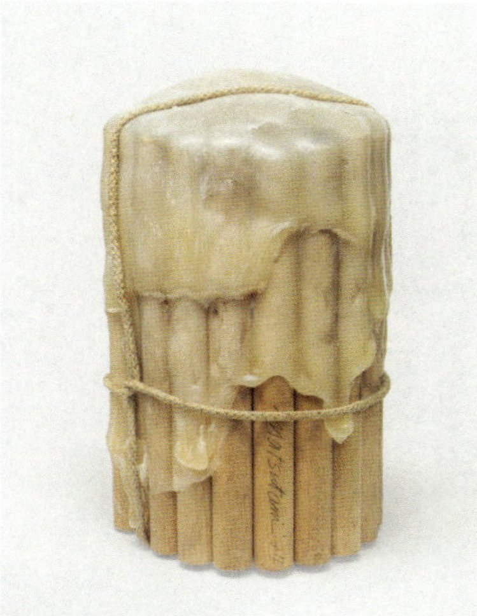

Make a Toy of Object, 1974.
Vinyl adhesive, wood, and cord,
8⅞ × 6¼ × 5½ in. (22.5 × 16 × 14 cm)

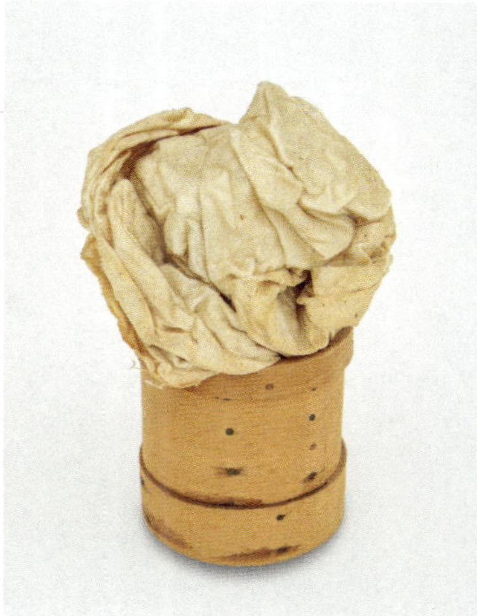

Double Decilitre, 1973. Wood, canvas,
and vinyl adhesive, 5⅞ × 4⅛ × 3⅞ in.
(15 × 10.5 × 10 cm)

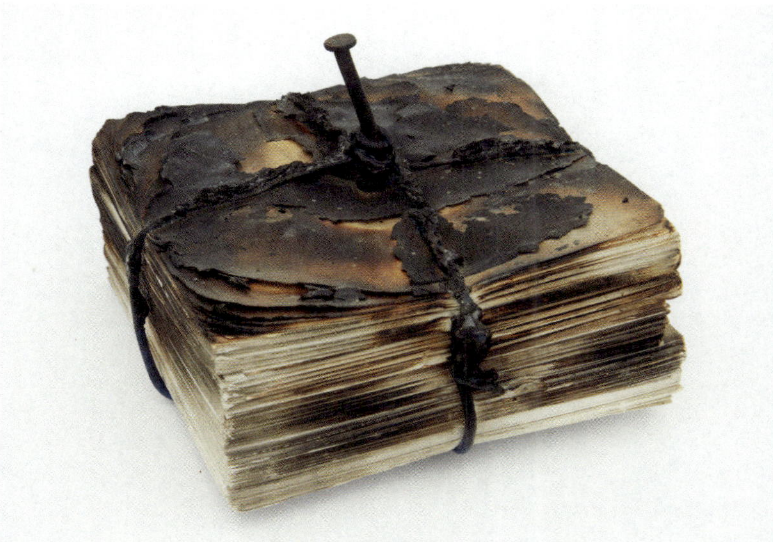

Pile 80, 1980. Paper, wire, and nail, 4¾ × 5⅛ × 3½ in. (12 × 13 × 9 cm)

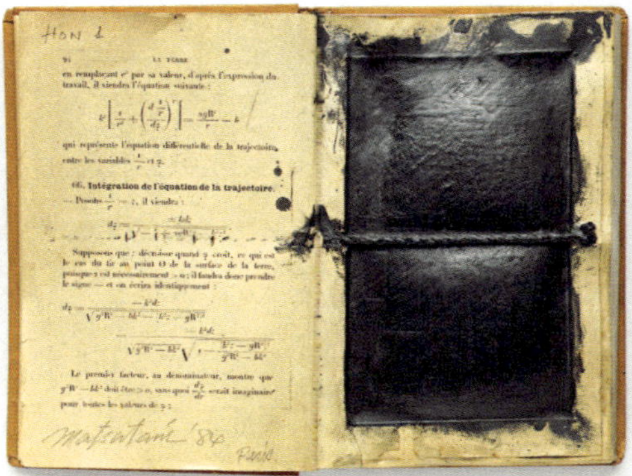

Metafiction/Book 1, 1984. Vinyl adhesive, graphite pencil, and cord on secondhand book, 7¼ × 4⅞ × 1¾ in. (18.5 × 12.4 × 4.5 cm)

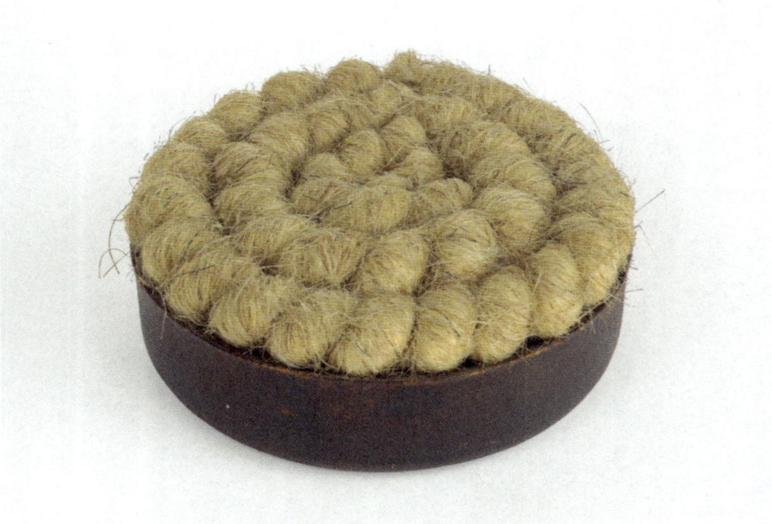

Work-O, 1973. Leather, vinyl adhesive, and jute rope, 2⅛ × 5⅛ × 5⅛ in. (5.5 × 13 × 13 cm)

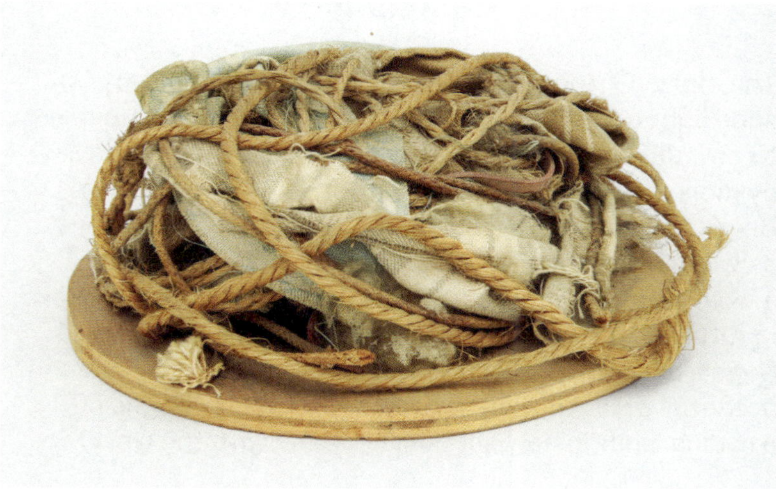

Untitled, 1973. Wood, string, bedding cotton, wool stuffing, and hemp cord, 3⅜ × 7⅝ × 7⅝ in. (8.5 × 19.5 × 19.5 cm)

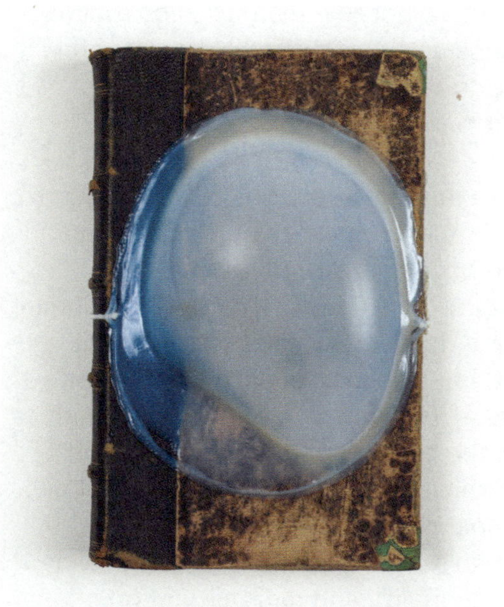

Metafiction, 2018. Vinyl adhesive and thread on secondhand book, 7⅛ × 4⅝ × 2⅛ in. (18 × 11.9 × 5.4 cm)

Resonances

The shared interests and affinities of artists often shed light on one another's ideas or provide an impulse to new developments in ways unlike those prompted by more explicit or publicly avowed influences (p. 64). Breakthroughs can occur through chance encounters, as when Matsutani saw John Cage drop a coin onto a work by Yūko Nasaka at the Gutai Pinacotheca in Osaka in 1964. In this seemingly simple act, which revealed Cage's belief in indeterminacy, spontaneity, and the potential of ordinary gestures, Matsutani recognized a radical shift in how art could engage with the world.

Above all, however, Matsutani's bold experiments with vinyl glue align him with a number of artists who were experimenting with visceral material languages after the end of World War II. To borrow from the vocabulary of psychoanalysis, these artists sought to activate the unconscious by mediating psychic and bodily realities through uncanny material transformation.

Louise Bourgeois, for example, had in the 1960s begun to use latex, plaster, and fabric to create anthropomorphic forms articulating the body as a site of memory and transformation through repetitive acts of sewing, binding, and molding. That same decade, Eva Hesse was starting to work with latex and fiberglass to create forms that sag, stretch, or collapse, evoking skin, flesh, and organic growth and revealing the tension between vitality and decay. Also of note in this context is Alina Szapocznikow, whose late 1960s *Lampe-Bouche* (Illuminated Lips) series of polyester resin sculptures depicts lips glowing from within, evoking sensuality and mortality at once.

Other figures who can productively be considered alongside Matsutani include Gutai artist Atsuko Tanaka, who externalized energy as luminous networks of color and circuitry in her performances and paintings. Like Matsutani, but in a different idiom, she transformed material into living form, revealing the pulse of continuity between the body, technology, and nature.

The psychic dimension of Matsutani's innovations in form and material also resonates with the work of Tetsumi Kudō, who lived in Paris from 1962 to 1980. While they did not meet often, Matsutani remembers being drawn to the intensity of Kudō's work when he first saw it. Kudō meticulously assembled strings, artificial flowers, and synthetic forms inside birdcages and domed terrariums to create works that often feature fragmented bodies, decaying faces, and crawling, slug-like creatures that blur the boundaries between life and decay.

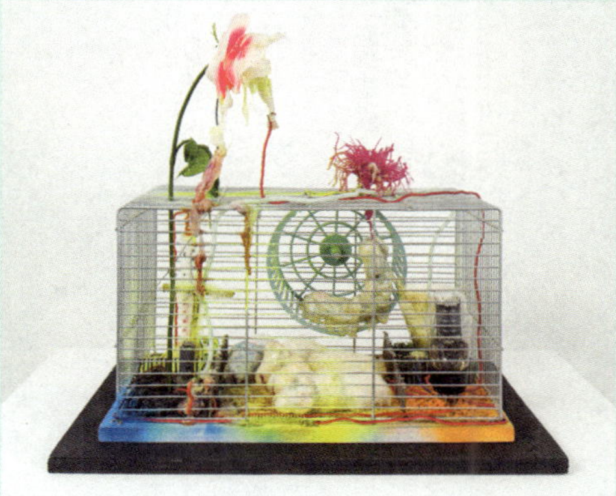

Tetsumi Kudō, *La vie confortable, cinq pièces, calme, chauffage central, électro regulateur, appareil gymnastique, plein soleil, petit jardin avec fleurs et pollution, taxes, TVA, et tout compris* (The comfortable life: five rooms, quiet, central heat, electricity, exercise equipment, direct sun, small garden with flowers and pollution, taxes, VAT, all included), 1972–73

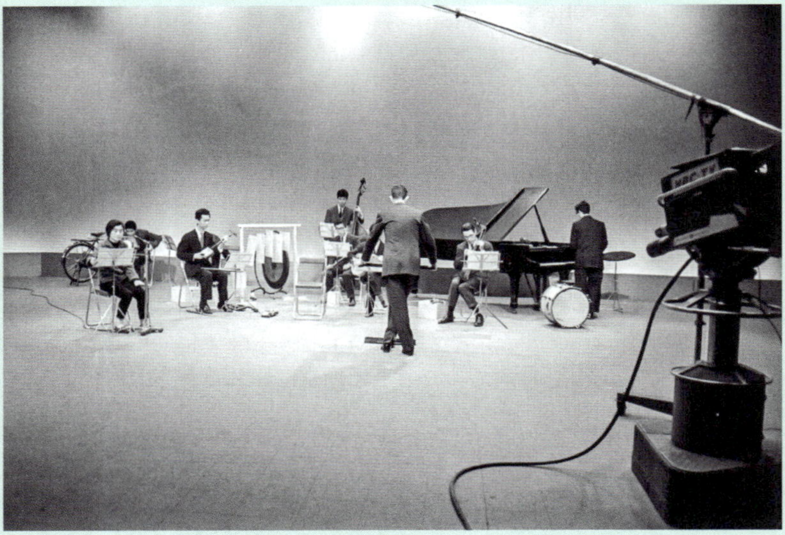

John Cage leading an ensemble on Japanese TV, 1962

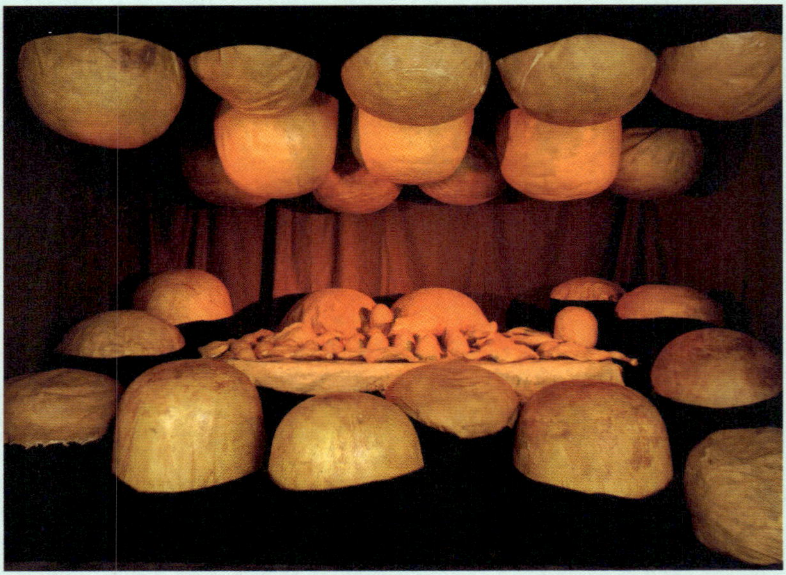

Louise Bourgeois, *Destruction of the Father*, 1979

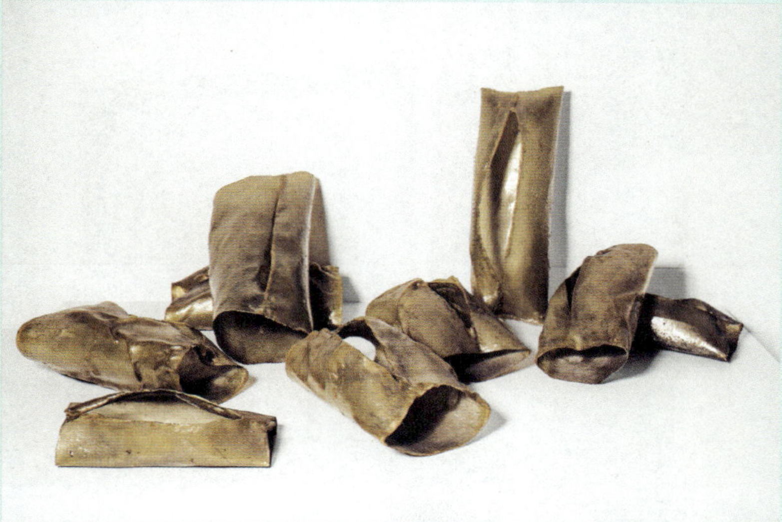

Eva Hesse, *Tori*, 1969

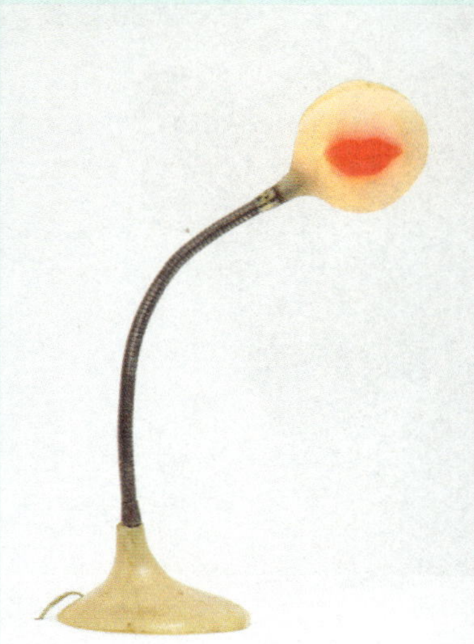

Alina Szapocznikow, *Lampe-bouche* (Illuminated Lips), 1966

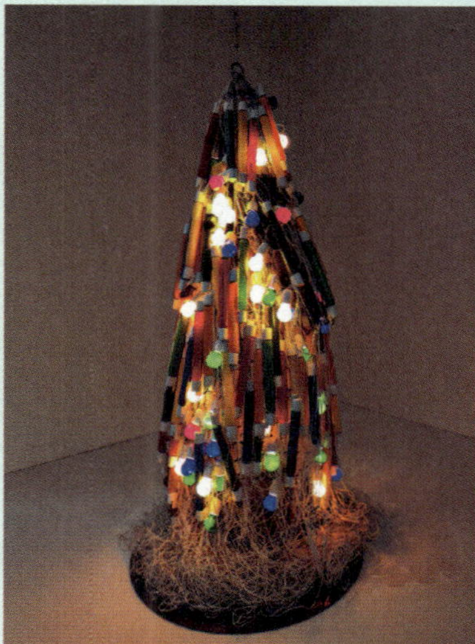

Atsuko Tanaka, *Denkifuku* (Electric Dress), 1956/1999

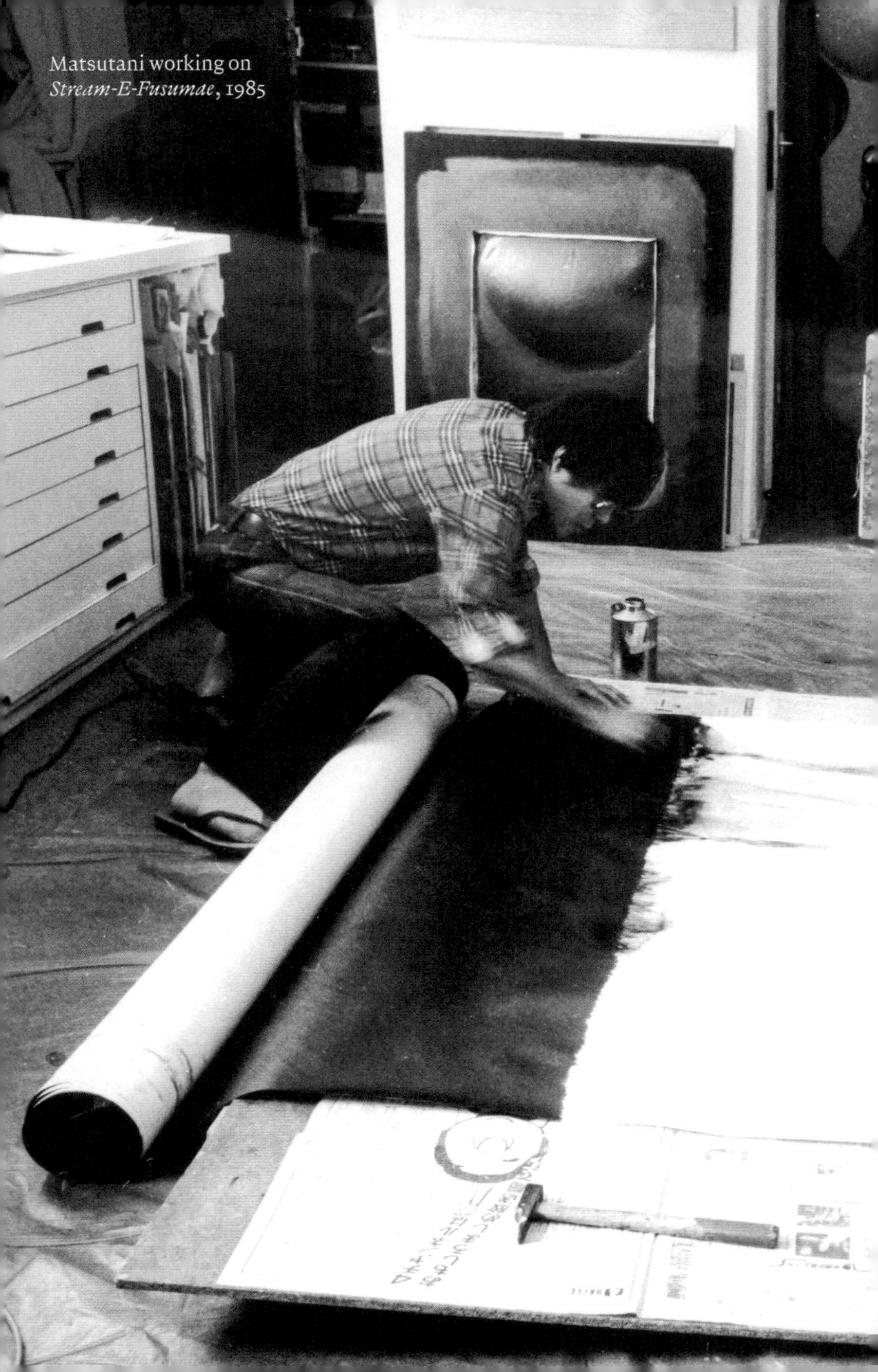

Matsutani working on
Stream-E-Fusumae, 1985

Time, Repetition, Meditation

A persistent theme in Matsutani's practice from the late 1970s onward is the notion of time, manifested through meditative repetition and accumulation. After his long foray into printmaking, Matsutani wanted to return to the foundations of drawing and, with the encouragement of Van Houten, who reminded him of the simple power of drawing a line, he began to shift into a new medium: graphite. *Untitled* (1977; p. 111), is one of Matsutani's earliest drawings of a long, rectangular vertical bar in graphite. The bottom edge has been mixed with turpentine to create the illusion of its disappearance, as if into water.

Matsutani was returning to Japan more regularly, taking renewed interest in calligraphy and immersing himself in Buddhist studies, visiting many temples, museums, and rock gardens. Although he concluded that he was "too full of desire to adhere to Zen," he posed a simple, Zen-like question to himself: "What can you do with just paper and pencil?" He felt that art was not about efficiency, and concluded that he wanted to use his time "to draw deeply." He was filling in sheets of drawing paper with pencil lines one day when a friend, the artist Shigeo Shinjō, dropped by and said: "Matsutani, this black is mysterious. If it were ten meters long, it might have power."

The French paper manufacturer Canson did, in fact, produce ten-meter (or thirty-three-foot) rolls of paper, and Matsutani proceeded to draw a wide black band across its entire length with a soft pencil. This marked the beginning of a long period in which Matsutani worked almost exclusively with graphite on paper in the first phase of a new series he called *Streams*, which involved the slow, repetitive act of rubbing a soft, dark graphite pencil across paper by hand in diagonal strokes that filled the paper in long bands. The dense, silvery-black fields of overlapping strokes in these works shimmer with subtle tonal variations. The process is highly labor-intensive and meditative, requiring hours, even days, of continuous motion. Over time, the accumulation of marks creates both a physical sheen and a visual depth, evoking the flow of water in motion or the endless passage of time.

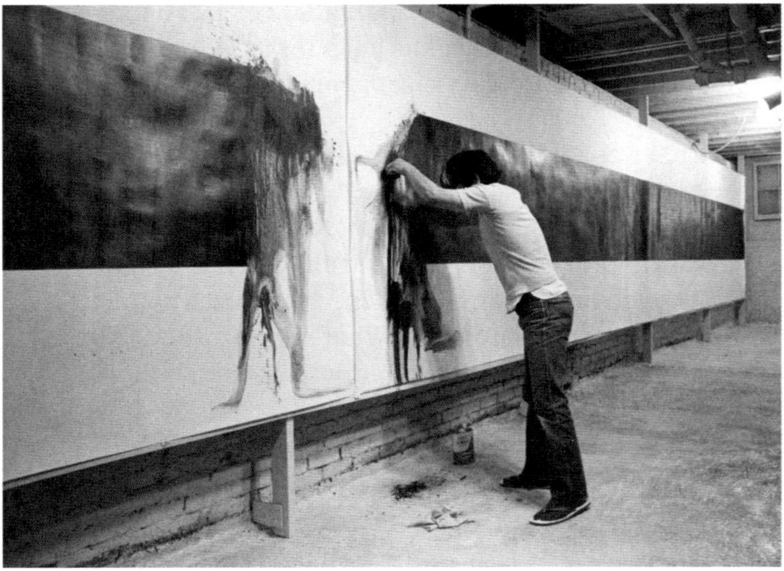

Matsutani performing *Stream-7* at Gallery Don Soker-Kaseman, San Francisco, 1982

In these years, Matsutani was also following the work of Joseph Beuys. Beuys's practice extended far beyond traditional art objects, emphasizing social transformation and ecological responsibility. He viewed art as a vehicle for shaping society, famously advocating that "everyone is an artist" in the sense that all people can contribute creatively

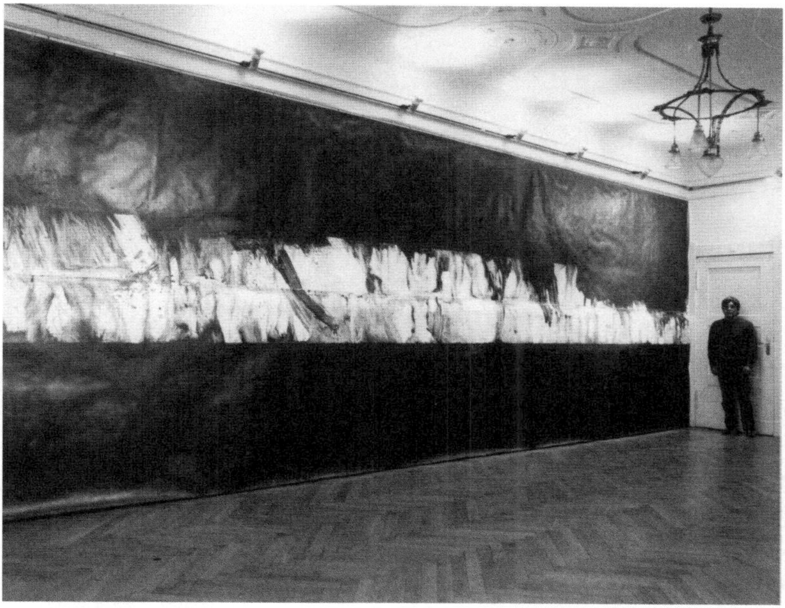

Stream-8, 1983. Graphite pencil on Canson paper with white spirit dilution. Galerie Marina Dinkler, Berlin, 1983

to social life. His projects often integrated performance, pedagogy, and activism, addressing environmental issues, human rights, and communal healing. Beuys's work indirectly encouraged Matsutani to reconsider both his materials and his working methods, and helped motivate him to consciously limit his material palette. While supporting himself by producing prints for others, he began to dedicate his mornings to drawing, treating the practice almost as a form of daily meditation or diary-keeping. Using only pencil and rolls of Canson paper, Matsutani embarked on a minimalist yet rigorous exploration of mark-making. With the *Streams* works (1977–), Matsutani aimed to achieve an emotional resonance—what Beuys might have described as tapping into an "intuitive function."

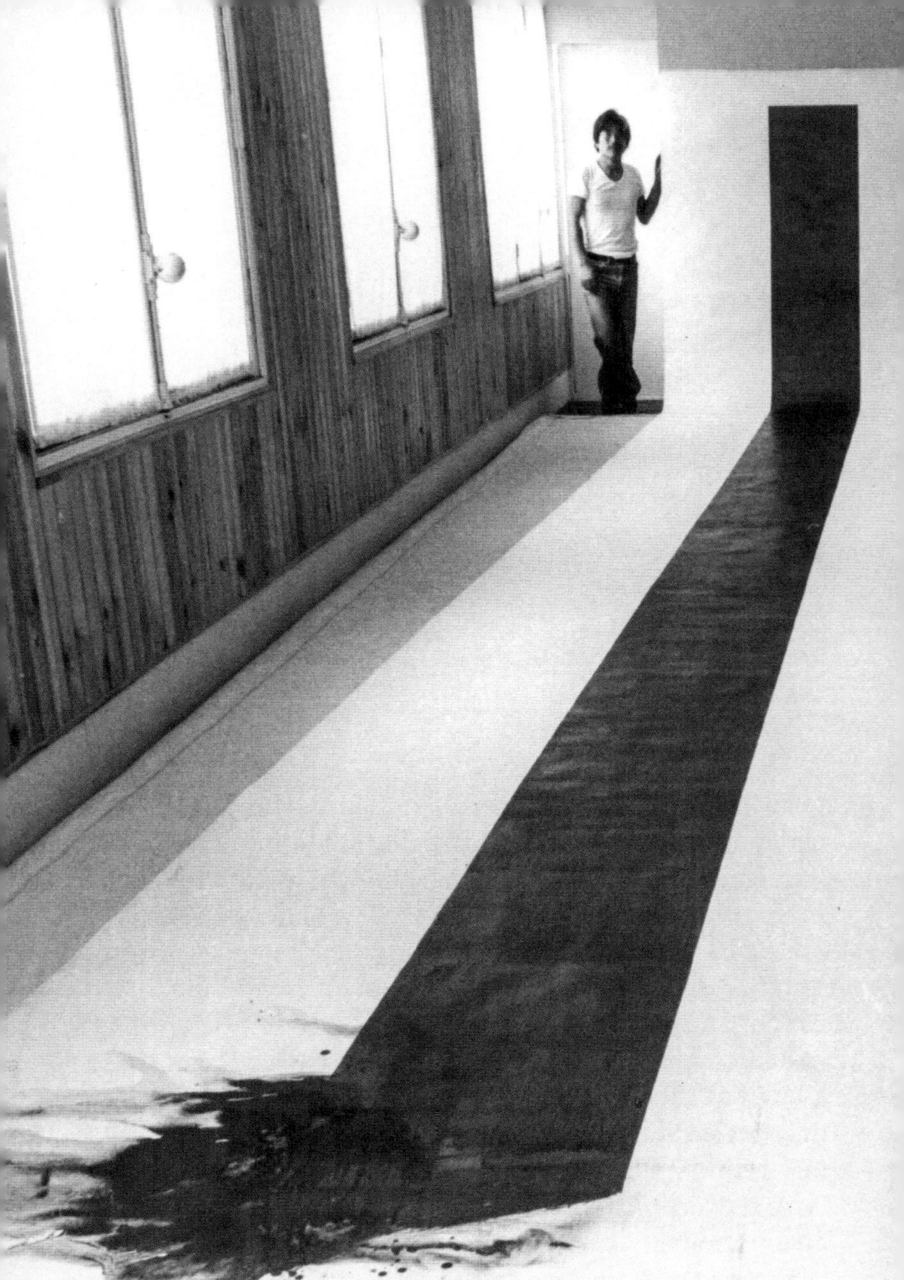

Matsutani with *Stream-1* (1977) and *Stream-2* (1978), Martial Arts Dōjō, Paris, 1978

“This work is rigorous, precise, sometimes painful, but for me there is meaning in this kind of trial by disciplined, repetitive movement.”

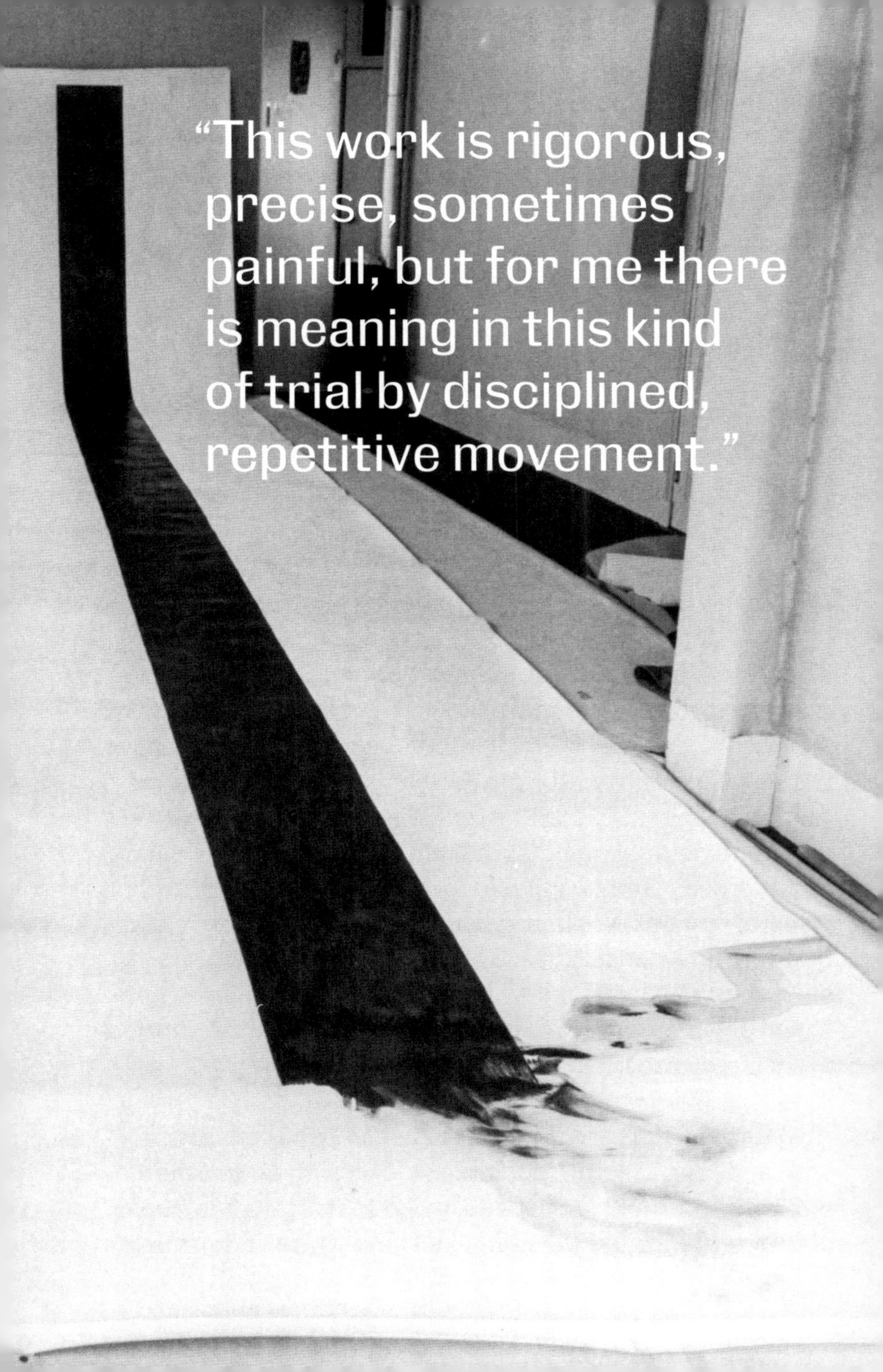

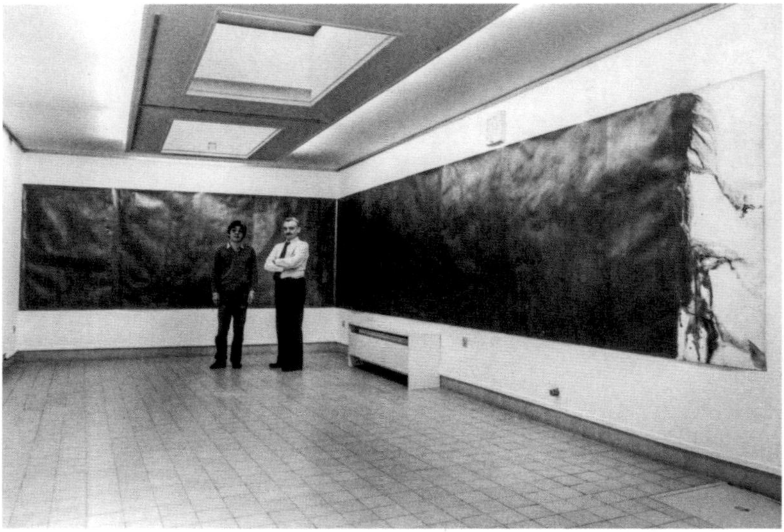

Matsutani (on left) in front of *Stream-6*, 1982. Galerij S65, Aalst, Belgium, 1983

This pared down yet emotionally charged aesthetic garnered new attention, and Madeleine Deschamps, a curator at the American Center in Paris, invited Matsutani to participate in the 1982 group exhibition *Sols, voûtes, espaces entre deux* (Floors, Vaults, Spaces Between Two). Even if made by apparently simple means, the tactile, labor-intensive nature of the process imbues these works with a vitality that elicits visceral responses. Their repetitive, hand-drawn strokes, building up a dense surface over time, force viewers to shift their expectations from a representational to a time-based engagement with materials, encompassing emotions associated with contemplation or even sorrow.

Also in the late 1970s, Matsutani began to experiment with applying graphite pencil to surfaces made of inflated vinyl glue. Earlier that decade, when Matsutani had been photographing glue works in black and white and turning

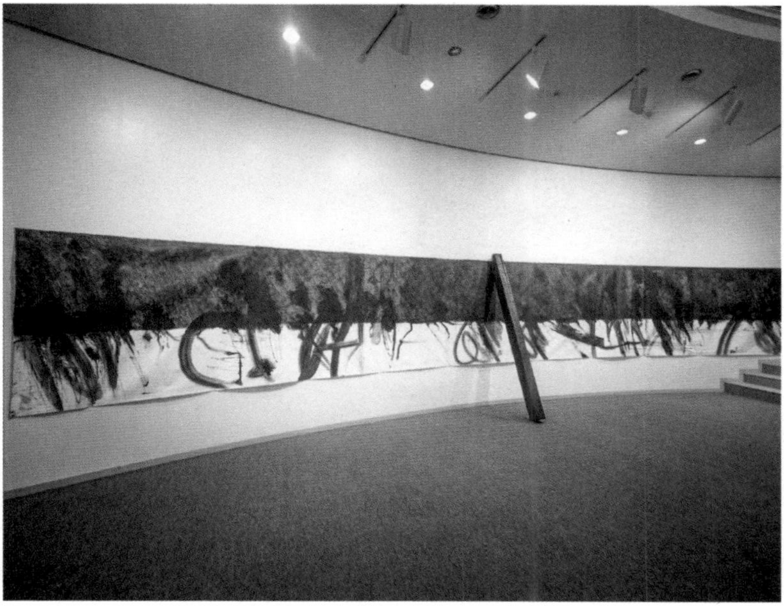

Stream-K-2, 1987. Graphite pencil, canvas mounted on paper, old beam blackened with graphite. Ashiya City Museum of Art and History, Ashiya, Japan, 1992

them into prints, his friend Chung Sang-Hwa, a Korean artist living in Japan, visited his studio in Paris. He had given Matsutani some harsh feedback: "Why print from a photo? Do the original." A few years later, Matsutani read Jun'ichirō Tanizaki's 1933 essay *In Praise of Shadows*, which deeply resonated with him (p. 134). "There is a part," he later recalled, "where [Tanizaki] talks about how the varying intensity of light can make things beautiful or mysterious. . . . It was then that I arrived at the combination I had been seeking, of the long roll of Canson paper and the organic undulations of glue." When he drew on top of this glue, the shadows suddenly appeared in the black surfaces. His conclusion at the time was: "One needs logic; mere action cannot continue."

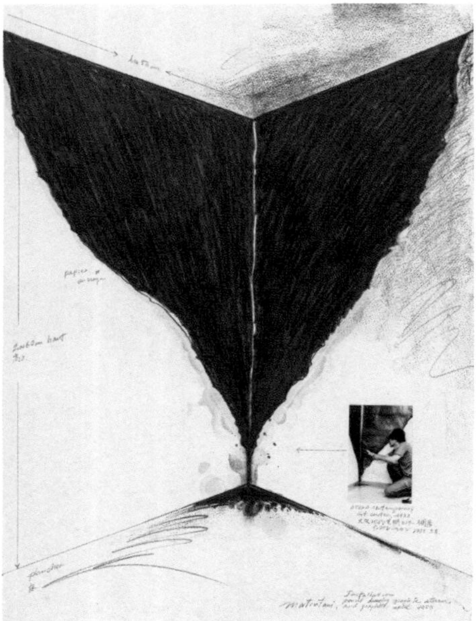

Untitled (Graphite stream and graphite spill, Osaka Contemporary Art Center, May 1983), 1983. Graphite pencil and collage on paper with white spirit dilution, 25¾ × 19⅝ in. (65.5 × 50 cm)

A similar logic led Matsutani to his large-scale graphite drawings, made by meticulously building up layers through rhythmic, almost ritualistic hand movements. In 1979, he presented *Stream-2* (pp. 94–95, at right) in Berlin. Here, a ten-meter-long band of graphite on paper was lifted vertically upon against the wall to evoke a black river that streams down and across the floor. At the opposite end, Matsutani used turpentine to distil the graphite into ephemeral smoke. Matsutani's bands of graphite often appear to drift and merge, suggesting currents that are at once fluid and monumental.

One of Matsutani's primary inspirations for this body of work was the sixteenth-century Japanese ink master Tōhaku Hasegawa and his legendary screen painting *Pine Trees* (ca. 1580; p. 65). But whereas Hasegawa employs vast areas of blank space to evoke mist, depth, and the unseen, Matsutani introduces elements of chance and expression in his splashes, providing a striking counterpoint to the repetitive regularity of the graphite strokes.

This method, in effect, represented a new variation on the dichotomous imagery ("soft and hard") that he had explored throughout the 1970s. Another precursor can be found in the work of fifteenth-century Zen painter Sesshū Tōyō, whose *haboku* (broken or splashed ink) technique uses faint gradations of ink to suggest atmospheric space without the need for discrete outlines.

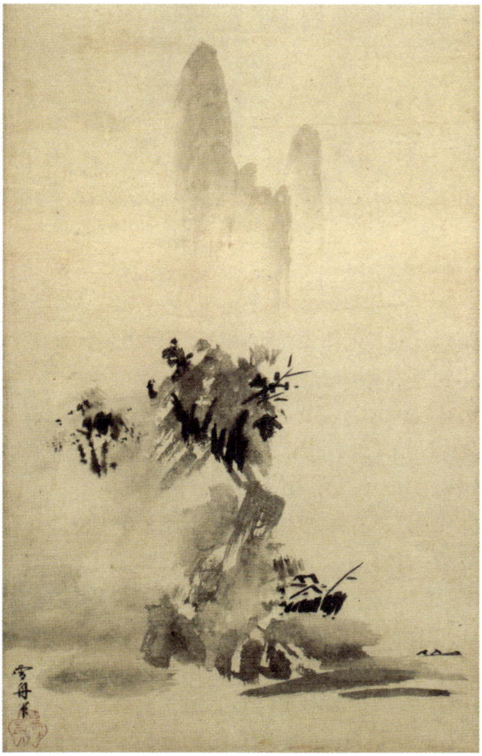

Sesshū Tōyō, *Splashed-Ink Landscape*, 1495

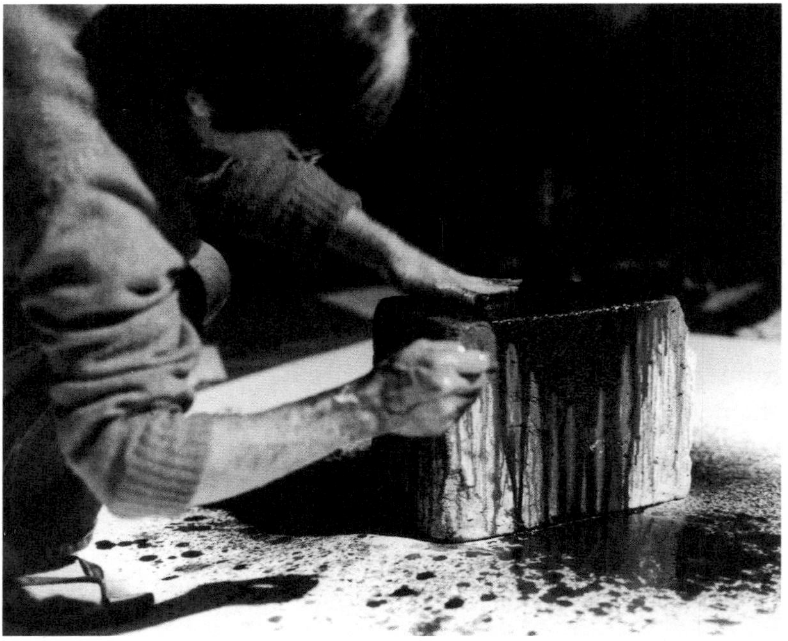

Courant Continu (Continuing Current), 1983. Cord, cotton sack, white spirit, graphite, Canson paper, and stone. Performance with music by Isao Matsushita. Galerie Marina Dinkler, Berlin

Starting in 1983, Matsutani introduced another dynamic aspect to the *Streams*, rubbing graphite on stones before diluting it with white spirit dripping from a sack suspended from the ceiling—as in *Courant Continu* (Continuing Current, 1983). Notions of the impermanence of all things, breath, and the physicality of the body in a cycle of life and death here correlate directly with core Buddhist teachings. From the mid-1980s on, the white spirit was replaced with water and the graphite by solid sumi ink (pp. 120; 126–27). In a group of distinct yet related works, begun in 1986, liquid ink drips from cotton sacks onto stones (p. 102), canvas (p. 105), paper, cloth, or wooden balls (pp. 123–25).

In 1985, Matsutani made *Stream-E-Fusumae* for Temple Kaikōsan in Kobe. Reminiscent of *Stream-7*, another large-scale work presented in San Francisco in 1982 (p. 92), the work features two horizontal graphite bands that almost converge at a central void, where white spirit has diluted the graphite and dissolved it into a splash. The graphite emphasizes discipline, repetition, and duration, each stroke being a trace of bodily action, layered until the surface itself becomes a meditation on time, persistence, and flow. In further variations on these horizontal bands, Matsutani added crossbeams that lean against the wall (p. 97), or black cords to link a graphite wall work with a zinc basin on the floor (p. 105).

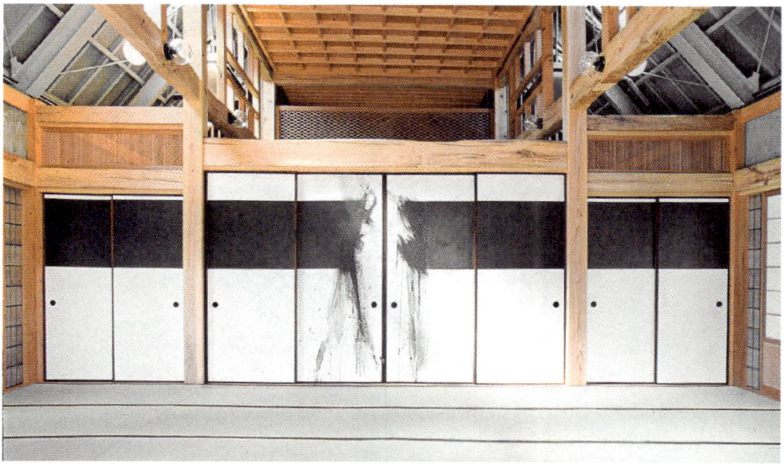

Stream-E-Fusumae, 1985. Graphite pencil on Canson paper mounted on plywood with white spirit dilution. Temple Kaikōsan, Kobe

Among the artist's most impressive presentations of graphite was *Stream-Ashiya-92*, staged at Ashiya City Museum of Art and History, Hyōgo Prefecture, in 1992. The work, in graphite on canvas, descended from the high

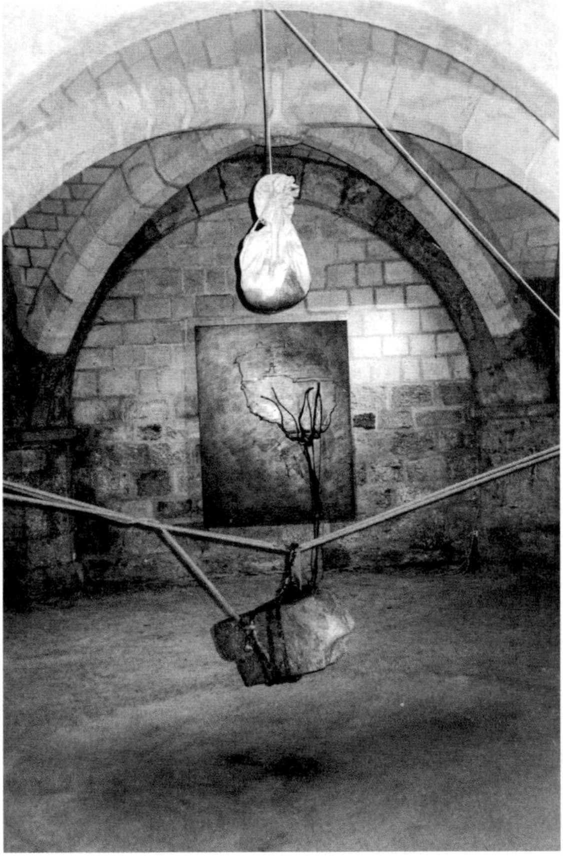

Stream-Mortagne-au-Perche, 1991. Cords, stone, cotton sack, and water. Crypt of the Church of All Saints, Mortagne-au-Perche, France

ceiling, while white spirit applied to its end produced a dramatic graphite splatter on the white circular canvas at its base. The graphite shimmered in the natural light from the skylight above, like a waterfall streaming down the museum's central rotunda, before the dense graphite was transformed into weightless splashes as it met the floor.

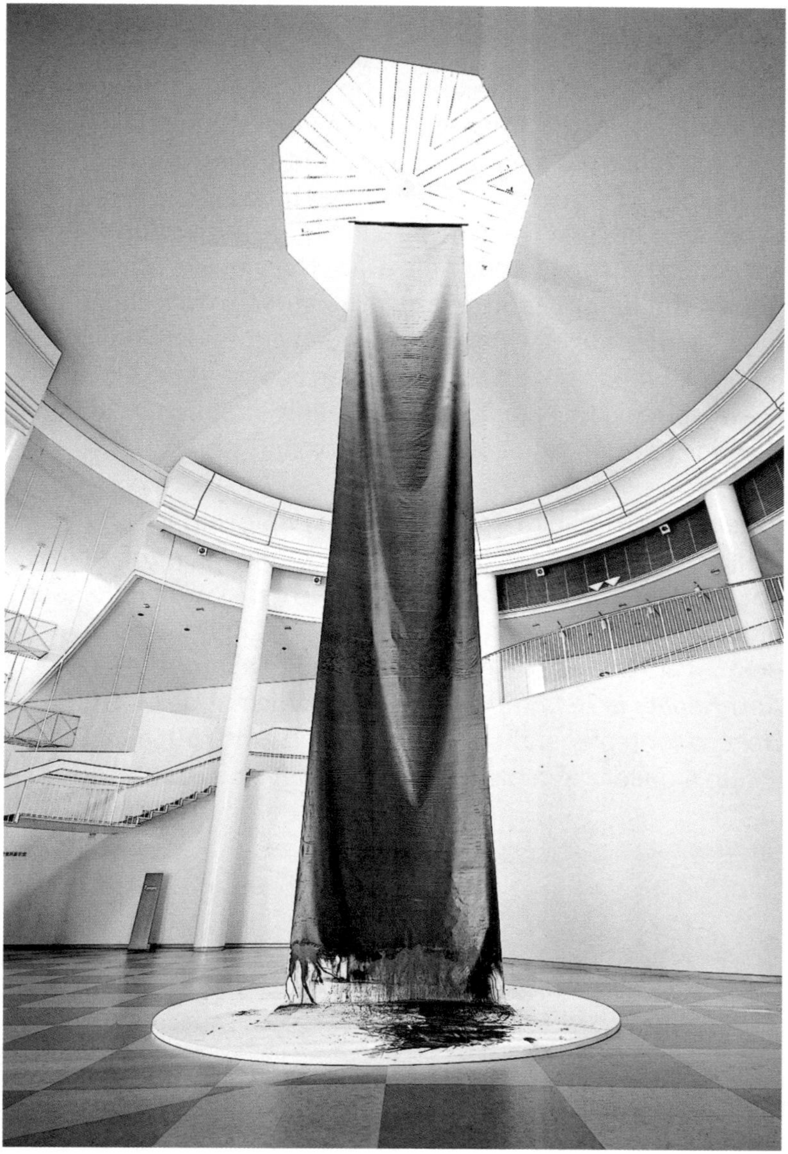

Stream-Ashiya-92, 1992. Graphite pencil and white spirit dilution on canvas and canvas mounted on plywood. Ashiya City Museum of Art and History

Stream-87-P (1987)

Stream-87-P, first installed at the Chapelle Saint-Louis de la Salpêtrière in Paris in 1987, involves masses of rope hanging from the surface of a graphite-filled canvas and dropping onto the floor. The rope extends the work's dynamism beyond the canvas's surface, activating the surrounding space and implicating the viewer. Materially, it links the flat, graphite-saturated surface to a three-dimensional world, where a leaky canvas sack filled with sumi ink bleeds onto a white canvas rectangle in a zinc basin below. The rope forms a conduit of energy within the work's quiet equilibrium of black and white.

Stream-87-P—one of several pieces deploying similar techniques—is conceptually reminiscent of Jirō Takamatsu's pivotal *Point* series (1961–64) where masses of lacquered wire or string "swelled out" from a central point. This body of work culminated in Takamatsu's *On Anti-Reality in Relation to a Trunk* performance in 1962. Here, a long piece of string stretched out from a suitcase inside a gallery in a museum all the way to Tokyo Station.

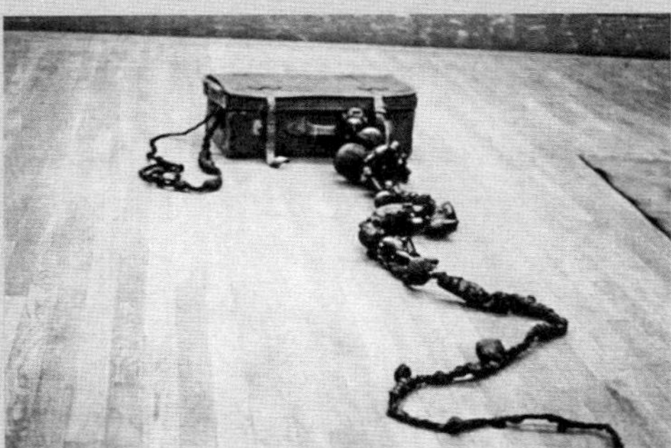

Jirō Takamatsu, *On Anti-Reality in Relation to a Trunk* (detail), 1962

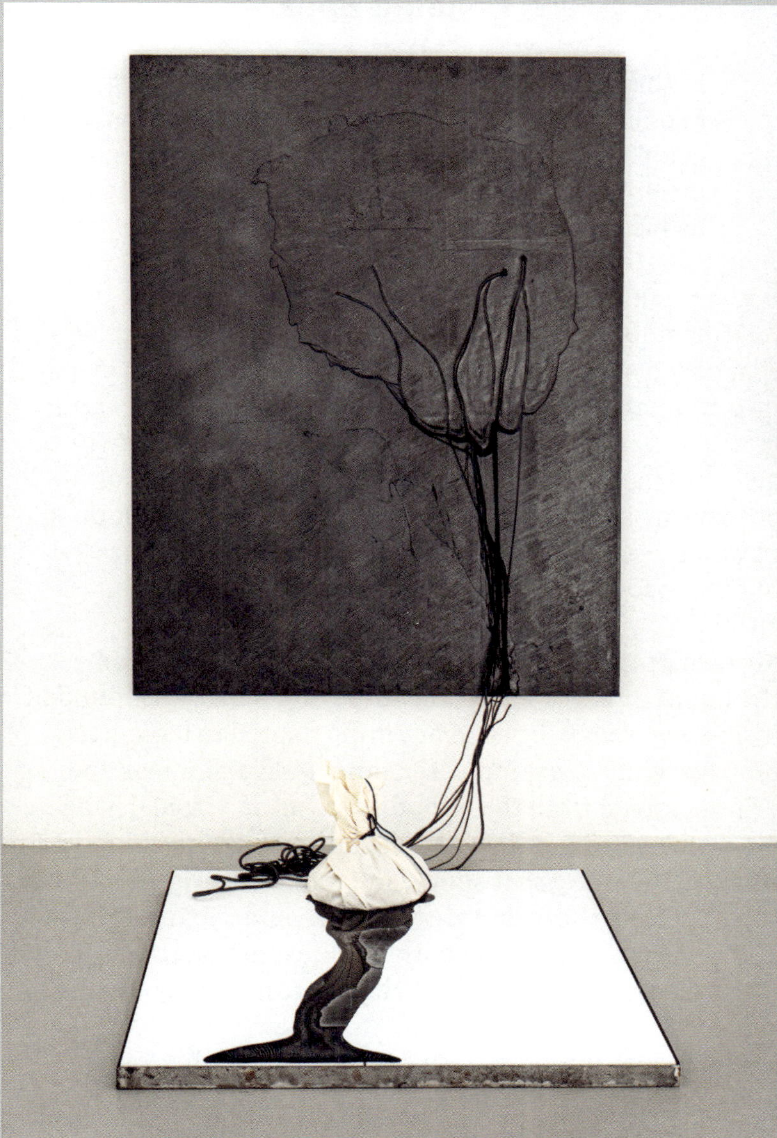

Stream-87-P, 1987. Vinyl adhesive, graphite pencil, and paper mounted on plywood; cord; zinc basin, canvas, canvas sack, and sumi ink. Galerie Jean Brolly, Paris, 2018

Looking Back

In this excerpt from "Searching for a Starting Point: From Any Place, From Any Thing" (2015), Matsutani recalls his turn to graphite in the 1970s and gives insight into how he arrived at this juncture as well as his broader philosophy.

It was at such a time when I began to reconsider my relationship with art. I recalled the streaks of straight grain that called on me and gradually transformed themselves into an image of a face. I remembered the sensuality and tactility that I felt through the use of the material of vinyl glue. In other words, I began to feel the importance of possessing an inner image and using that as a medium in which to shape the work. I realized the significance of the process, its depth, and the story it tells.

My own inner images include visual forms drawn from the liquid forms of waves and drips, organic forms rounded by my own sensuality and anything related to biological propagation. For example, the inner image of waves and drips emerged from the structures resulting from drying vinyl glue, letting it flow and then drip. While the tension of seeing something that should fall remain still is suggestively incorporated, the round vinyl forms could expand and contract, suggesting both hardness and softness, when the temperature was changed or air was injected.

In any case, I arrived at a level of control over my material where I could make the best use out of the vinyl glue. Still, I wanted to take a step further. I wanted to reconsider Gutai's statement: "Do something no one's ever done before." In the 1970s, when issues of humanity and ecology were discussed, I was encouraged to think about the honest and natural feelings of people. In an age where the development of industry limited the use of hands, I wanted to discover an anti-productive, natural, and personal expression.

As I wasn't making much money at the time, I seriously considered a way I could express myself while spending as little as possible. Again, the same thought went through my head: "Do something no one's ever done before." I asked myself, "What is the origin of drawing?" The answer to which I arrived was a pencil and paper. Rather than sketching as I had done before, I wanted to see what sort of "surface" would emerge out of an accumulation of repeated pencil line strokes. Sure enough, a surface with a tone of black unlike oil painting or sumi ink made an appearance. As each line was drawn by hand, the angle of the light against it would show or hide the traces of the pencil marks and the shades of graphite. I thought to myself, "This is quite good. As I've arrived to this point in my life, I shall do what feels right." I promised myself that I would keep on drawing until the surface turned black.

While engaging with the sculptural forms made of vinyl glue and living between Japan and France, I began to seek the roots of the culture and history in the East, particularly Japan, that perhaps related to my own work. Firstly, blackness related to the sumi ink that I habitually used, and therefore, connected to writing. Such blackness is also accompanied by white margins. Secondly, our own disposition, predating Buddhism, replaces our own soul with nature while also incorporating nature into ourselves. Buddhism deepened thoughts on life and death further. A recognition of infinity.

Translating the cycle of life and death onto black bands on a hanging scroll, I began to draw line after line, day after day, until I reached the end of a ten-meter-long roll of paper. The daily, rule-based repetition and the concentrated action embedded time into the surface of the paper. The longer I continued the more I began to experience a certain physical and spiritual pain, which became a drive to go on further. After showering the resulting drawing with turpentine and violently rubbing the end of a pencil against it, the ingredients dissolved and flowed like a waterfall off the paper, onto the wall and the ground, only to disappear after dominating the space for a moment.

After challenging myself to draw using a pencil onto long rolls of paper, I began applying the same techniques onto the protrusions that I made out of vinyl glue. The accumulations of black lines created shadows and fused with my organic inner image. Continuing to make such works, I arrive to this day.

A person is born and eventually dies. There are many theories that exist to describe this flow of life. While it is an act that appeals to the visual sense, aesthetics has also experienced a proliferation of meaning that has inundated the public. If we position aesthetics within the flow of life and death, I firmly believe our mission as people who create and look at art is to respect one another and observe the truth, as human nature is about having an individual way of living and feeling.

Shinshō (Inner Imagery)

Combining the characters 心 (*shin*: heart, mind, feeling) and 象 (*shō*: image, form, phenomenon), *shinshō* refers to images, impressions, or visions that arise within the mind. In art and literature, it often points to the way reality is experienced internally rather than objectively depicted. Sakutarō Hagiwara's *Howling at the Moon* (1917) is credited as the first *shinshō-shi*, or poetry of inner imagery. Capturing psychological states via fragmented, dreamlike, and surreal images, *shinshō* poetry emphasizes the subjective and symbolic, breaking with tanka and haiku, earlier traditions rooted in seasonal imagery. In the visual arts, Japanese artists influenced by European modernism—among them Matsutani's mentor, Shōsaku Arao—invoked *shinshō* as they moved away from literal realism to instead depict internal visions, memory images, and dreamscapes as a way to explore psychological depth, emotion, and the subconscious.

For Matsutani, *shinshō* is not a preformed mental image that can be faithfully reproduced. Rather, it is a vivid yet indeterminate presence within consciousness, a compelling expression that evolves autonomously. It fluctuates in intensity and is continuously refined through deliberate engagement, retaining an independent force that guides his practice. Matsutani uses the term when describing his method, in relation to both his early paintings conveying anguished mental states and his later work with accumulations of black lines, which, he says, "fused with" his inner image. *Shinshō* is, for him, shaped by a heightened awareness of the senses, intertwining the body, space, experience, and perception.

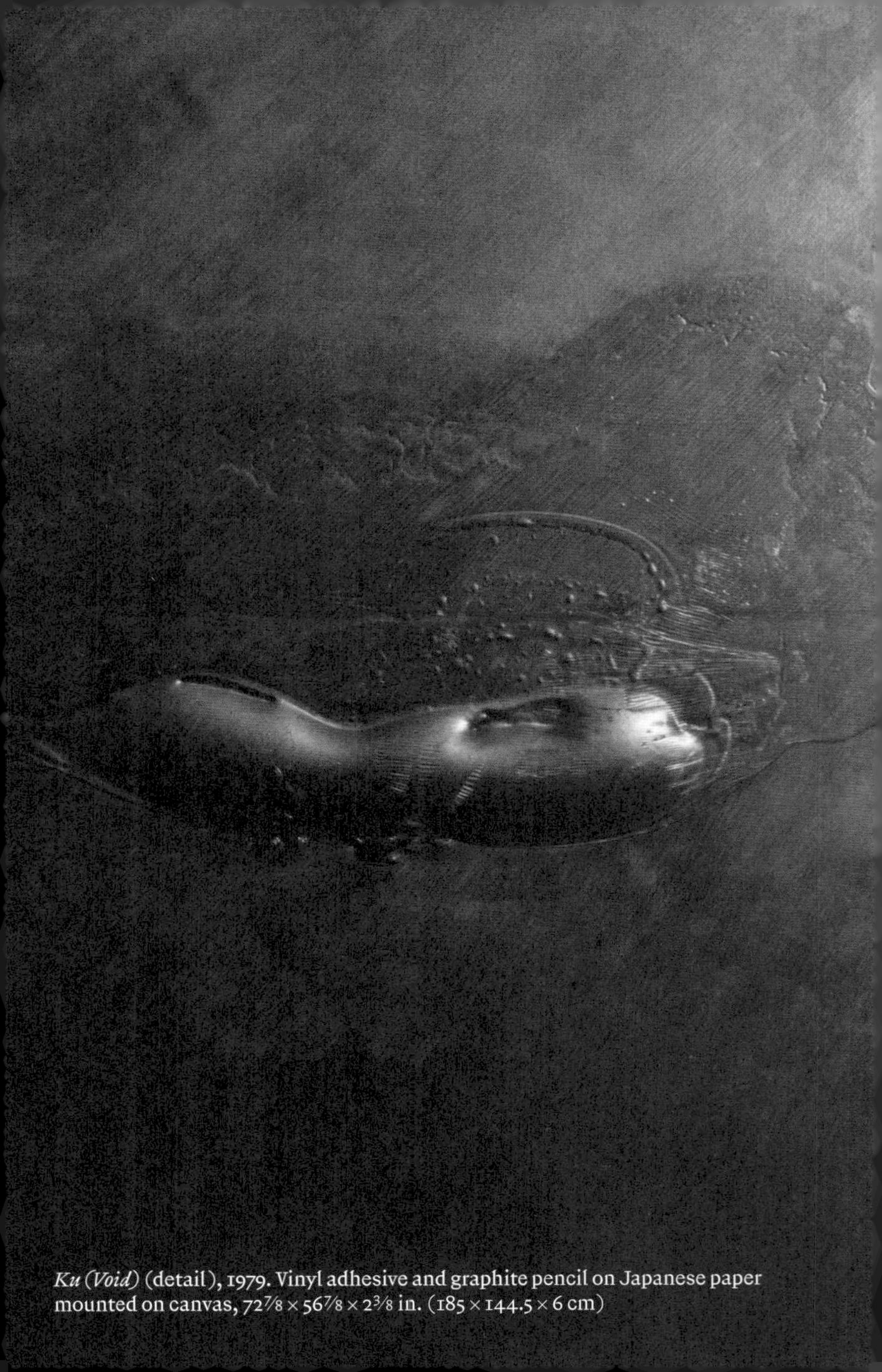

Ku (Void) (detail), 1979. Vinyl adhesive and graphite pencil on Japanese paper mounted on canvas, 72⅞ × 56⅞ × 2⅜ in. (185 × 144.5 × 6 cm)

The Color Black

For Matsutani, the color black embodies a convergence of material, cultural, and philosophical meanings. Rooted in the culture and history of the use of sumi ink, it is associated in his work less with darkness than with breath and flow, depth and subtle gradations. This blackness connects to calligraphy's unity of body, mind, and gesture (p. 116). Philosophically, it signifies an existential duality, its presence defined through contrast with the surrounding white void, echoing Buddhist ideas of interdependence and impermanence. Ultimately, for Matsutani, blackness does not describe a color but rather is a state of being—a condensation of breath, time, and presence in which the corporeal and the metaphysical converge.

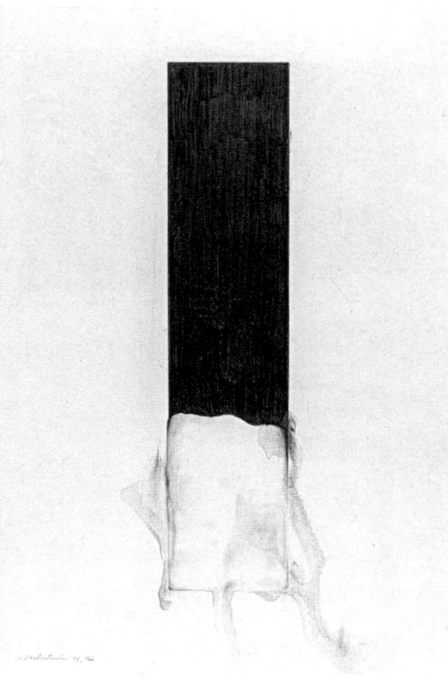

Untitled, 1977. Graphite pencil and turpentine on BFK paper, 40¼ × 27½ in. (102.2 × 70 cm)

“I wanted to explore the richness of shadow. I also liked the fact that black, the graphite pencil line, retains the trace of the hand.”

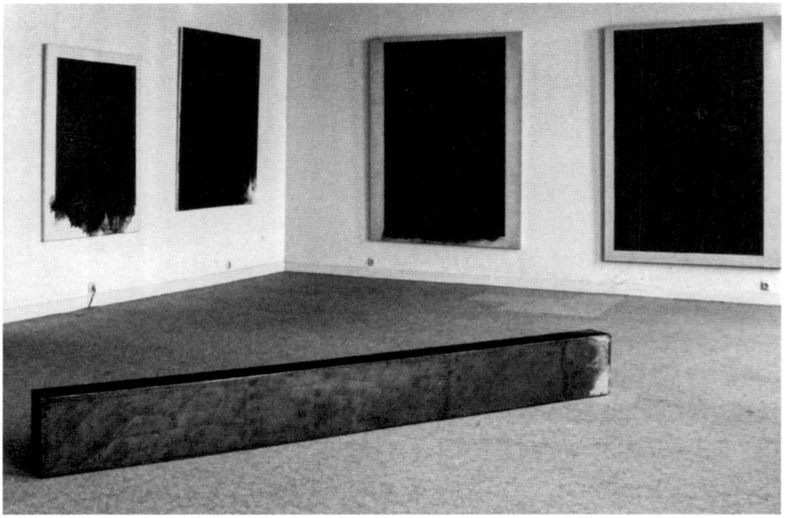

Matsutani’s solo show at Galerie Alain Oudin, Paris, 1978

Stream of One-P-7; Suggestion-11-'78, 1978. Graphite pencil on paper with white spirit dilution, mounted on canvas, 57½ × 44⅞ in. (146 × 114 cm)

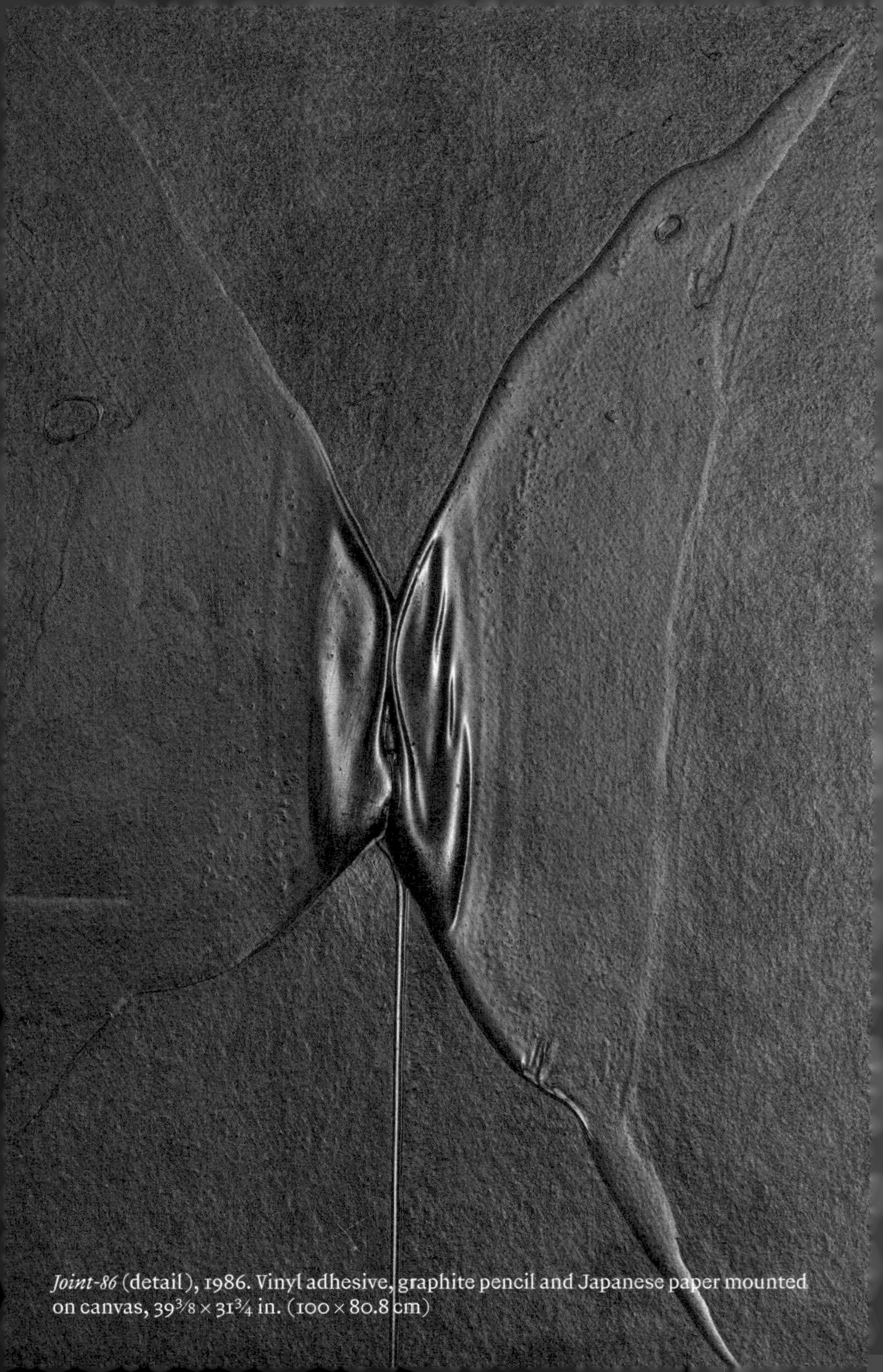

Joint-86 (detail), 1986. Vinyl adhesive, graphite pencil and Japanese paper mounted on canvas, 39 3/8 × 31 3/4 in. (100 × 80.8 cm)

Following a period of introspection and experimentation in the mid-1970s, Matsutani reached a turning point that called for a more direct, tactile dialogue with matter. Around 1976, he returned to the familiar materials of paper and pencil, methodically layering surfaces with strokes of graphite. The blackness of graphite differed from the sumi ink of his youth as well as the rich blacks of his printmaking at Atelier 17—it was coarser, more mutable, and more responsive to touch. Depending on application pressure, speed, and surface, its material properties proved astonishingly variable, and when worked to density, it took on a metallic sheen that reflected not color but substance.

Matsutani came to see blackness as a return to his cultural and spiritual roots, a grounding force amid the material experimentation of his Paris years. When he went on to pour white spirit over areas of compacted graphite, allowing the particles to liquefy and flow, the unpredictable rivulets and splashes introduced chance and movement, counterbalancing the geometric precision of his repeated strokes.

From the late 1970s on, Matsutani further extended the dialectical interplay—between order and spontaneity, softness and hardness—that had long defined his practice as he began again to work with vinyl glue on canvas, now drawing graphite over thick, bulbous drips of vinyl. In the *Wave* series from the late 1990s, he continued to investigate the layering of graphite, drawing out its capacity to shimmer and occasionally offsetting it with white. In drawings and sketches he also introduced strokes of light, picking up on the graphite's dissolution in white spirit in the *Streams* series and accentuating questions of interplay and balance.

Calligraphy

In Japanese aesthetics, calligraphy is regarded as an embodiment of the self, a direct manifestation of one's inner state (heart, spirit, or mind). Each brushstroke reveals one's rhythm, energy, and presence at the moment of inscription. A line is not merely drawn but breathed into existence. Calligraphy reflects both impermanence (*mujō*) and mindfulness (*mushin*), the state of "no-mind" in which the artist acts without ego or premeditation. Because each stroke is irreversible, the act of writing becomes a meditation on time and transience, a record of a singular, unrepeatable moment. At a conceptual level, calligraphy transforms language into abstraction. The surrounding void (*yohaku*) carries equal weight to the ink, demonstrating the interdependence of presence and absence, fullness and emptiness.

From an early age, Matsutani "used a brush as we use a ballpoint pen today." The practice of *shūji* (traditional calligraphy) would inform his Gutai-era experiments with vinyl glue as well as his later works with graphite and ink. The sweeping, fluid forms of his poured and stretched vinyl glue surfaces recall the gestural flow of brushstrokes, while his *Streams* works are, no less than calligraphy, centered on controlled gesture, repetition, and the meditative discipline of mark-making. The later *Streams* often incorporate sumi ink, the traditional medium of calligraphy, for which inksticks with pigments are ground against a stone with water to create liquid ink. In Matsutani's work, sumi ink is something alive, breathing, and fluid—a substance that, rather than being opaque or static, embodies transformation.

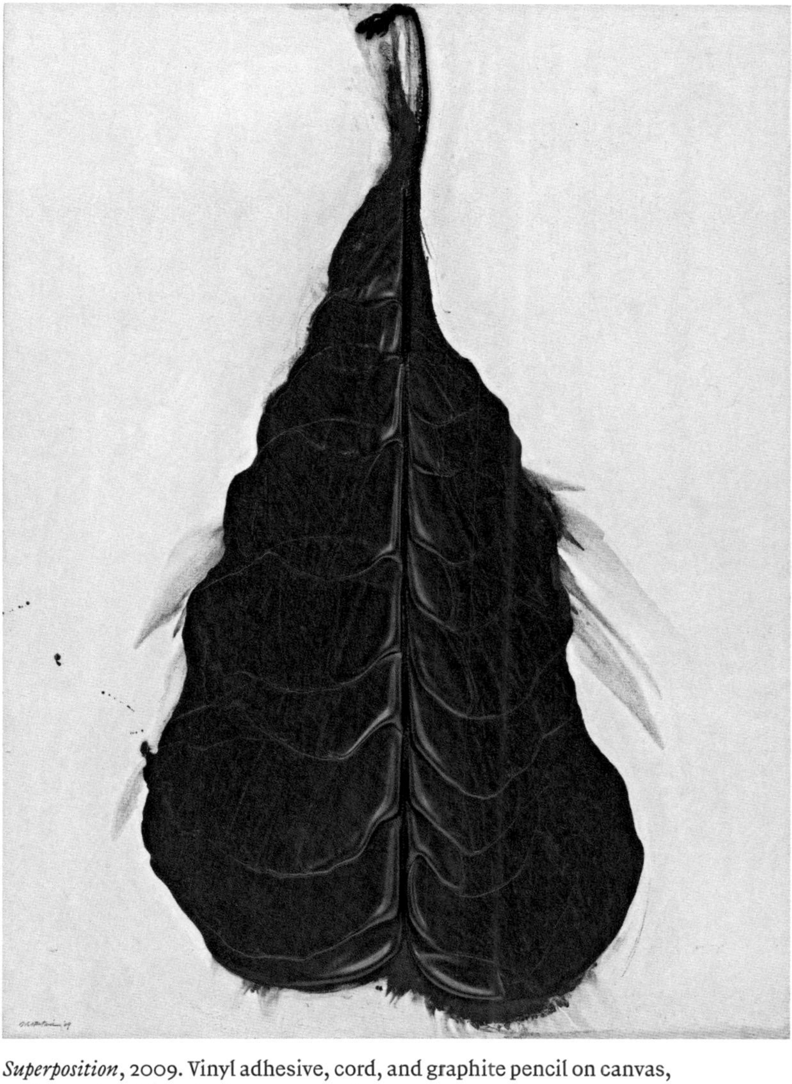

Superposition, 2009. Vinyl adhesive, cord, and graphite pencil on canvas, $57\frac{1}{2} \times 44\frac{1}{8} \times 1\frac{5}{8}$ in. (146 × 112 × 4 cm)

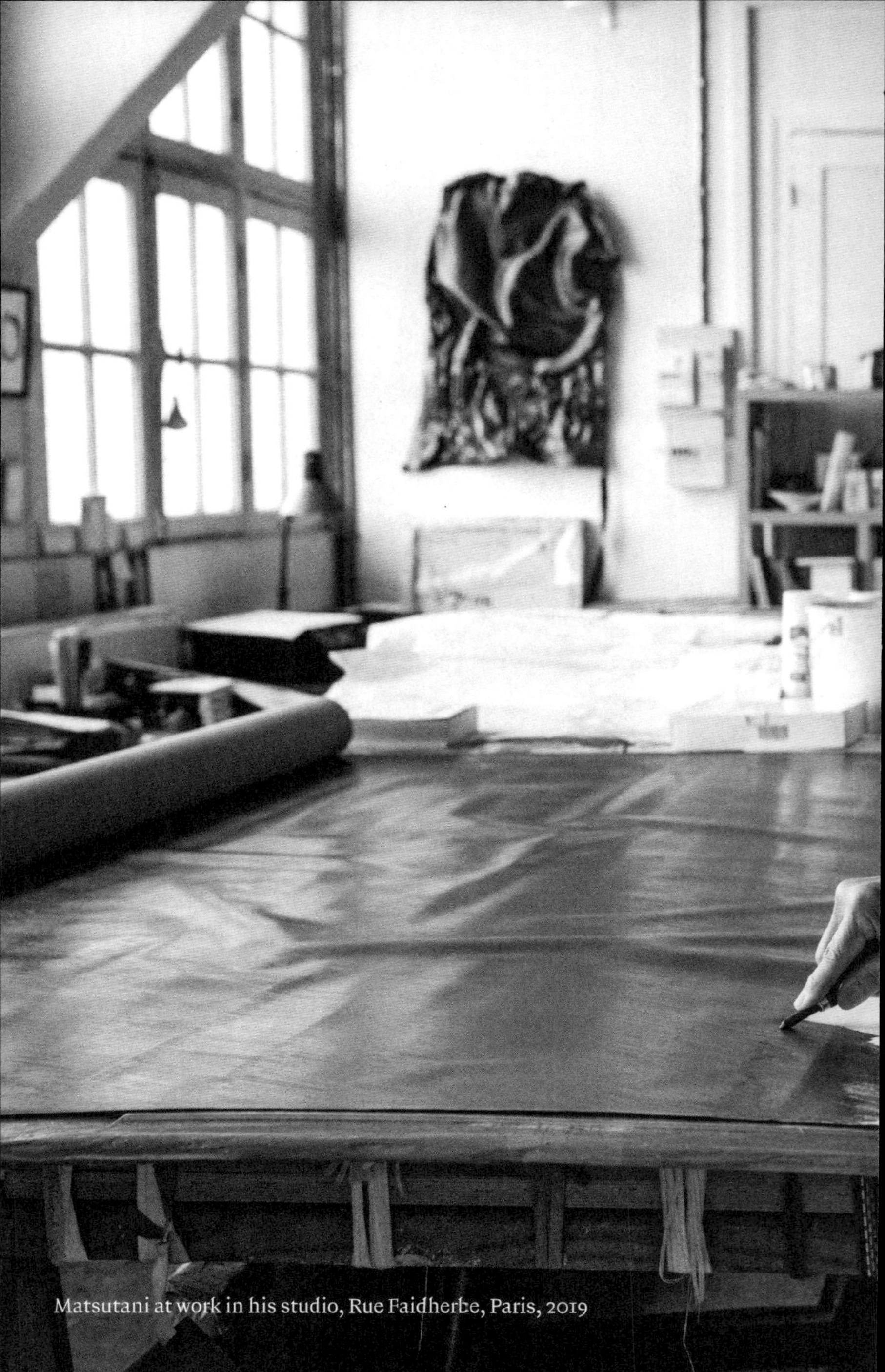

Matsutani at work in his studio, Rue Faidherbe, Paris, 2019

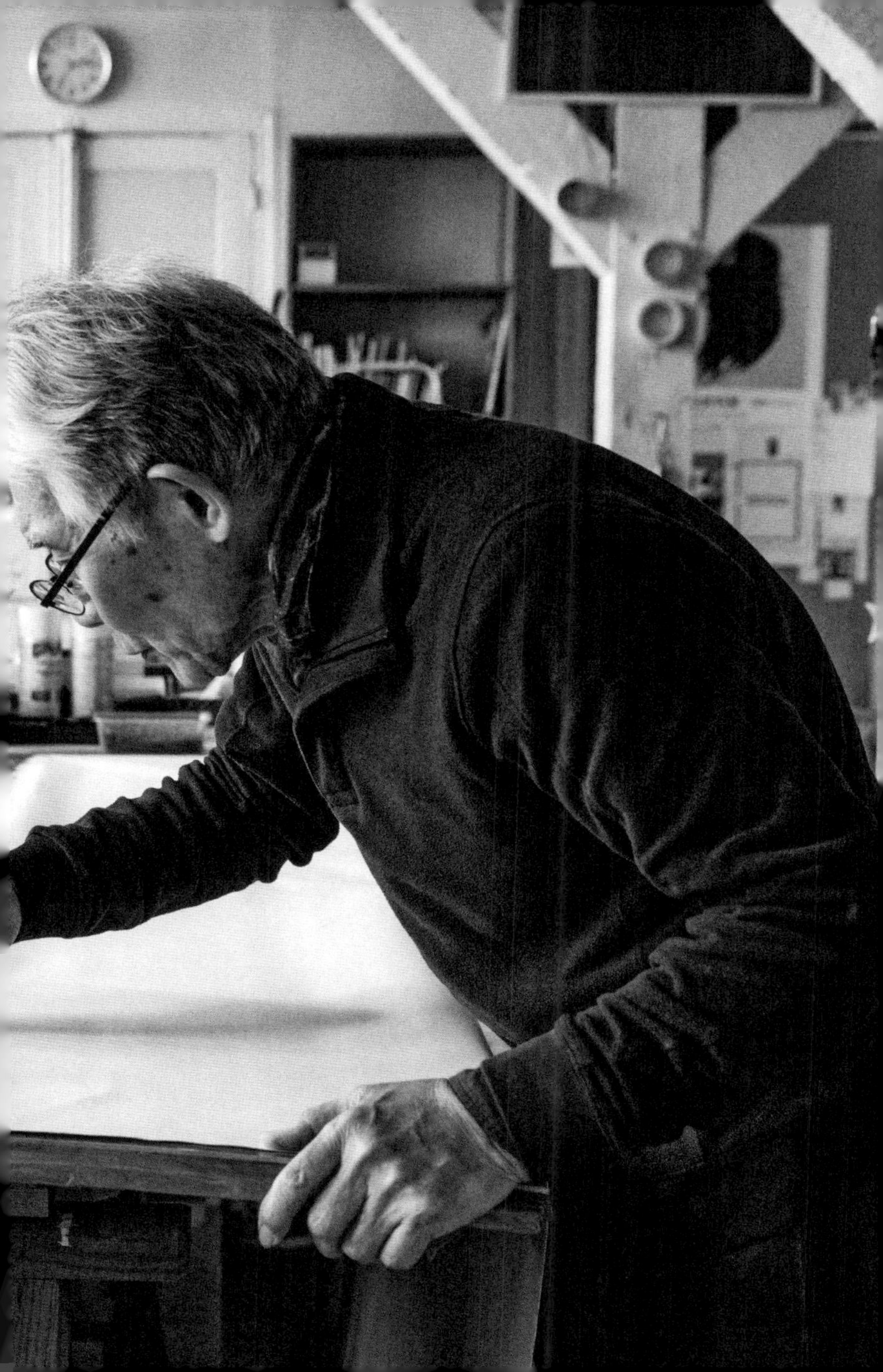

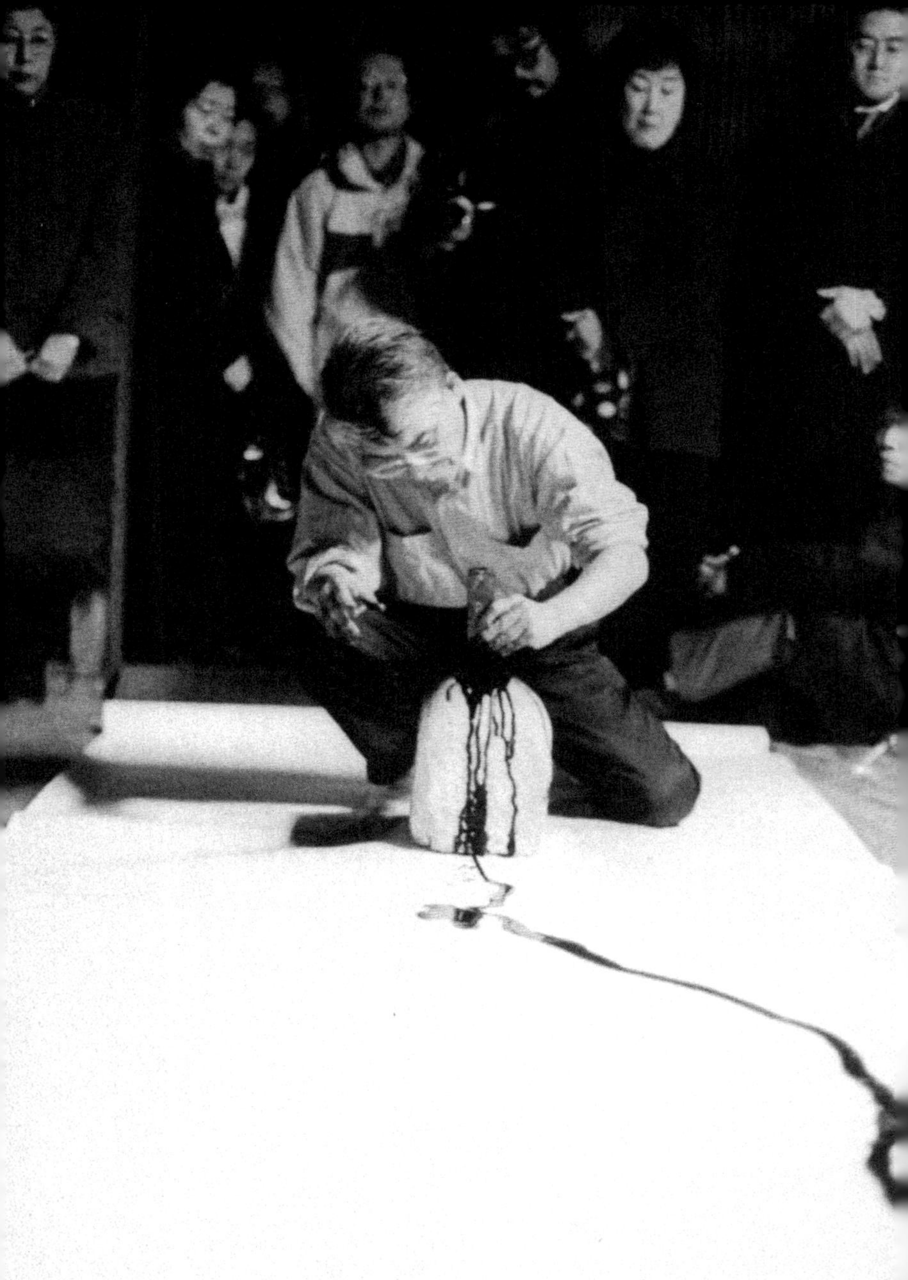

Stream-Konishi House, 2001. Performance with sumi ink and water on stone and Canson paper. Konishi House, Osaka

Spatial Awareness and the Five Senses

Matsutani's works from the late 1970s onward reflect a new strategy that addresses and negotiates the five senses. In the artist's own words: "In order to express the image in my mind as art in a concrete form, I felt that the material and my own thinking had to be properly aligned. As I was considering the five senses of the human body (sight, hearing, touch, smell, and taste) while reflecting on the five senses within myself, the terms 'sensual' and 'organic' first came to my mind."

Matsutani's performances center on a deep engagement with the senses alongside materiality, gesture, and temporality. His performative interactions with graphite, sumi ink, water, and occasionally vinyl glue foreground process over outcome. The performance itself becomes a durational act of making, where the artist's physical presence and sensory awareness are central. Time plays a significant role: Materials are allowed to drip, pool, and move gradually, revealing transformations that cannot be entirely predicted or controlled. These performances often culminate in a decisive act—a moment that serves as a final gesture—signaling completion and release. The intentional interruption disrupts the meditative rhythm that precedes it, highlighting both control and surrender in his artistic process.

At the 2017 Venice Biennale, Matsutani presented the largest surface yet entirely covered in graphite. Against this vast backdrop of shimmering graphite, evoking a monastic atmosphere, *Stream-Venice* featured a sack filled with sumi ink suspended above a wooden ball positioned atop a large square zinc basin. With a long wooden stick, the artist pierced the sack, allowing the ink to drop onto the wooden ball below, completing the work. For Matsutani, the evolution of *Streams* transformed his drawing practice into a performative and durational act, fusing material, gesture, and time into a unified expression. Similarly, the resulting works are not merely images but records of sustained presence—embodied time rendered visible.

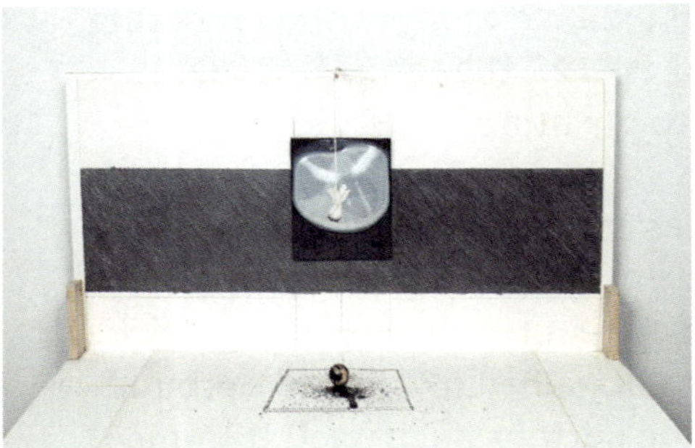

Maquette for *Stream-Pompidou*, 2019. Graphite pencil, vinyl adhesive, sumi ink, wood, cotton, and cord on paper and cardboard, 16⅜ × 31½ × 16½ in. (41.5 × 80 × 42 cm)

Rather than adopting overtly theatrical or dramatic movement, Matsutani's performances are characterized by a deliberate, ritual-like quality. His actions—rubbing an inkstick onto stone, piercing a bag of ink, or slowly guiding materials across a surface—are restrained yet resonant. These gestures draw attention to the tactile and temporal qualities of matter, inviting the viewer to consider the shifting boundaries between drawing, painting, and performance. Often site-responsive, Matsutani's performances are presented within specific spatial contexts, where the remnants of the action—stained paper, an ink trail, a blackened stone—remain as physical documentation. These traces serve both as records of an event and as independent works in their own right.

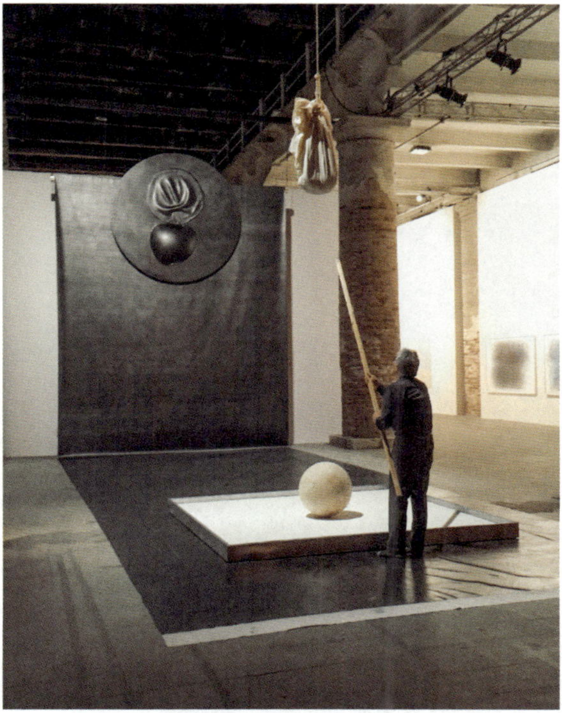

Matsutani performing *Stream-Venice* (2016–17) at the Venice Biennale, 2017

Matsutani's performances are deeply aligned with his broader artistic practice. The longstanding interest in repetition, accumulation, and material transformation evident since the beginning of the *Streams* series is here extended and made visible through live action. While less overtly physical than the body-centric work of some of his Gutai peers, Matsutani's performances nonetheless emphasize corporeal presence. They are acts of both endurance and reflection, where attention to the inner image and the unfolding of process converge in subtle, resonant forms.

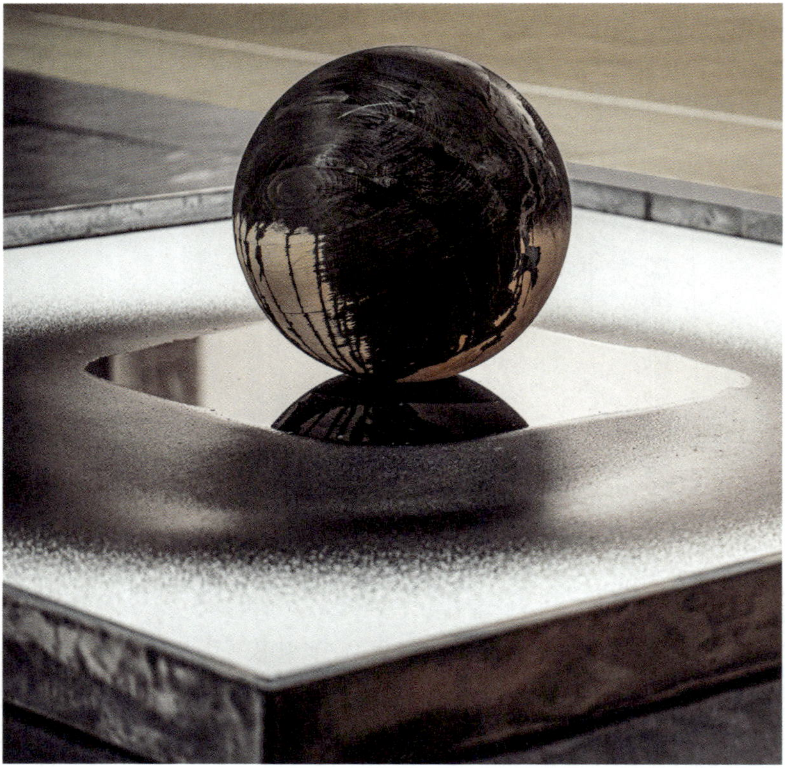

Stream-Venice (detail), 2016–17

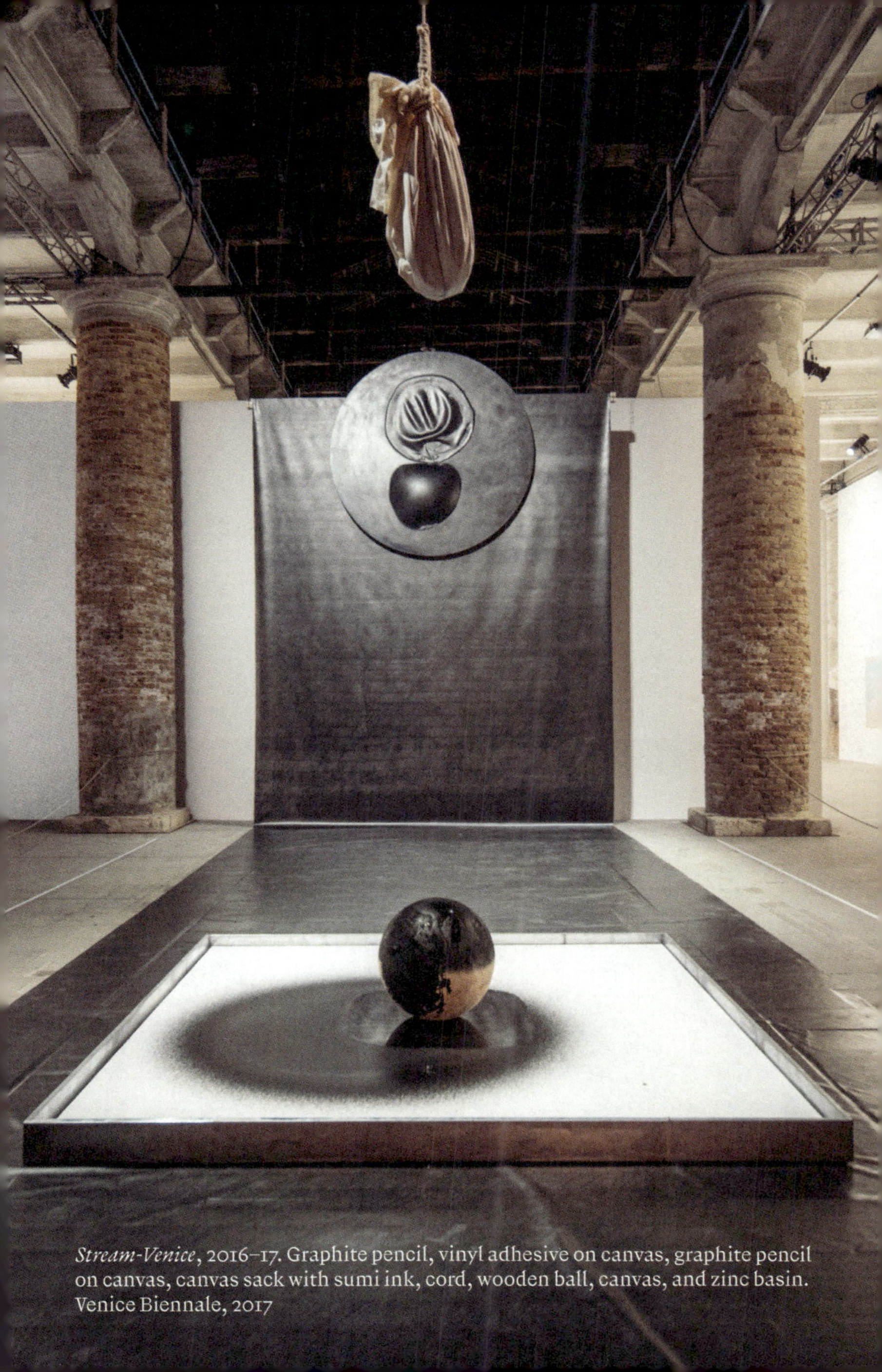

Stream-Venice, 2016–17. Graphite pencil, vinyl adhesive on canvas, graphite pencil on canvas, canvas sack with sumi ink, cord, wooden ball, canvas, and zinc basin. Venice Biennale, 2017

A *Stream* Performance

On May 17, 2023, as part of the exhibition *Takesada Matsutani: A Matrix*, the artist staged a performance with sumi ink and a block of stone from Somerset, at Hauser & Wirth London. The stills here come from footage of this performance, which is available online.

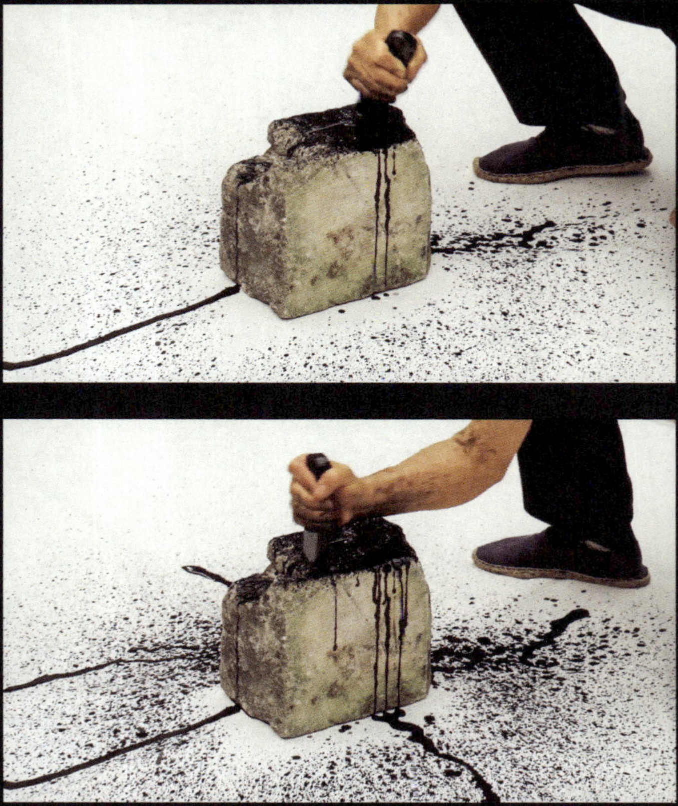

Stream-Hauser & Wirth London, 2013

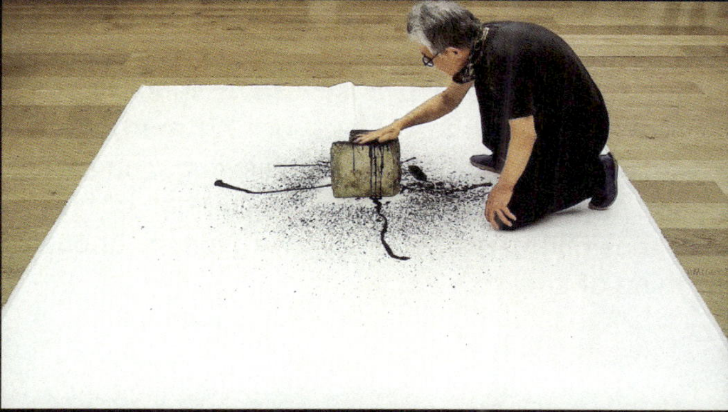

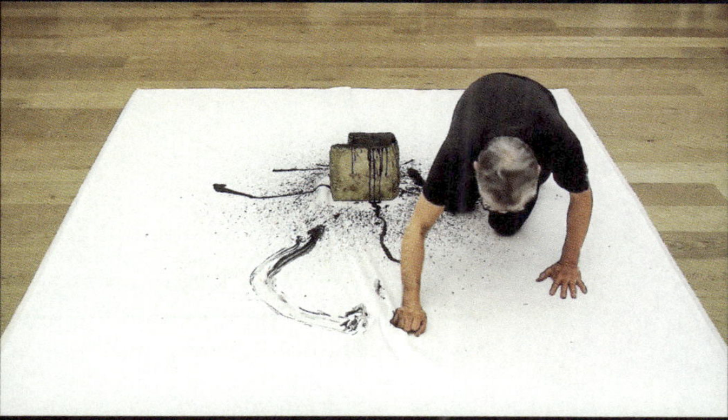

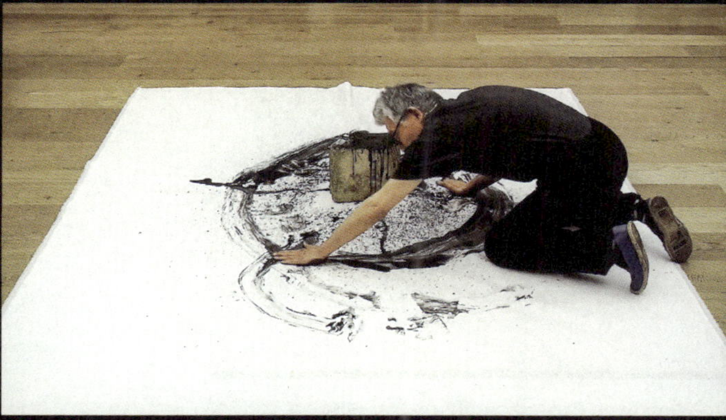

In Pictures

Sketchbooks and Drawings

Matsutani's sketches are prisms into his inner imagery that reveal how he probes and refines his methods. His extensive archive of sketches, drawings, conceptual notes, and studio diaries reveal the evolution of his visceral sensibilities, engagement with binary oppositions, and probing of space.

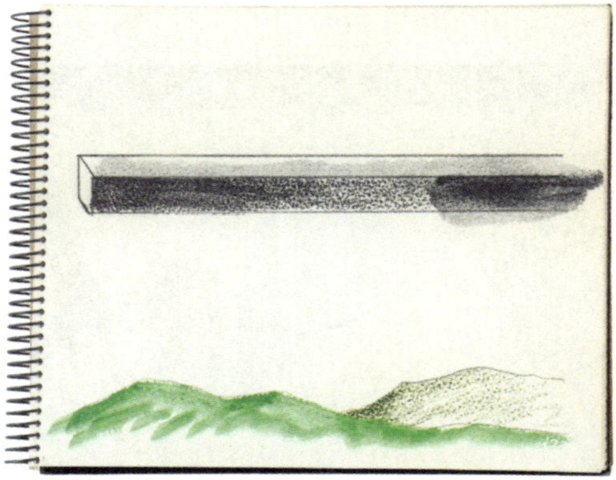

Drawing from Paris sketchbook, 1980

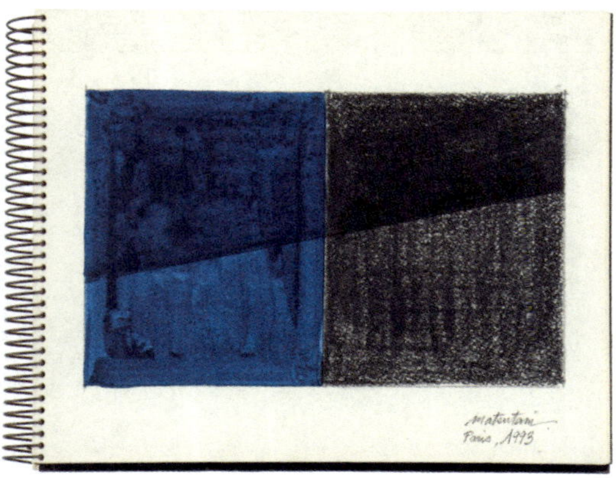

Drawing from Paris sketchbook, ca. 1989–93

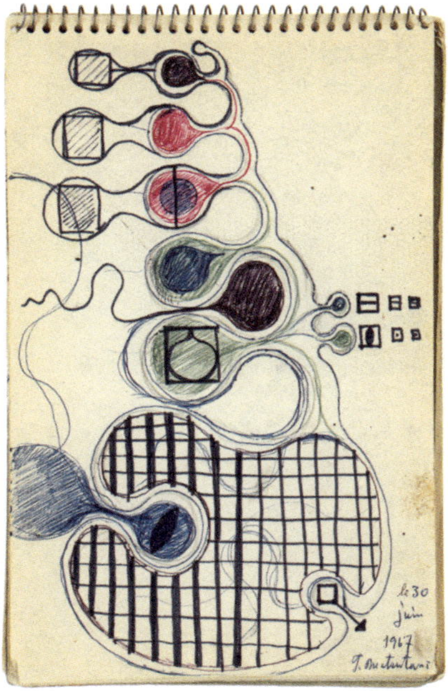

Drawing from Atelier 17 sketchbook, 1967

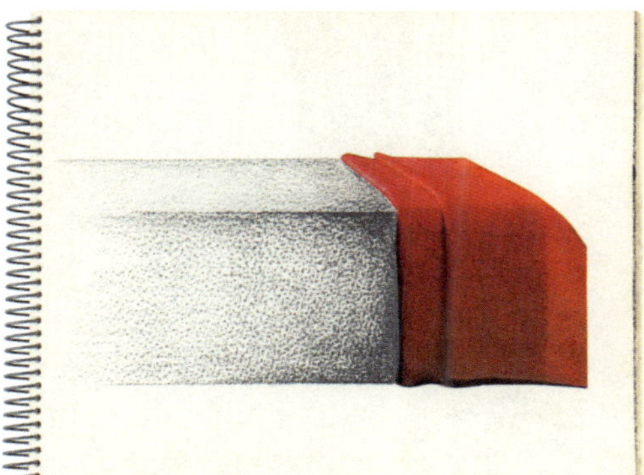

Drawing from Paris sketchbook, ca. 1984–86

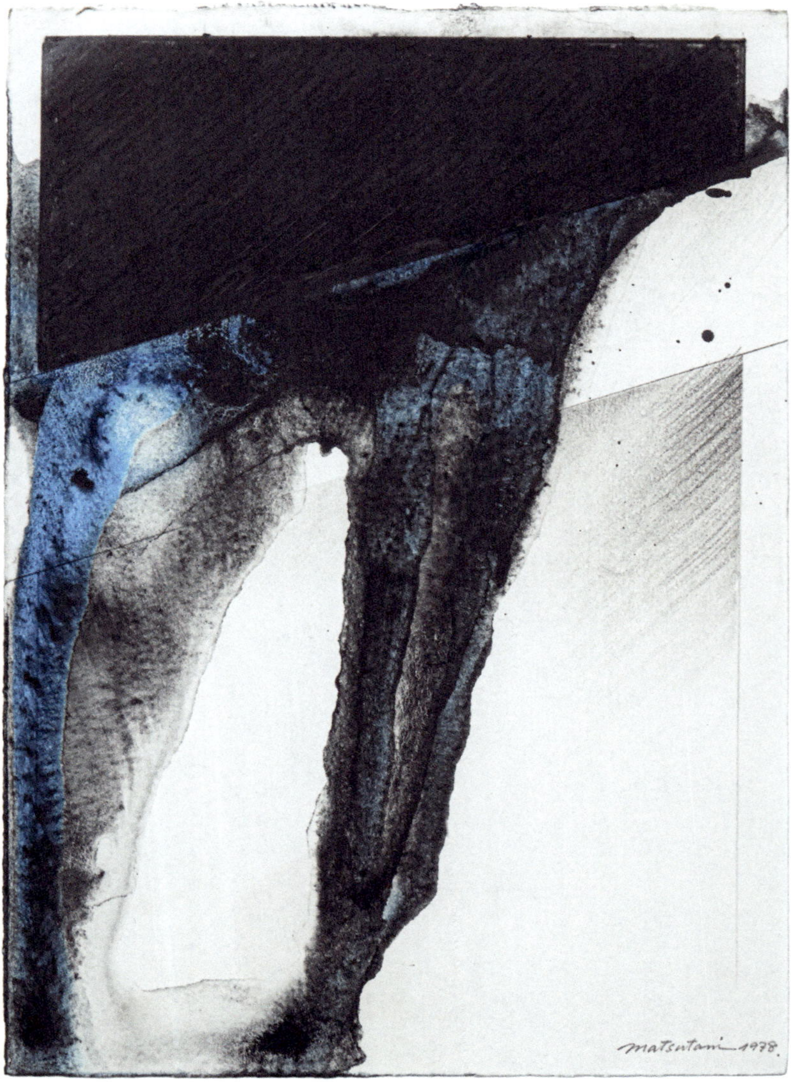

Stream-78, 1978. Graphite and oil on paper, 16⅞ × 12⅜ in. (43 × 31.5 cm)

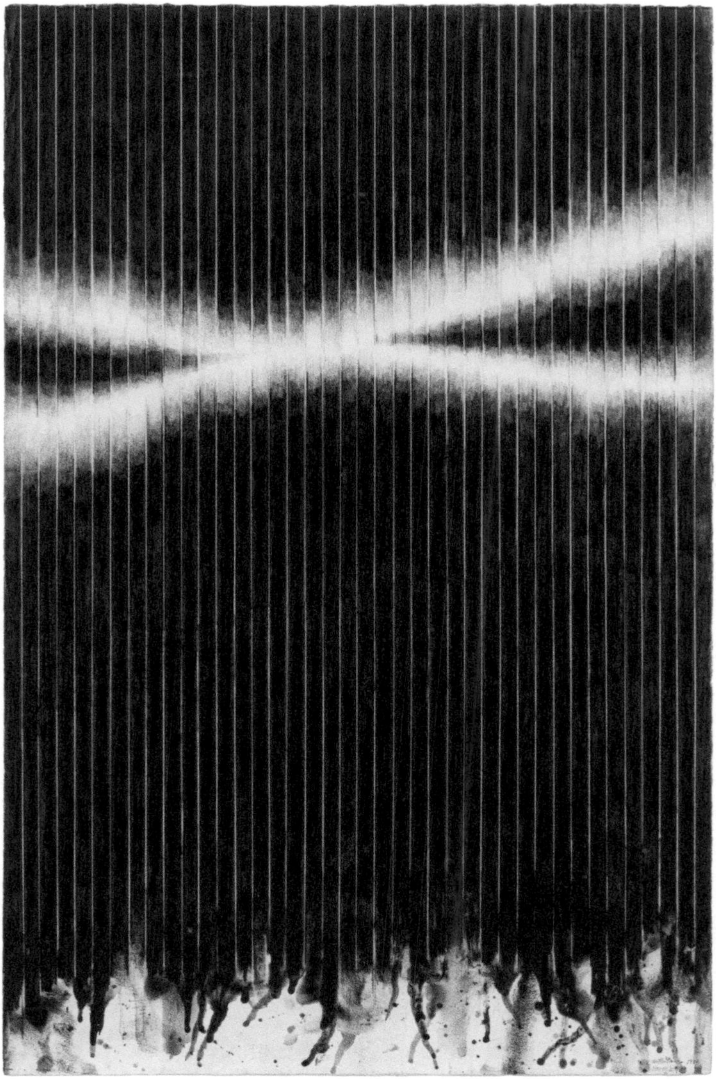

Stream 84-A, 1984. Graphite pencil and turpentine on paper, 47⅛ × 31½ in. (119.7 × 80 cm)

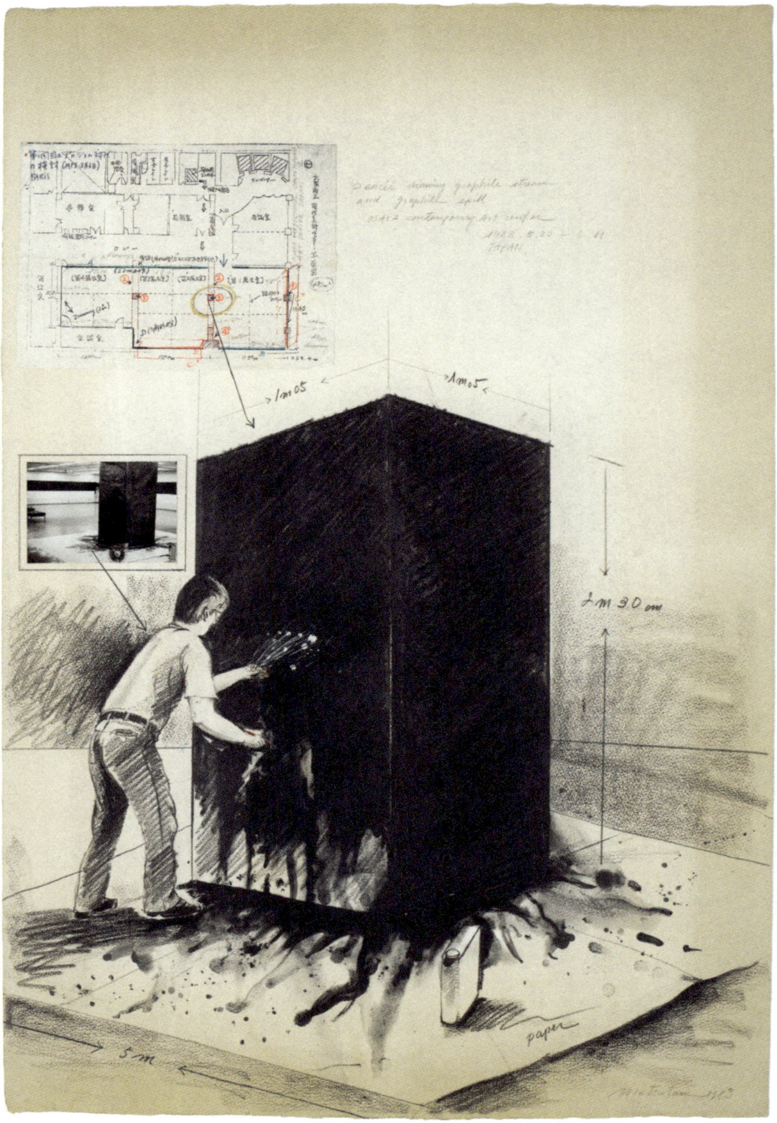

Stream-On That Day, 1983. Graphite pencil with turpentine dilution and collage on paper, 35½ × 24¾ in. (90.2 × 63 cm)

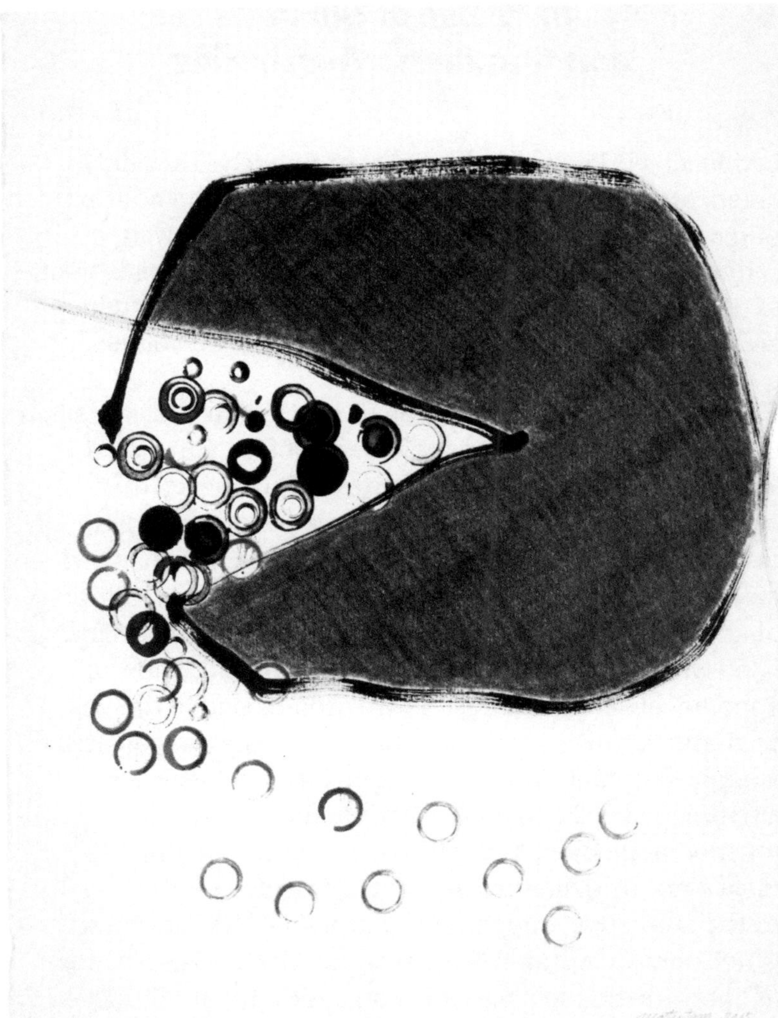

Untitled, 2015–20. Graphite pencil and sumi ink on paper, 15 × 11¼ in. (38 × 28.5 cm)

In Praise of Shadows and "Japanese Aesthetics"

In Jun'ichirō Tanizaki's *In Praise of Shadows*, a widely celebrated essay first published in 1933 in the context of a rapidly modernizing Japan, the author—a writer otherwise known for his sharp wit and erotic obsessions—articulates a distinctly Japanese aesthetic grounded in subtlety, obscurity, and the activation of the senses.

Tanizaki seems at times to play with the (self-)orientalism in his advocacy of a "Japanese" sensibility. But there is sincerity too, as when he writes, "The quality that we call beauty . . . must always grow from the realities of life." Emphasizing that aesthetic appreciation is often mediated through the sensory and atmospheric effects of shadows, he reflects on the tactile warmth of a bowl filled with soup, the silent presence of liquid, and the ephemeral scent that rises with steam. Under the veil of shadow, these seemingly mundane experiences attain a quasi-spiritual significance. Similarly, in describing a hanging scroll and a flower arrangement within a dim *tokonoma* (alcove), Tanizaki notes that these objects "serve not as ornament but rather to give depth to the shadows," suggesting that visual indistinctness is not only acceptable but essential. Rather than a lack of light, the shadow becomes an aesthetic condition.

Tanizaki's contemplative examination of the interplay of light and shadow deeply resonated with Matsutani, whose intensely corporeal artistic practice invites a meditative stillness that allows viewers to oscillate between sensory immediacy and imaginative distance. Like Tanizaki's shadows, Matsutani's surfaces are meant not to reveal but to withhold—to become, in Tanizaki's words, "a delicate surface upon which the faint, frail light can play."

Translated into French and English in 1977 and 1978, respectively, *In Praise of Shadows* was read as a compelling alternative to Western rationalism. It was seen as a prescient critique of modernity, gently warning against the sterilizing effects of excessive illumination and the obsession with perfection. With its reflections on the tactile beauty of the muted sheen of lacquerware or the nuanced interplay of light and shadow in traditional architecture, Tanizaki's essay was widely praised for its exploration of imperfection and restraint and for opening a window to the natural and sensory richness of "Japanese aesthetics." It resonated deeply within French intellectual and artistic circles and had a lasting influence on art, design, and cultural reflection.

The essay's critique of Western emphasis on clarity and brightness, contrasted with the Japanese appreciation for shadow and subtlety, mirrors the challenges faced by Matsutani. Navigating between Japanese and European influences and aesthetic paradigms, Matsutani's art can be seen as a response to the perceived binary tensions between Eastern tradition and Western modernity and as a direct challenge to any exoticized representation of "Japaneseness." His deep engagement with a wide range of practices, from nihonga, Surrealism, and Gutai to Minimalism and performance, as well as his participation in international exhibitions, has allowed him to combine global contemporary art practices with elements of traditional Japanese aesthetics, presenting a more complex, uniquely transcultural practice.

The Target (detail), 2021 (p. 139)

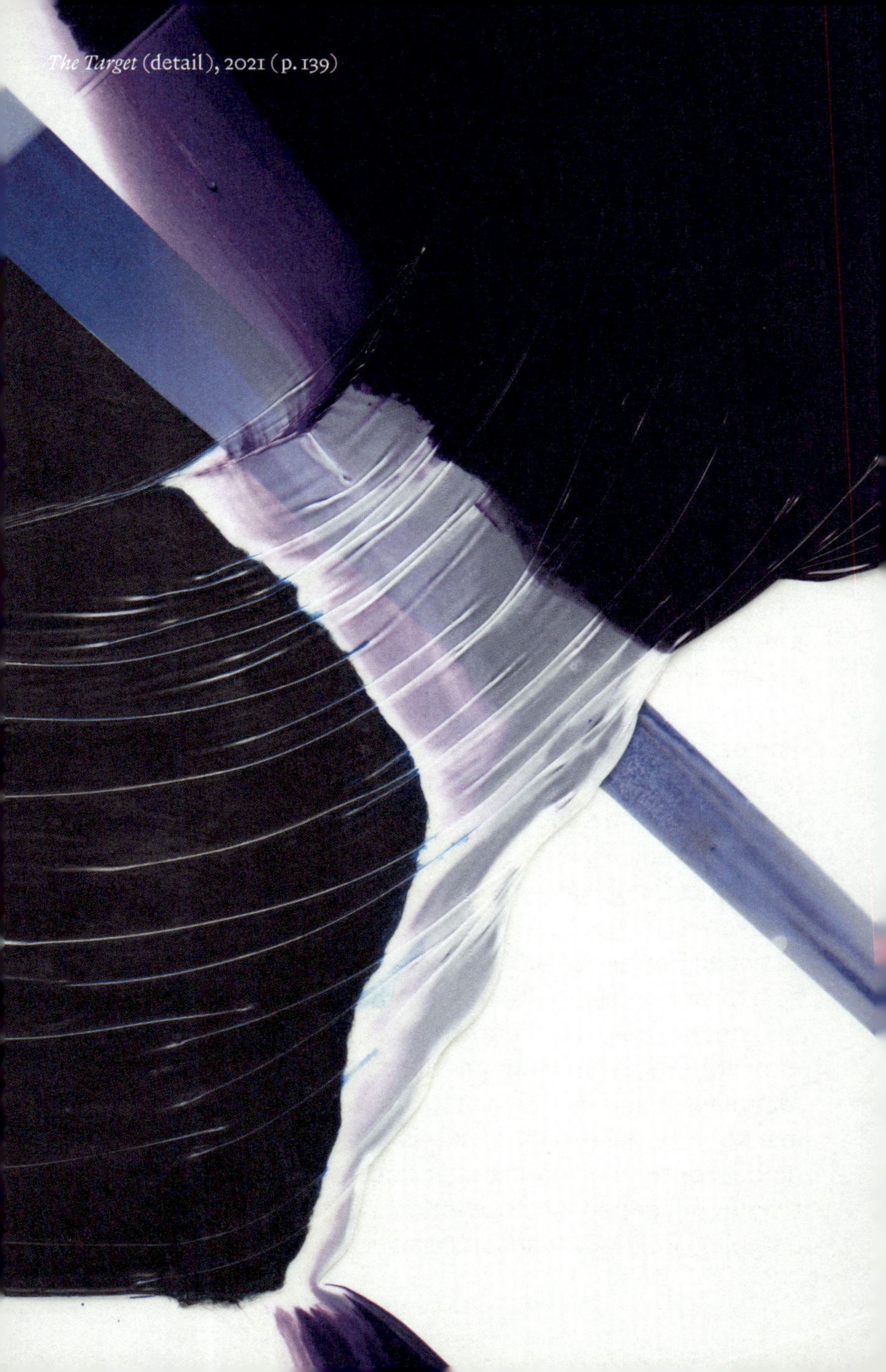

Emptiness and Openness

What has become more prominent within Matsutani's evolving practice is the recurrence of emptiness. Like Hasegawa's compositions (p. 65), his works often explore the dynamic relationship between form and void, presence and absence. Across Matsutani's installations and works on paper, vast fields of blankness set off concentrated zones of activity, heightening the viewer's awareness of silence, breath, and emptiness as active components of the work. This sensibility is also, in part, deeply resonant with Zen philosophy, which prizes emptiness as a generative space—an interval that invites contemplation and self-reflection. In this sense, Matsutani's works function as meditative objects, encouraging a state of mindful engagement and perceptual openness.

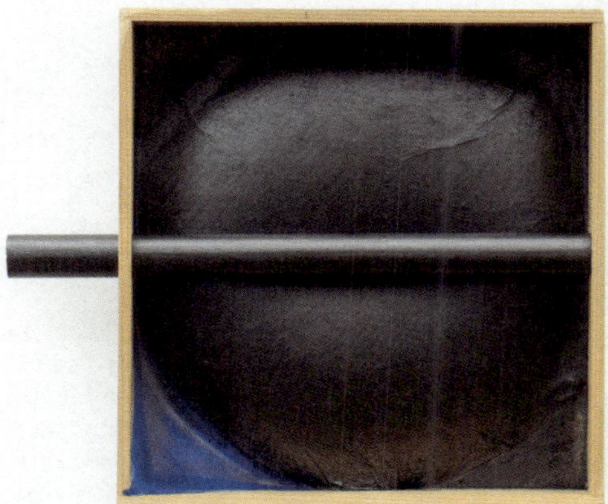

Soft and Hard 9-11-2010, 2010. Vinyl adhesive and graphite pencil on paper, acrylic, and wooden stick in a wooden box, 9⅞ × 12 × 2⅛ in. (25 × 30.5 × 5.5 cm)

In recent years, Matsutani has adopted a more liberated and versatile approach, eschewing adherence to any single technique or mode of expression. His practice has expanded in both scope and complexity, characterized by a synthesis of boldness and nuanced subtlety. Drawing inspiration from quotidian experiences and sensory perceptions, he repurposes books, sticks, ropes, soft fibers, wood, and other objects that he has accumulated over the past fifty years in his studio. He combines them with glue or bright pigments to make works that sometimes function as a form of visual diary. Through continued engagement with his own body and sensory faculties, Matsutani generates artworks that are marked by ongoing exploration, innovation, and unexpected revelation.

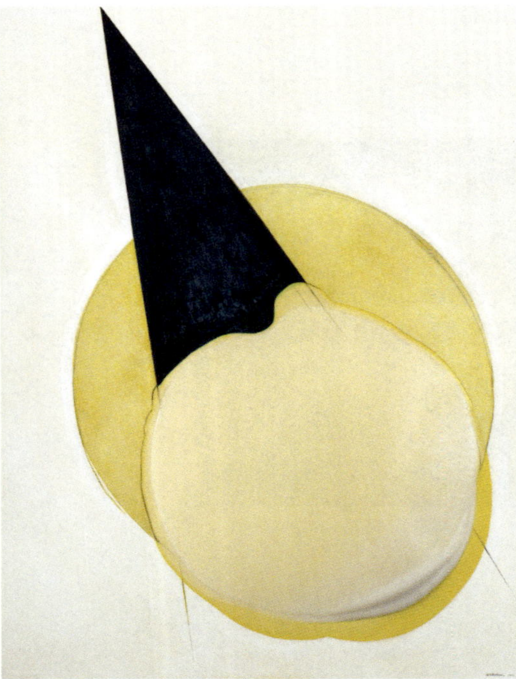

C, Yellow-2022, 2022. Vinyl adhesive, graphite pencil, and acrylic on canvas, 57⅝ × 45⅛ × 2¾ in. (146.5 × 114.5 × 7 cm)

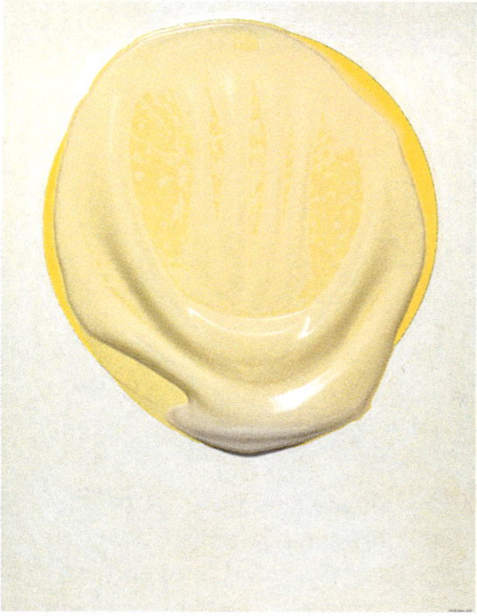

Propagation 15-2, 2015. Vinyl adhesive and acrylic on canvas and plywood, 57½ × 44⅞ in. (146 × 114 cm)

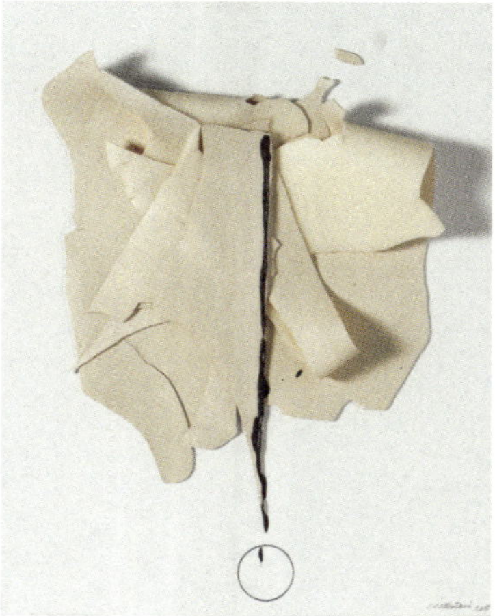

Work-15, 2015. Vinyl adhesive, graphite pencil, and acrylic on canvas, 16⅛ × 13 in. (41 × 33 cm)

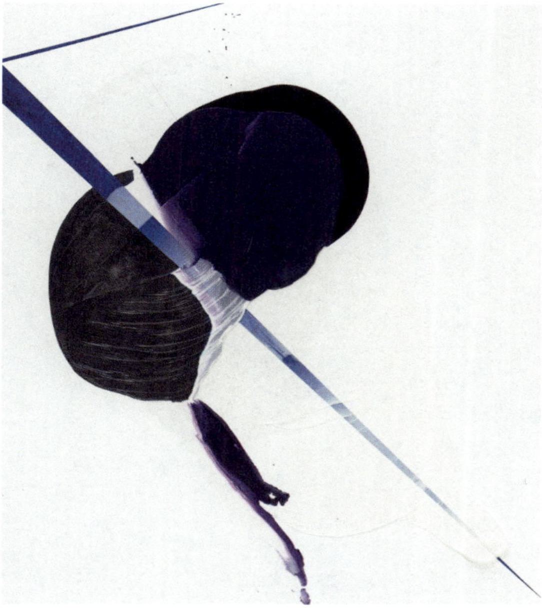

The Target, 2021. Vinyl adhesive, acrylic, and graphite pencil on canvas mounted on plywood, 86½ × 78⅞ × 1½ in. (219.7 × 200.3 × 3.8 cm)

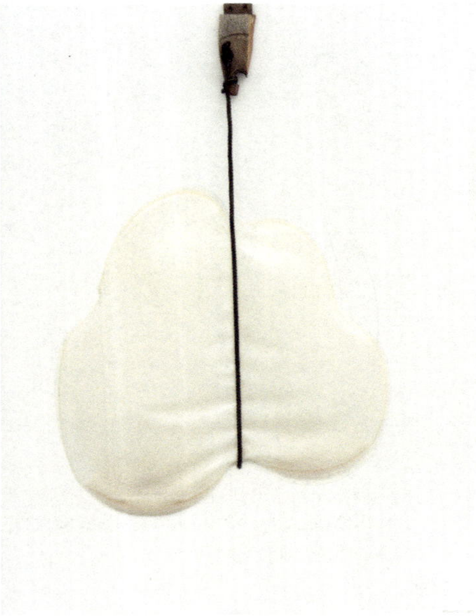

Suspend, 2023. Vinyl adhesive, graphite pencil, acrylic, wood, and cord on canvas, 57½ × 44⅞ × 4⅜ in. (146 × 114 × 11 cm)

Circle-Blue and Black, 2022. Vinyl adhesive, graphite pencil, and acrylic on canvas mounted on plywood (in two parts), 63 × 57⅛ × 2 in. (160 × 145 × 5 cm)

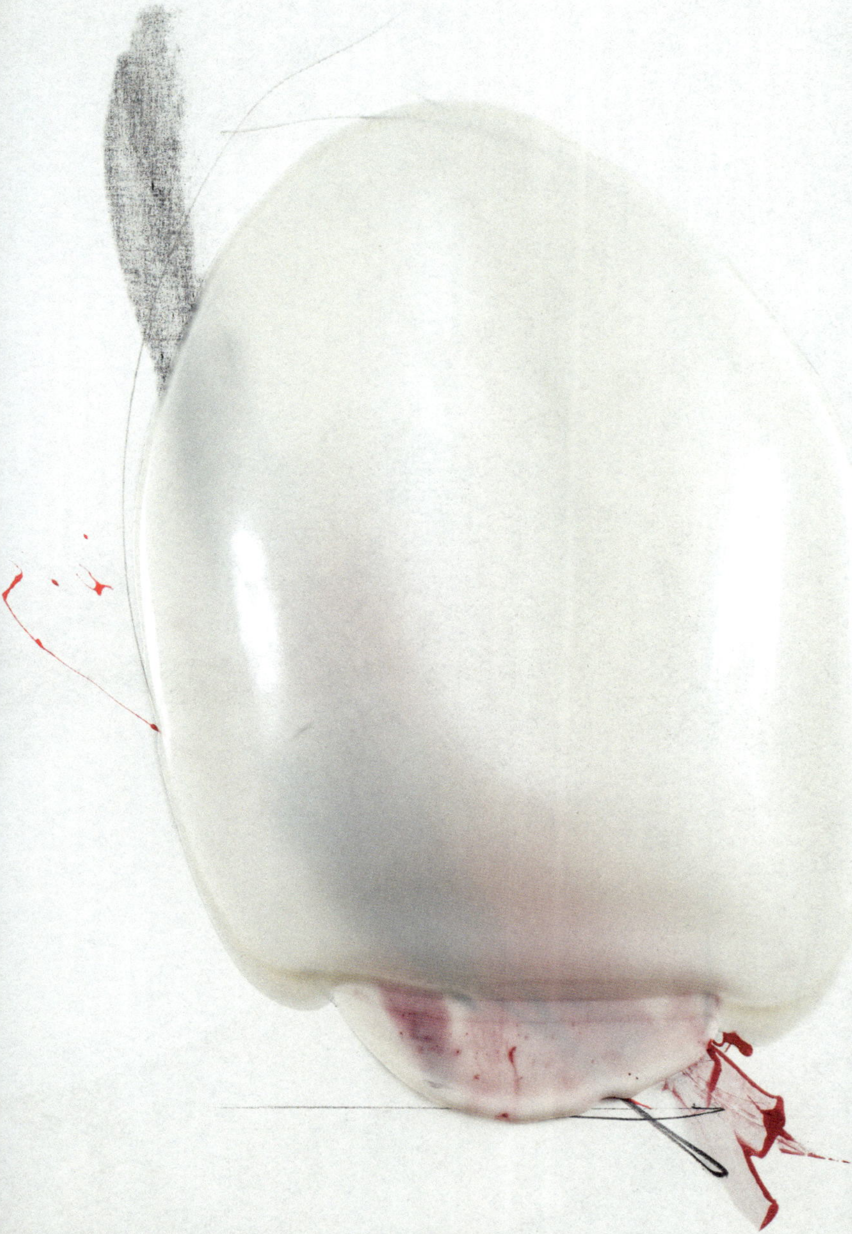

Puffed up-2, 2020. Vinyl adhesive, graphite pencil, and acrylic on canvas mounted on plywood, 36 × 24¾ × 4⅛ in. (91.5 × 63 × 10.5 cm)

Matsutani at work in his studio, Rue Faidherbe, Paris, 2025

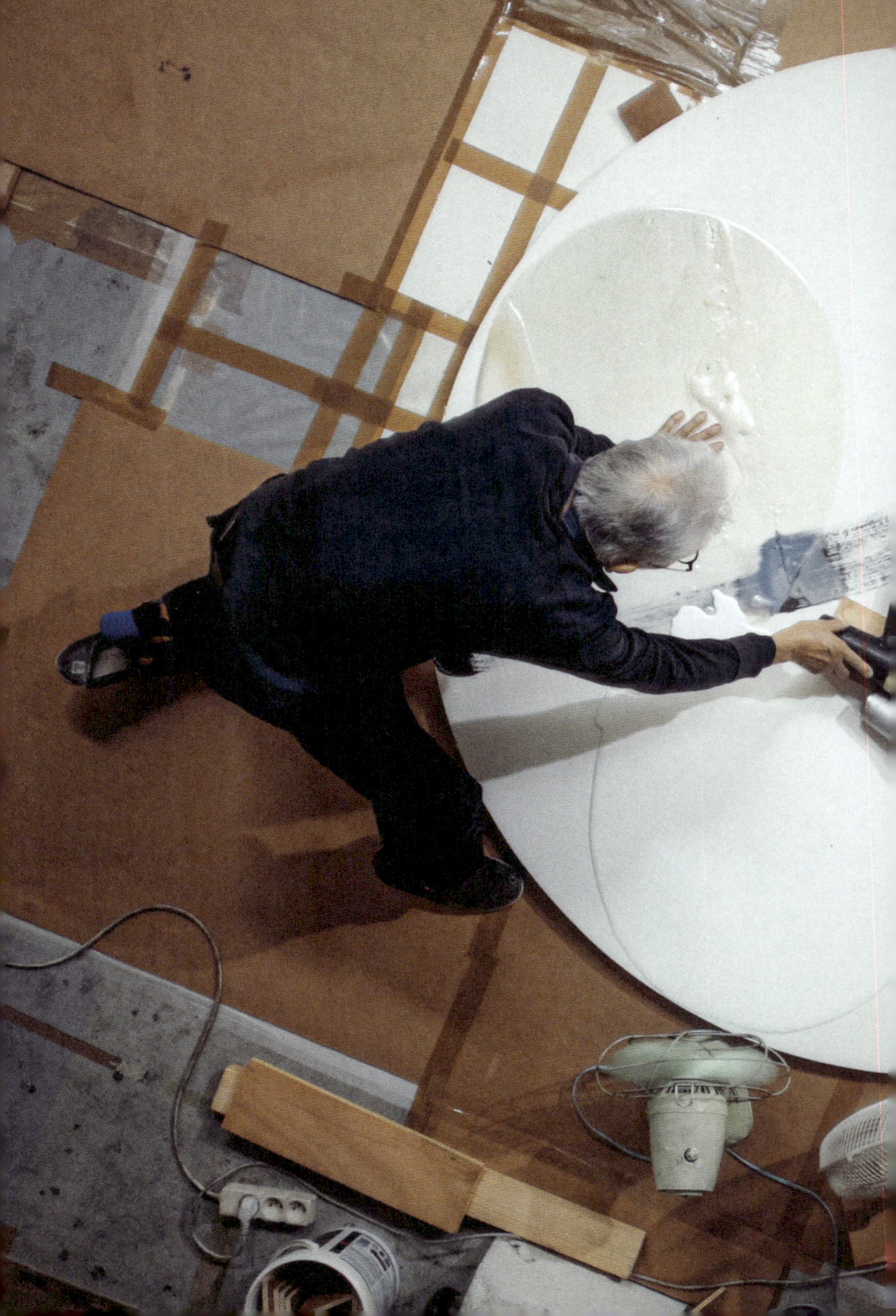

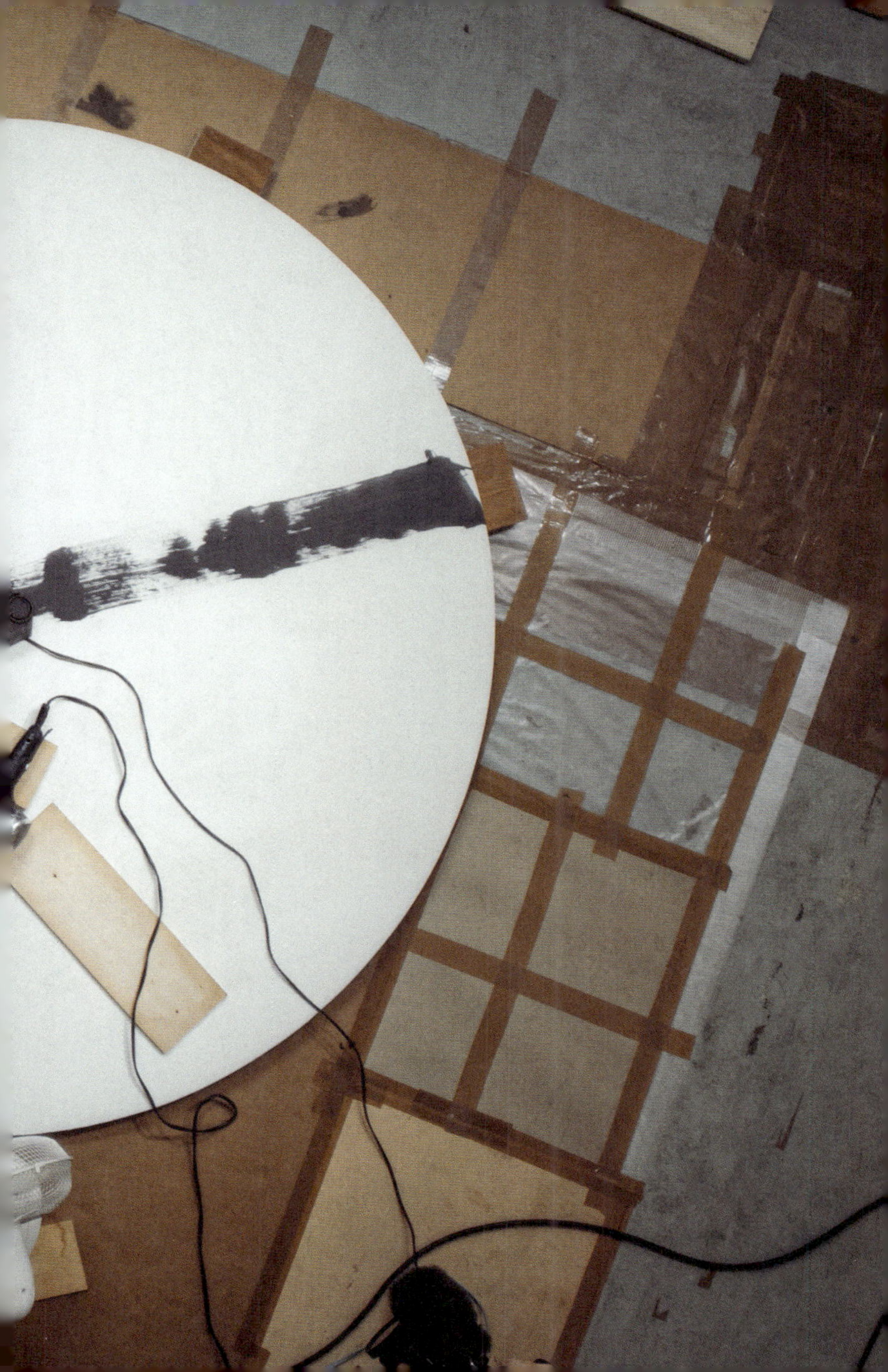

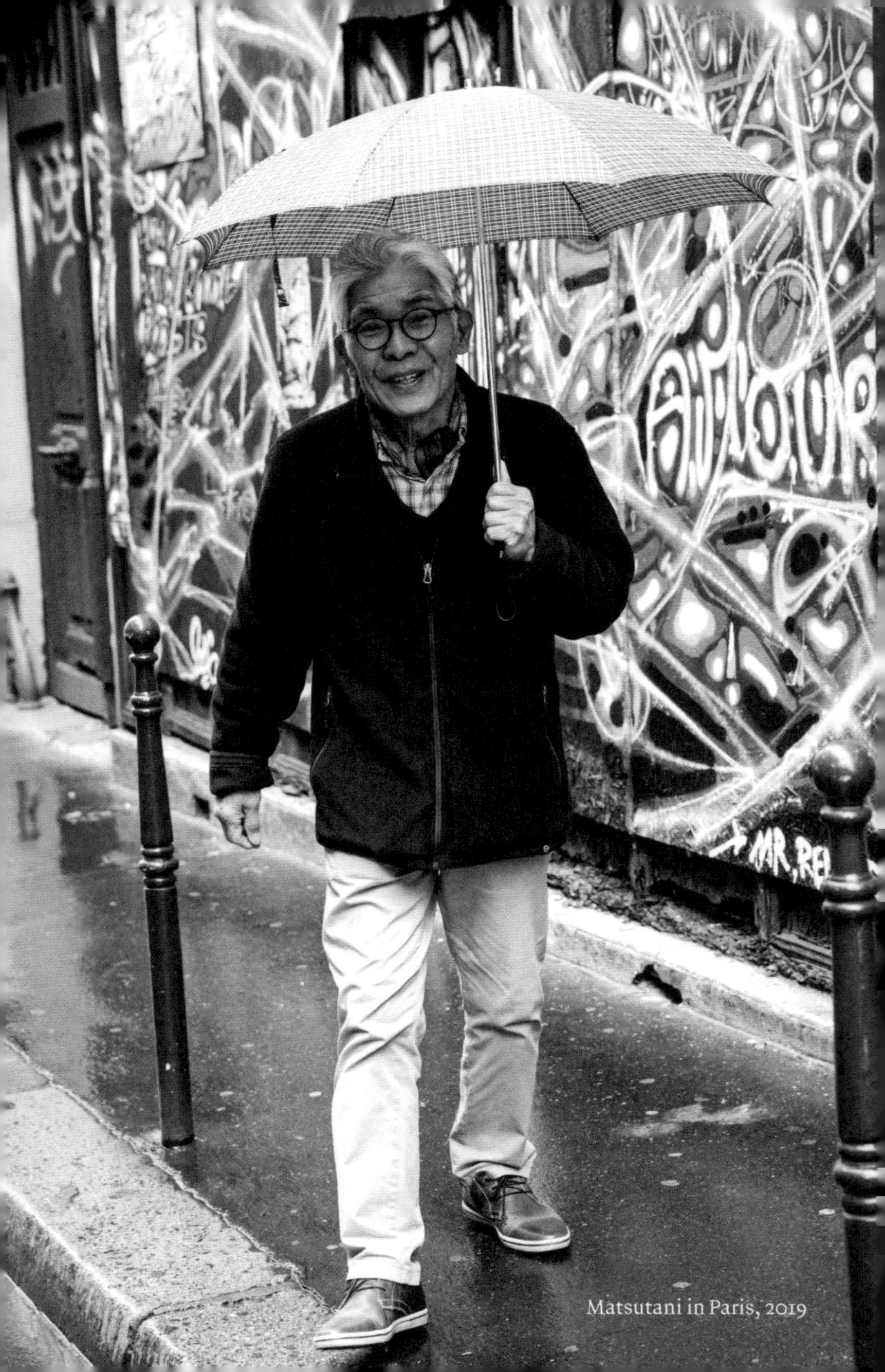

Matsutani in Paris, 2019

Memory, Impermanence, Resilience

Beneath much of Matsutani's art is an undercurrent of memory, impermanence, and the search for continuity. Having suffered from tuberculosis as a young man, and later experiencing the tumult of postwar Japan and the disbanding of the Gutai group, he often grapples with themes of vulnerability and endurance in his work. The surfaces of his paintings bear traces of rupture and repair—bulges are punctured and sealed, graphite is abraded and reapplied—signaling the perpetual negotiation between damage and healing.

This motif resonates with both personal and collective histories, transforming individual memory into a universal meditation. His works record both the immediacy of touch and the endurance of process, embodying the slow passage of existence through the accumulation of marks, folds, and surfaces. The rupturing of materials mirrors Matsutani's own perseverance through illness, displacement, and loss, while also evoking Japan's postwar struggle to recover its cultural and moral equilibrium.

At its core, Matsutani's work confronts the transience of existence and the fragile lines of its emergence and disappearance. The swelling and deflating forms of his early works recall the pulse of living tissue, while their contraction and collapse signal the quiet inevitability of decay. In his later graphite works, repetition becomes both a discipline and a meditation on mortality: Each stroke is a gesture of continuation, yet also an acknowledgment of impermanence. His practice embodies the cyclical nature of being—birth, growth, erosion, and renewal—rendering death not as an end but as an essential transformation

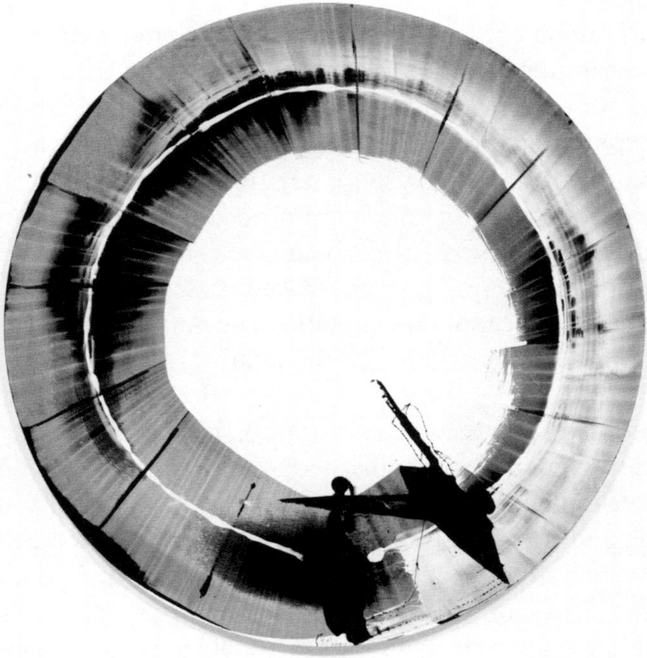

Abstrait LA BOVERIE, Liège, Belgique, 2024. Vinyl adhesive and acrylic on canvas mounted on plywood, 72⅝ × 72⅝ × 1⅜ in. (184.5 × 184.5 × 3.5 cm)

within the continuum of existence. Ultimately, Matsutani's oeuvre stands as an elegy to impermanence and endurance alike. In the face of inevitable dissolution, each mark and scar becomes a quiet affirmation of life's continual unfolding. His accomplishment is an eloquent testament to survival, adaptation, and the dignity of persistence, a place where transformation itself becomes an enduring form of life.

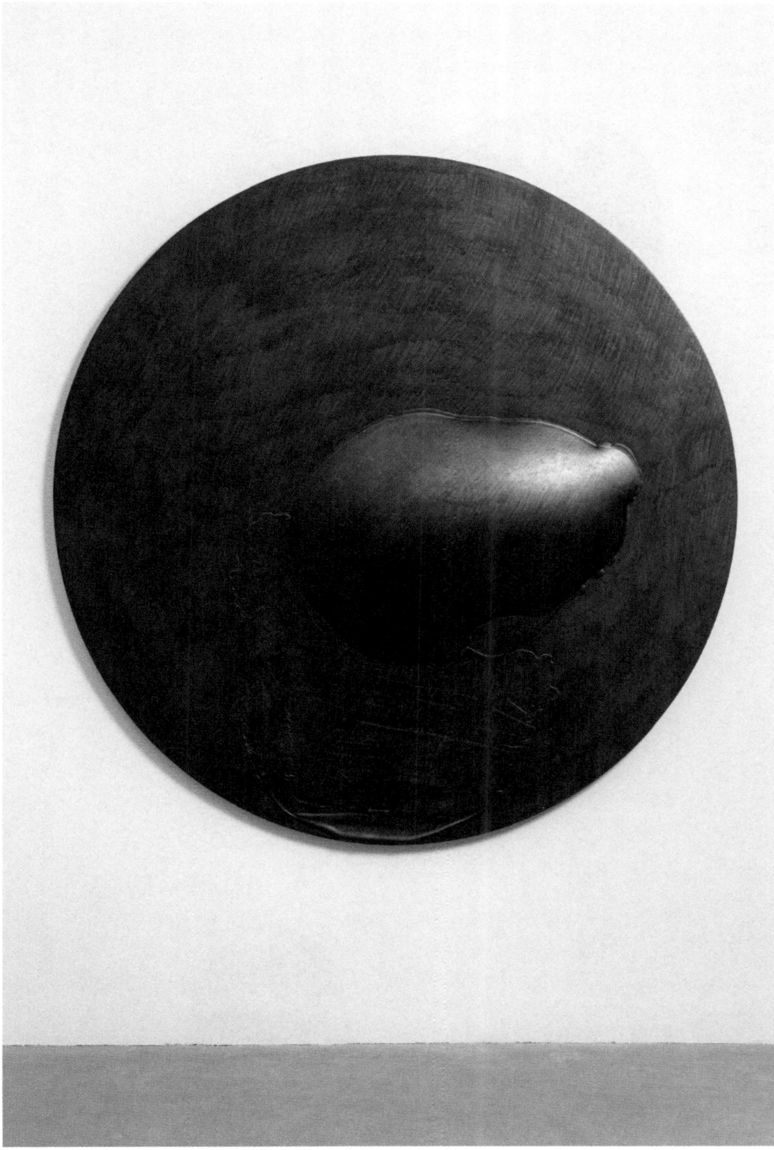

Circle 17-11, 2017. Vinyl adhesive and graphite pencil on canvas, 69¼ × 69¼ in. (176 × 176 cm)

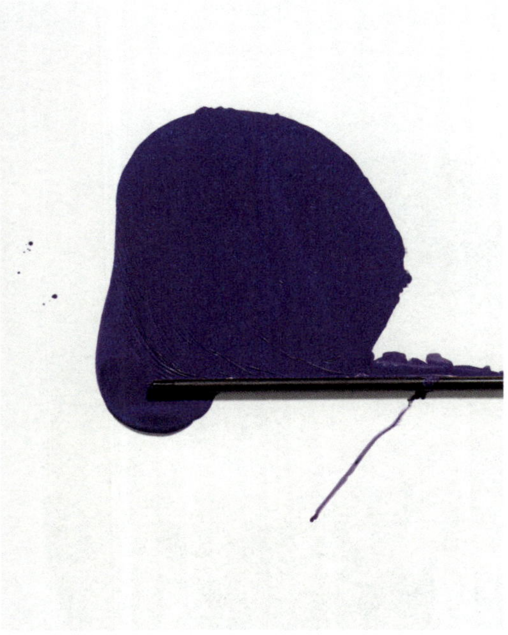

Propagation 25-B, 2025. Vinyl adhesive, acrylic, and wooden stick on canvas mounted on plywood, 63¾ × 51⅛ × 2½ in. (162 × 130 × 6.4 cm)

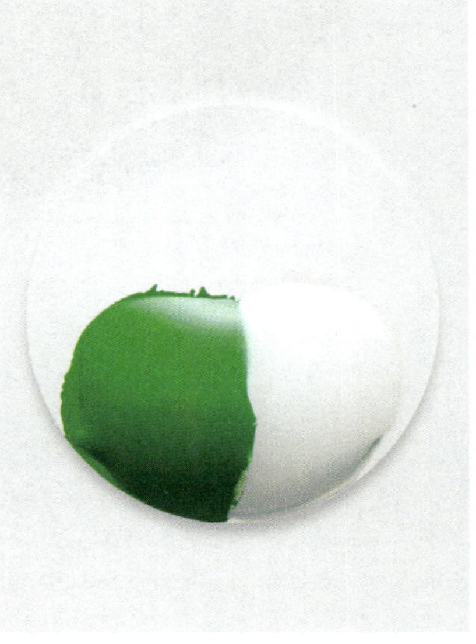

Circle Green-2, 2019. Vinyl adhesive, acrylic, and canvas mounted on plywood, 63⅞ × 63⅞ × 6¾ in. (162.2 × 162.2 × 17 cm)

Moments/Time

For Mr. Minoru Onodera

A flow—the flow of time. When did it start? When will it end?

Within this almost unimaginable flow, we try to create some kind of visual form.

Even if we are truly able to stop time through the act of making a picture, time continues to flow on without end. The human race has survived for thousands of years. Our consciousness is fragmented and our thoughts expand limitlessly. Human beings are living things. Our instincts dwell somewhere deep within us.

Before human society became mechanized, working with our hands, feet, and bodies was important, as were emotions like laughter, sorrow, and anger.

Based on logical convenience, today's machine civilization shows no signs of slowing down. It was also created by human beings, but we have now sunken into an absurd mental abyss.

Unfortunately, those of us living in the present age are the ones who must cope with such contradictions.

We cannot return to primitive times, but instinctive work performed by hand enables us to display our individuality and enriches our powers of expression. We cannot allow ourselves to be used by machines.

Paris, April 2018

Chronology

1937 Takesada Matsutani is born on January 1 in Osaka, as the eldest child of his father, Yoshio, and his mother, Kiyoko. His father works for a life-insurance firm and is often relocated, so Matsutani's childhood involves frequent moves within Japan's Kansai region.

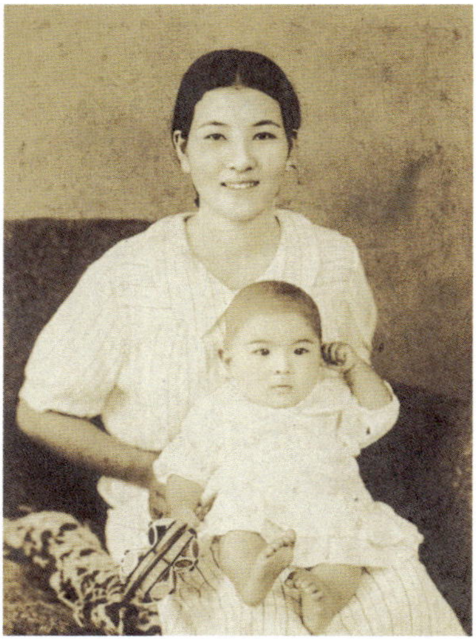

Matsutani and his mother posing for a photo, 1937

1945 Matsutani is nine years old when the United States drops atomic bombs on Hiroshima and Nagasaki.

World War II ends.

1951 Matsutani contracts tuberculosis, of which he is not cured completely until 1959. He remains homebound for long periods of time, during which he discovers Western contemporary art through books and magazines.

1952 In response to his son's wish to avoid repeated moves, his father requests a transfer and the family settles in Nishinomiya. Matsutani grows roses and lilies in the garden of their home and also keeps animals such as birds, dogs, and rabbits, which he sketches, deepening his interest in art.

1954 Enrolls in the traditional painting (nihonga) department at the Osaka Municipal High School of Crafts and Arts, but drops out after two years due to illness.

The Gutai Art Association is founded. Matsutani hears about its first exhibitions, but, in his own words, "In all honesty, I did not like what they were doing and thought, 'This is not art.'"

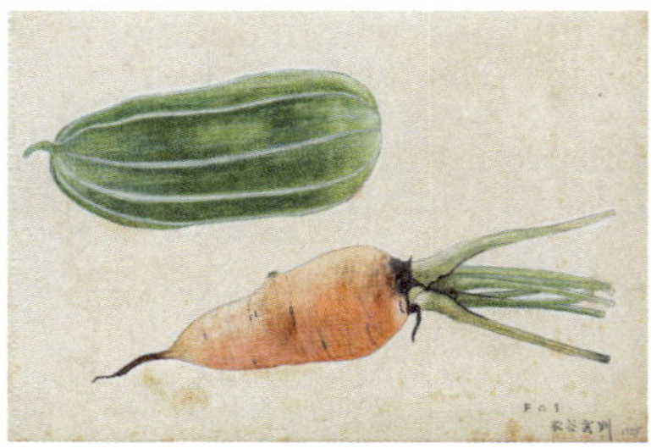

Untitled, 1955. Mineral pigments on paper, 9½ × 14½ in. (24 × 36.7 cm)

1957 Matsutani's landscape painting *The Rock's Surface* (1956) is included in the Eighth Nishinomiya City Exhibition (nihonga). One of the jurors, Shōsaku Arao—a traditional painter open to foreign influences—writes to Matsutani and invites him to visit. They go on to meet often to talk about art.

1958–59 Paints works using mineral pigments on paper, among them *Résistance (Pressure)* (1958), and other paintings that convey a sense of inner conflict and states of anxiety or distress.

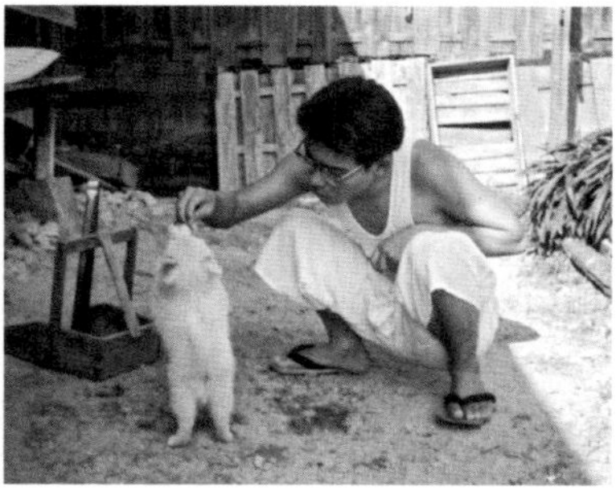

Matsutani petting his dog, 1958

1959–60 Meets Sadamasa Motonaga at a municipal school for drawing. A friendship begins, and Motonaga—an artist who was, in Matsutani's words, "always in good spirits and claiming he was the best in the world"—soon introduces him to Jirō Yoshihara, the Gutai group's founder and mentor. But when Matsutani shows him his new action-based works, Yoshihara tells him "This is no good" and "You have another week. Try again."

1960 Has a single work accepted for the Ninth Gutai Art Exhibition. It is displayed in a corner, which Matsutani finds so frustrating he destroys all the rejected works.

1962 Following the Gutai credo "Do something no one's ever done before," begins to experiment with a newly developed material—vinyl adhesive—which becomes his primary medium. He applies the glue to his canvases, covering them with reliefs or bubbles that spread or burst over the surface, developing a unique technique of breathing air into the material.

First solo show takes place at the YMCA Annex in Kobe, Japan.

Early to mid-1960s Makes a living giving drawing classes to children.

Matsutani's palette at the time ranges from vivid reds to almost monochromatic works in tones of white.

Experiments with techniques to emphasize gravity, such as cutting a slit in drying glue or tilting the support and letting it drip. Starts to be regularly invited to show his work in exhibitions, both in Japan and, from the mid-1960s on, internationally.

1963 Granted membership in the Gutai Art Association.

Solo exhibition of vinyl glue works takes place at the Gutai Pinacotheca in Osaka. He continues to show in all Gutai exhibitions until the group's dissolution in 1972.

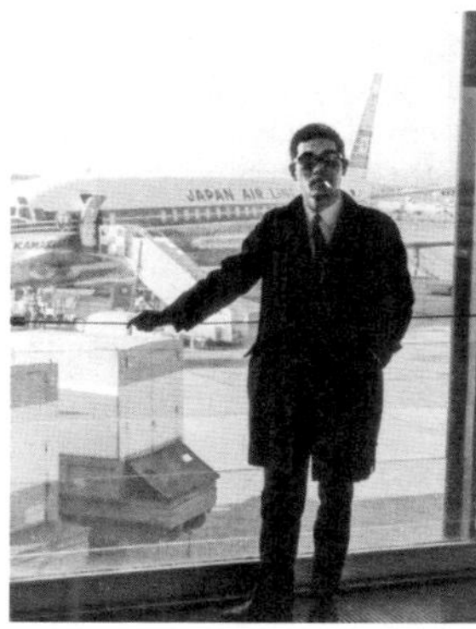

At the airport in Rome, on his way to Cairo, 1966

1966 Shows several objects, among them a flask containing water and oil-based white paint slowly rotating with a motor, at the Gutai Pinacotheca.

Wins first prize in an art competition organized by the newspaper *Mainichi* and the Institut Français.

The award includes a six-month stay in France, and on November 23 he arrives in Paris, where he experiences culture shock. He then travels extensively—to Egypt, Greece, Italy, and Southern France.

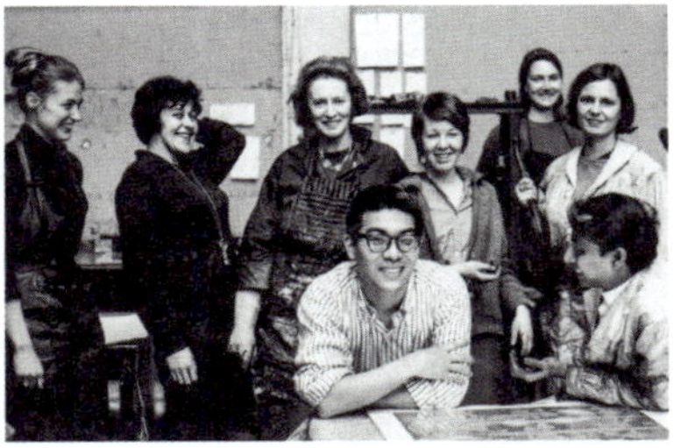

Matsutani (center) and Kate Van Houten (fourth from left) with friends at Atelier 17, Paris, 1967

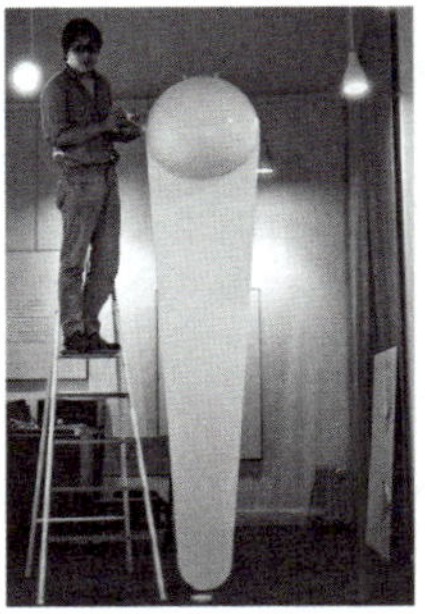

Installing at Galerie Zunini, Paris, 1968

1967 Begins printmaking at Stanley William Hayter's Atelier 17, Paris, taking language classes in the evenings.

Meets his future wife, American artist Kate Van Houten, beginning a lifelong personal and professional relationship. "We stuck together like glue," he later recalls. She asks him on their first date: a trip to the cinema for a Buster Keaton film.

Influenced by Ellsworth Kelly, Matsutani begins working on hard-edge style drawings and paintings, with clearly defined shapes, lines, and vivid colors on flat surfaces, which would become the chief tendency of his work in the 1970s.

1968 Matsutani's first exhibition outside Japan takes place at Galerie Zunini in Paris: a two-person show with Mittsu Sugai. He presents two-dimensional works created using glue shipped from Japan, as well as two sculptures.

Catherine Millet, critic and editor of the magazine *Art Press*, writes a long review for *Les lettres françaises*.

Late 1960s Begins to work with silkscreen in a studio opened by Van Houten and Lorna Taylor in 1968 in Montparnasse. Continues to work on silkscreens with etching through the 1970s.

1970 While still involved with Atelier 17, Matsutani begins working independently as a printer, earning his income by printing silkscreens for other artists, such as Kumi Sugai.

From this time through the 1980s, his own prints are widely exhibited and he wins numerous awards at international print exhibitions.

Takes the opportunity of a solo exhibition at Gallery Shinanobashi, Osaka, to return to Japan for the first time since leaving for France in 1966.

1972 Two of Matsutani's screenprints and one lithograph are shown in the graphic arts section of the Venice Biennale.

Concurrently to their regular live-work studio in the Passage de la Bonne Graine, near Bastille, Van Houten and Matsutani take on a nearby silkscreen studio on Rue Saint-Nicolas, which they use until 1979.

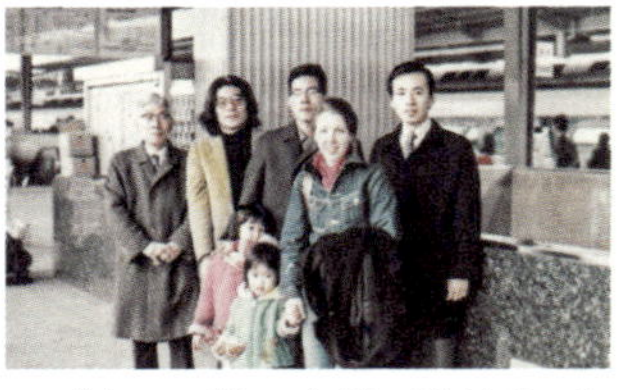

Matsutani (second from left) with his family, 1973

Mid-1970s Confronted with a lack of funds, but time to think, Matsutani reconsiders his relationship to art and to the history of Gutai, and devotes renewed attention to process and communicating an "inner image." He also studies Buddhism and visits numerous temples and rock gardens on trips to Japan. This spiritual exploration is accompanied by a return to the origin of drawing, as Matsutani begins covering paper with graphite pencil strokes, exclusively in black, exploring immobility and movement in time. As he would recall after making this step: "I thought to myself, 'This is quite good. As I've arrived at this point in my life, I shall do what feels right.'"

1976 Matsutani and Van Houten get married.

Late 1970s Standard-format drawings and canvases morph into a series of ten-meter (thirty-two-foot) works in graphite on paper. With a trajectory potentially stretching to infinity, the series *Streams* begins in 1977 and becomes increasingly important. To finish these "bands of blackness," Matsutani frees the graphite with splashes of solvent. He also revisits organic forms made from vinyl adhesive, breaking new ground in his layered graphite-stroke works. In the ensuing years, Matsutani continues to produce a wide variety of works, moving between various series and motifs. He exhibits widely in Europe and Japan.

1978 Matsutani's *Japan Sea-5*, a print of his and Van Houten's cat Neko arching its back, proves a bestseller; Van Houten later recalls, "That cat provided us with a meal for years."

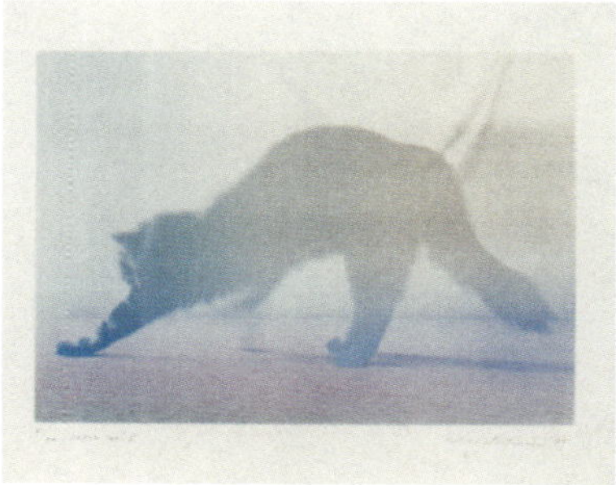

Japan Sea-5, 1978. Photo-silkscreen on paper, $14\frac{3}{8} \times 20\frac{7}{8}$ in. (36.5 × 53 cm)

1979 Matsutani further develops the *Streams* series, creating site-specific installations that enter into a silent dialogue with the surrounding space.

Matsutani starts renovating the studio on Rue Faidherbe where he still works today.

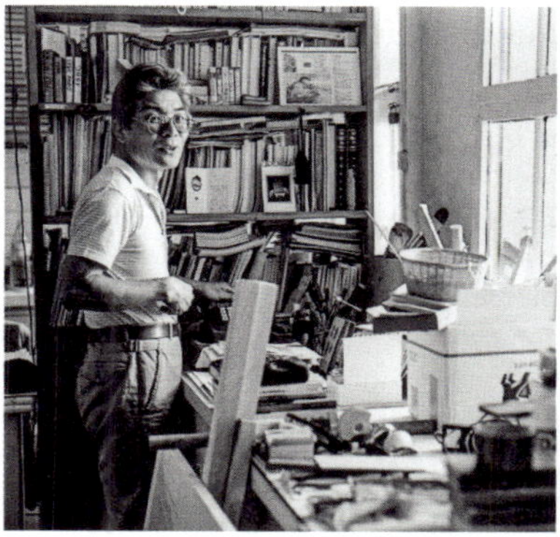

Matsutani in his studio, Passage de la Bonne Graine, Paris, 1981

Early 1980s The *Streams* installations begin to be accompanied by performances, often including an element of chance.

Starts the *Wave* series, applying layers of graphite as a way to experiment with the material's essential character and expressive possibilities.

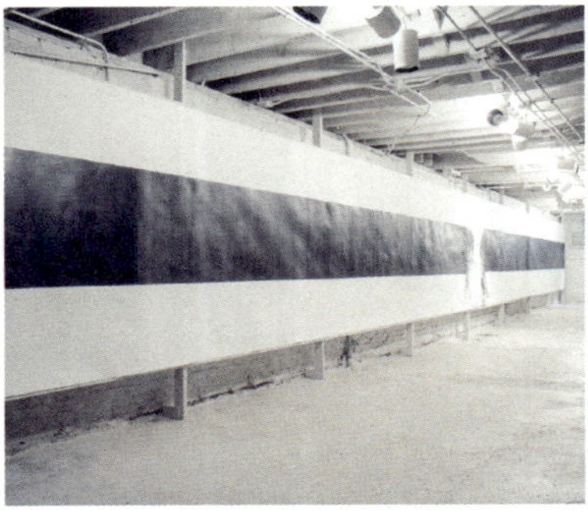

Stream-7, 1982. Graphite pencil on paper with white spirit dilution. Gallery Don Soker-Kaseman, San Francisco

1985 Thanks to Matsutani's efforts, a comprehensive exhibition of Stanley William Hayter's work is held in Kobe and Tokyo.

Begins work on an eight-meter (twenty-six-foot) piece in graphite on paper mounted on wood, commissioned for the sliding screens in the main hall of the reconstructed Temple Kaikōsan in Kobe.

1993 *Takesada Matsutani: Works from the 1960s to Today* opens at the Otani Memorial Art Museum, Nishinomiya.

1996 Van Houten establishes the small independent press Estepa Editions in Paris.

2000 *Matsutani: Waves* takes place at the Otani Memorial Art Museum, Nishinomiya, accompanied by a comprehensive catalogue.

2002 Receives the City Cultural Award in Nishinomiya, where he spent much of his childhood.

2010 *Matsutani Takesada: Stream* opens at the Museum of Modern Art, Kamakura, Japan.

2011–12 Initially using smaller formats, Matsutani revisits his earlier palette and increasingly uses green, yellow, and blue in vinyl glue works on canvas.

2012 Participates in the first major Gutai retrospective in Tokyo, *Gutai: The Spirit of an Era*, at the National Art Center.

2013 *Takesada Matsutani: A Matrix* is published, featuring an extensive interview previously published in Japanese.

Matsutani's work is presented in major Gutai exhibitions around the world, most notably *Gutai: Splendid Playground* at the Solomon R. Guggenheim Museum, New York, which revives international interest in the movement.

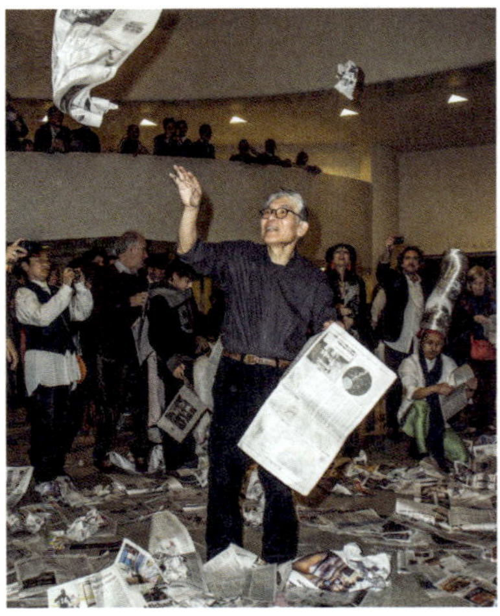

Matsutani performing at the Solomon R. Guggenheim Museum, New York, 2013

2015 *Matsutani: Currents* opens at the Otani Memorial Art Museum, Nishinomiya, accompanied by a comprehensive catalogue.

Matsutani and Van Houten create SHŌEN, a Paris-based endowment with three main objectives: the preservation and study of Matsutani's and Van Houten's work; supporting research and care in the field of visible and invisible handicaps; and encouraging artistic and cultural creation.

2017 SHŌEN launches the Prix Matsutani, an annual award that aims to support artists in developing their work.
Exhibits the large-scale installation *Stream-Venice* as part of the Venice Biennale.

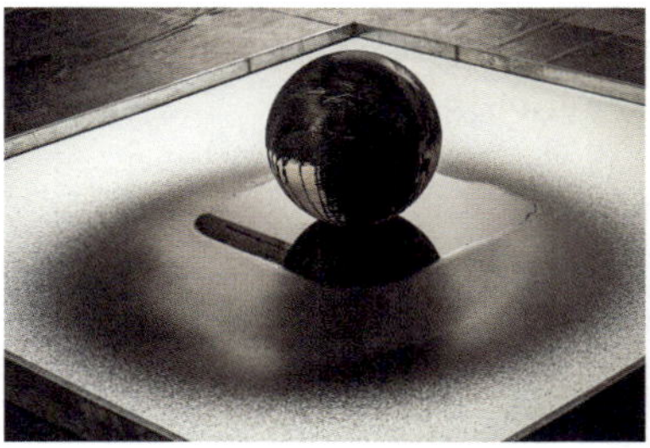

Stream-Venice (detail), 2017

2019 A major retrospective featuring works from the late 1950s to 2019 takes place at the Centre Pompidou, Paris.
Matsutani and Van Houten make an important donation of works to the Musée National d'Art Moderne – Centre Pompidou.

2020 Matsutani and Van Houten initiate a major donation of Matsutani's prints to the Institut National d'Histoire de l'Art (INHA), Paris, completed in 2024–25. INHA now has the most important corpus of the artist's printed works. A large part of the first donation is presented in *Takesada Matsutani: Estampes, 1967–1977* at Les Abattoirs, Toulouse, France.

2023 Japan's Wakayama Prefecture, where the artist lived for four years, awards him its Culture Prize.

2024 The artist's largest retrospective exhibition to date opens at the Tokyo Opera City Art Gallery, featuring more than two hundred works.

2026 The Prix Matsutani celebrates its tenth laureate.
Exhibitions in London and Paris mark the sixtieth anniversary of Matsutani's arrival in Paris.

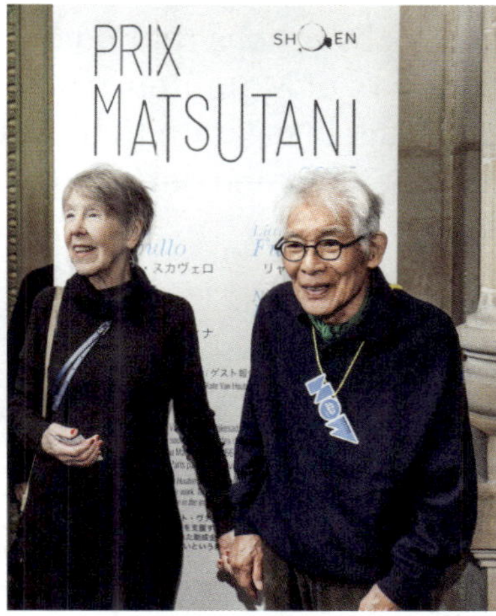

Matsutani with Kate Van Houten at a ceremony for the Prix Matsutani, 2025

Additional Resources

As is apparent from his own texts in this volume (pp. 44, 106, 149), Matsutani is gifted in finding words both candid and profound to express his attitudes toward art and life. His early Gutai experiments and the startling shifts in his work in the 1970s are particularly worth reading about, whether through his own recollections or in scholarly essays by others that address the historical and aesthetic contexts of Matsutani's practice and the significance of his art in relation to both the perception of reality and the communication of inner worlds.

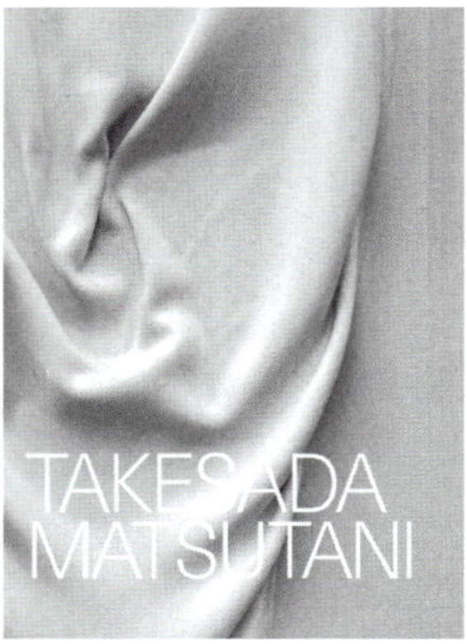

Takesada Matsutani (Tokyo Opera City Art Gallery, 2025)
Thanks to its chronological arrangement, this book allows readers to trace the development of Matsutani's art, aided by texts in Japanese and English. Among them is a "message" by an old friend of Matsutani's, the architect Tadao Ando, and an essay by the exhibition's curator, Osamu Fukushi, who writes on "spatial awareness and the geometry of life" in the artist's work.

Matsutani: Currents (Otani Memorial Art Museum, 2015)
This bilingual catalogue for Matsutani's 2015 exhibition at the Otani Memorial Art Museum, Nishinomiya, Japan, includes, among much else, the full version of the text excerpted on pp. 106–8, "Searching for a Starting Point: From Any Place, From Any Thing."

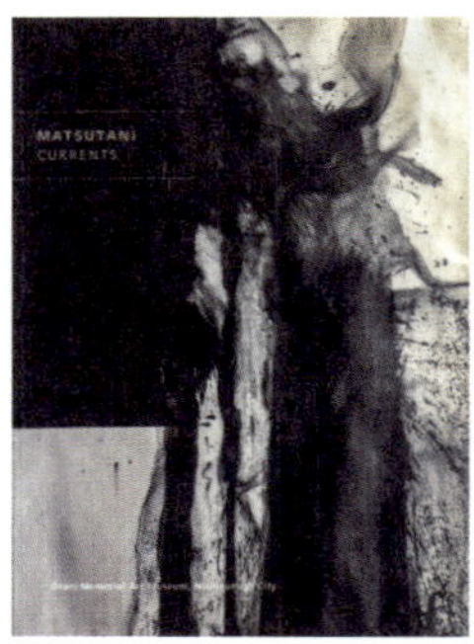

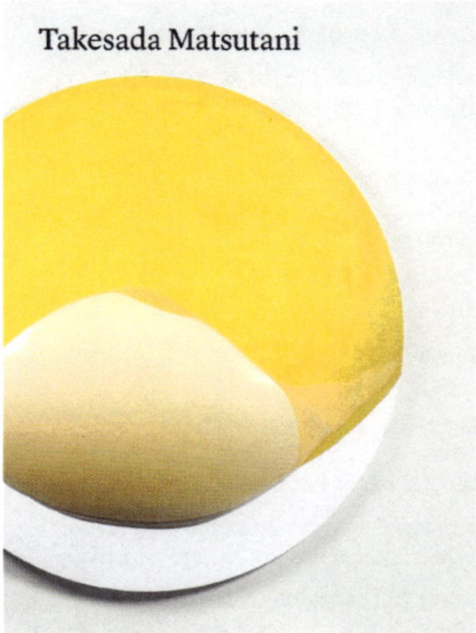

Takesada Matsutani (Hauser & Wirth Publishers / Centre Pompidou, 2019) The texts in this bilingual French / English book, published on the occasion of a major retrospective at the Centre Pompidou in Paris, include an insightful essay by the show's curator, Christine Macel; a survey of the *Streams* works by Valérie Douniaux, who has been working with Matsutani's archive since 2014; a reflection on the artist's relationship to Japanese traditions by Yves Peyré; and an essay exploring the themes of his work by Toshio Yamanashi, director of the Osaka National Museum of Art.

Takesada Matsutani: A Matrix (Hauser & Wirth / JRP | Ringier, 2013) Co-edited by Kate Van Houten and Midori Nishizawa, this book features, among other texts and plentiful images of key works, the English translation of a 2009 interview with Matsutani, as well as Van Houten's notes on early *Streams* pieces. It also includes a translation of Sadamasa Motonaga's assertion, in the pamphlet accompanying Matsutani's 1963 Gutai Pinacotheca exhibition, that "Matsutani is a bit of a chicken, but there is a strong spirit deep inside him."

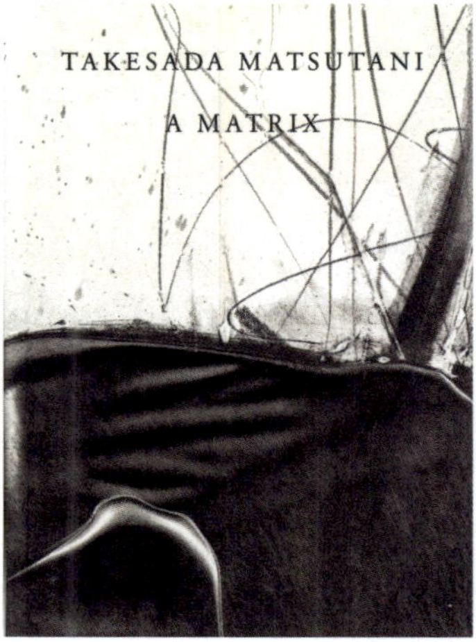

Scan this QR code to access additional material, including videos of Matsutani at work and footage of recent performances, including the one illustrated on pp. 126–27. A particular highlight is Lisa Rovner's 2022 short *Takesada Matsutani: Glue*, commissioned by *Ursula* magazine, showing the artist both talking about and making a vinyl glue piece in his studio in Paris.

Additional Captions

Cover, pp. 4–15: Matsutani in his studio, and views of the studio, Rue Faidherbe, Paris, 2020–25

p. 16: *Untitled*, 1964. Wood, acrylic, and mop, 4 3/8 × 9 1/4 × 2 in. (11 × 23.5 × 5 cm)

p. 17, left: *Make a Toy of Object*, 1974. Vinyl adhesive, wood, and cord, 8 7/8 × 6 1/4 × 5 1/2 in. (22.5 × 16 × 14 cm)

p. 17, right: *Metafiction*, 2018. Vinyl adhesive and found book, 7 × 4 5/8 × 3 in. (17.7 × 11.7 × 7.5 cm)

p. 160: Matsutani with *Stream-Venice* (2016–17) at the Venice Biennale, 2017

Sources

Translations of *shinshō* have been silently standardized, throughout, to "inner image(ry)."

p. 15: "Art is special . . ." is from an interview with Hans Ulrich Obrist, *Mousse*, Fall 2018, p. 132.

pp. 23–25: "I spent my uneasy adolescence . . ."; "For a twenty-year old . . ."; and "One evening . . ." are from "Searching for a Starting Point: From Any Place, From Any Thing," in *Matsutani: Currents* (Nishinomiya, Japan: Otani Memorial Art Museum), p. 21. The first quotation has been lightly adjusted by the artist.

p. 26: Matsutani's "severe" is quoted in Christine Macel, "Be Careful Not To Think Slightingly of This One Grain of Rice," in *Takesada Matsutani* (Zurich / Paris: Hauser & Wirth Publishers / Centre Pompidou, 2019), p. 40, note 16.

p. 30: "the human spirit . . ." is from Jirō Yoshihara, *Gutai Art Manifesto* (1956), trans. Reiko Tomii, http://web.guggenheim.org/exhibitions/gutai/data/manifesto.html.

p. 32: "In all honesty . . ." is from a conversation with Tsutomu Misizawa and Sawako Inaniwa in *Takesada Matsutani: A Matrix* (Zurich: Hauser & Wirth / JRP | Ringier, 2013), p. 17.

p. 37: "By chance . . ." is from an interview with Lucija Šutej, *Sursuma*, September 9, 2022, https://www.sursuma.com/magazine/interview-with-takesada-matsutani.

p. 40: "I realized . . ." is from an interview by Matthew Wilcox, *Apollo*, July / August 2016, p. 56. "A lot of people were repelled . . ." is from *Matrix*, p. 25.

p. 43: "All of a sudden . . ." is from *Matrix*, p. 29.

p. 44: Published in the *Art Journal* (Tokyo) 54 (1965): p. 36. Translated by Christopher Stephens.

p. 51: "a 'work' of nature itself" is from Alexandra Munroe, "To Challenge the Midsummer Sun: The Gutai Group," in *Scream Against the Sky: Japanese Art After 1945* (New York: Abrams, 1994), p. 92.

p. 55: "The Europe I had in my mind . . ." is from "Searching," p. 24.

pp. 58–59: "is very heavily pressed . . ." is from *Matrix*, p. 32.

p. 68: "artistic creation . . ." is from Antoni Tàpies, "Japanese Art and the Cult of Imperfection," in *Kazuo Shiraga* (Paris: Galerie Stadler, 1992).

p. 80: "primal images" is from a conversation with the author via Zoom, August 27, 2025.

p. 91: "too full of desire . . ." is quoted in Macel, "Be Careful," p. 37. "What can you do . . ." and subsequent quotations are translated by the author from Oral History of Postwar Japanese Art [4], Osaka New Museum of Art Preparation Office, October 11, 2017, https://nakka-art.jp/wp10/PDF_ORAL/04_matsutani.pdf.

p. 95: "This work is rigorous . . ." is quoted in Valérie Douniaux, "*Stream*: The Possibilities of Black and White," in *Matsutani* (2019), p. 140.

p. 97: "There is a part . . ." is quoted in Toshio Yamanashi, "Pouring, Inflating, Filling In: 'Without These the Work Is Not Mine,'" in *Matsutani* (2019), p. 195. "One needs logic . . ." is from the Osaka Oral History interview.

p. 106: Published in full in *Matsutani: Currents*, pp. 21–25.

p. 109: "fused with" is from "Searching," p. 25.

p. 112: "I wanted to explore . . ." is from an interview by Valérie Douniaux, in *Perspective* 2020:1 (2020), https://doi.org/10.4000/perspective.17938.

p. 116: "used a brush . . ." is from *Matrix*, p. 44.

p. 121: "To express the image in my mind . . ." is quoted in Osamu Fukushi, "Takesada Matsutani: Spatial Awareness and the Geometry of Life," in *Takesada Matsutani* (Tokyo: Tokyo Opera City Art Gallery, 2025), p. 242.

pp. 134–35: Quotations from Jun'ichirō Tanizaki, *In Praise of Shadows*, trans. Thomas J. Harper and Edward G. Seidensticker (Sedgwick, ME: Leete's Island, 1977), pp. 19–20.

p. 149: Previously unpublished.

pp. 150–55: The chronology is indebted especially to Tokyo Opera City Art Gallery's 2025 publication.

p. 150: "In all honesty . . ." is from *Matrix*, p. 17.

p. 151: "always in good spirits . . ." is from *Matrix*, p. 21. "This is no good . . ." is from "Searching," p. 22.

p. 152: "We stuck together like glue" is from the *Sursuma* interview.

p. 153: "I thought to myself . . ." is from "Searching," p. 25. *Bands of Blackness* was the title of a traveling exhibition in 2004. "That cat . . ." is quoted in Marjon Carlos, "The Star of Hauser & Wirth's Most Recent New York Exhibition Is a Half-Century-Long Love Story," *Cultured*, March 12, 2024, https://www.culturedmag.com/article/2024/03/12/takesada-matsutani-kate-van-houten-hauser-wirth/.

Credits

All artwork and writing by Takesada Matsutani © Takesada Matsutani

Cover, 4–5, 142–43: Charles Devoyer. 6–7, 12, 14–15, 22, 24, 32–35, 45, 47 top, 48–50, 52, 53 left, 56–57, 61 left, 63–64, 71, 80, 82, 90, 92–96, 100–102, 112, 123, 151–52, 153 bottom, 154, 155 right, 160: Archives Matsutani. 8–11, 13: Matthew Avignone. 16, 83 top right and bottom, 85 top: Matthew Kroening. 17 top: Todd-White Art Photography. 17 bottom, 41, 46, 47 bottom, 60 top, 61 right, 83 top left: Alex Delfanne. 18, 21, 118–19, 144: Photo: Michel Lunardelli. 25, 28 top, 29 top and bottom left, 73, 150 right: Kaoru Minamino. 26 left: Reiko Nonaka © 2025, ProLitteris, Zurich. 26 right, 27, 98: Ken Kato. 28 bottom, 78–79, 97, 103: Ashiya City Museum of Art and History. 29 bottom right, 39, 74, 117, 131, 148 bottom: Stefan Altenburger Photography Zürich. 30: © Motonaga Archive Research Institution Ltd. 31: © Associazione Shozo Shimamoto. 36: Timothy Dyon. 37–38, 42, 54–55: © Takeru Koroda. 43, 72, 128–29, 137, 140 top, 146, 148 top: Nicolas Brasseur. 53 right: Hyogo Prefectural Museum of Art (the Yamamura Collection). 59, 85 bottom, 122, 132, 141, 150 left: Marc Domage. 60 bottom, 75, 153 top: Sarah Muehlbauer. 62 top, 84 top, 147: Ken Adlard. 62 bottom, 76–77, 136, 139 bottom: Thomas Barratt. 65: ColBase (https://colbase.nich.go.jp/collection_items/tnm/A-10471). 67: © Museum of Fine Arts, Boston. Gift of Bank of America Corporation, 2011 © Ellsworth Kelly Foundation. All rights reserved/Scala, Florence. 68: © Fondazione Lucio Fontana, Milan/2025, ProLitteris, Zurich. Photo: Kristopher McKay © Solomon R. Guggenheim Foundation, New York. 69: © 2026 The Solomon R. Guggenheim Foundation/Art Resource, NY/Scala, Florence. 70, 130: Archives Matsutani. Photo: Reiko Nonaka © 2025, ProLitteris, Zurich 81, 84 bottom: Genevieve Hanson. 87: Tetsumi Kudo © 2025, ProLitteris, Zurich. Photo: Pierre Le Hors. 88 top: Yasuhiro Yoshioka. 88 bottom: © The Easton Foundation/2025, ProLitteris, Zurich. Photo: Christopher Burke Studios. 89 top: Philadelphia Museum of Art. © The Estate of Eva Hesse. Courtesy Hauser & Wirth. Photo: Eric Pollitzer. 89 bottom left: Alina Szapocznikow © 2025, ProLitteris, Zurich. Courtesy The Estate of Alina Szapocznikow/Galerie Loevenbruck, Paris/Hauser & Wirth. Photo: Fabrice Gousset © 2025, ProLitteris, Zurich. 89 bottom right: © Kanayama Akira and Tanaka Atsuko Association. Photo: © Centre Pompidou, MNAM-CCI, Dist. GrandPalaisRmn/Georges Meguerditchian. 99: Cropped from the image on Colbase (https://colbase.nich.go.jp/collection_items/tnm/A-282). 104: © The Estate of Jiro Takamatsu. Courtesy of Yumiko Chiba Associates, Tokyo; Pace Gallery, New York; and Stephen Friedman Gallery, London. 105: © Patrick Rimond. 110: The Museum of Modern Art, Kamakura & Hayama, Japan. 111, 139 top left: © Centre Pompidou, MNAM-CCI, Dist. GrandPalaisRmn/Philippe Migeat © 2025, ProLitteris, Zurich, Christian Bahier. 113: Tokyo Museum of Contemporary Art. 114: Kitmin Lee. 120: Archives Matsutani. Photo: Yasushi Kanbe. 124–25, 155 left: David Levene/Guardian/eyevine. 126–27: BigFaceArt. 133, 138, 140 bottom: Benoît Fougeirol © 2025, ProLitteris, Zurich. 139 top right: Archives Matsutani. Photo: Sylvia Bataille. 156 top: Courtesy Tokyo Opera City Art Gallery. 156 bottom: Courtesy Otani Memorial Art Museum.

Illustrated works are held in the following public collections: Ashiya City Museum of Art & History, Japan; Museum of Modern Art, Wakayama, Japan; Himeji City Museum of Art, Japan; Institut National d'Histoire de l'Art, Paris; Miyagi Museum of Art, Sendai, Japan; Musée National d'Art Moderne – Centre Pompidou, Paris; Museum of Modern Art, Kamakura & Hayama, Japan; Otani Memorial Art Museum, Nishinomiya, Japan; Museum of Contemporary Art, Tokyo; Tokyo Opera City Art Gallery.

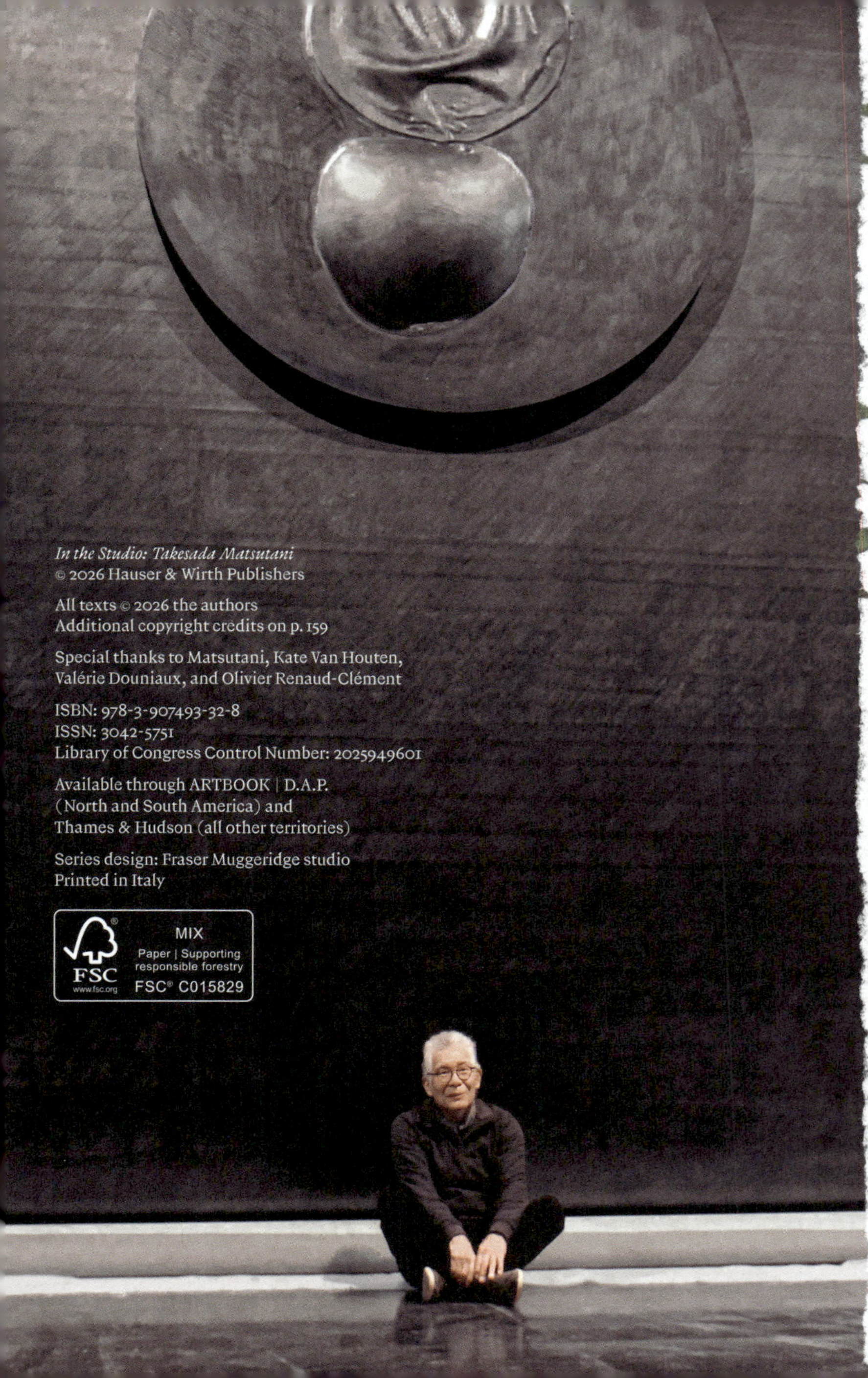

In the Studio: Takesada Matsutani

Additional copyright credits on p. 159

Special thanks to Matsutani, Kate Van Houten,
Valérie Douniaux, and Olivier Renaud-Clément

ISBN: 978-3-907493-32-8
ISSN: 3042-5751
Library of Congress Control Number: 2025949601

Available through ARTBOOK | D.A.P.
(North and South America) and
Thames & Hudson (all other territories)

Series design: Fraser Muggeridge studio
Printed in Italy

FSC www.fsc.org
MIX
Paper | Supporting responsible forestry
FSC® C015829